AA

TOURING ENGLAND

CENTRAL ENGLAND AND EAST ANGLIA

THE COMPLETE TOURING GUIDE

Cover picture:
River Witham at Waterside North, Lincoln.

Produced by the Publishing Division of the Automobile Association
Editor Allen Stidwill
Designer Neil Roebuck
Picture Researcher Wyn Voysey
Index by D Hancock

Tours compiled and driven by the Publications Research Unit of
the Automobile Association.

Photographs by Jarrolds Colour Library, J Hunter, C Molyneux,
S & O Mathews, J Allen Cash Photolibrary, Barnaby's Picture
Library, Woodmansterne Picture Library, British Tourist Authority,
R Corbett, D Cripps, The National Trust, AA Photolibrary, T Wood.

All maps by the Cartographic Department, Publishing Division of
The Automobile Association. Based on the Ordnance Survey Maps,
with the permission of the Controller of HM Stationery Office.
Crown Copyright Reserved.

Town plans produced by the AA's Cartographic Department.
©The Automobile Association.

Filmset by Senator Graphics, Great Suffolk St, London SE1
Printed and bound by New Interlitho SPA, Milan, Italy

Published by the Automobile Association, Fanum House,
Basing View, Basingstoke, Hampshire RG21 2EA

ISBN 0 86145 498 7
AA Reference 51910

Standing 46ft above the Suffolk countryside with its sails spanning almost 55 feet, the finely-preserved Saxtead Green Windmill is recognised as one of the finest post mills in the county.

Touring Central England & East Anglia

CONTENTS

INTRODUCTION

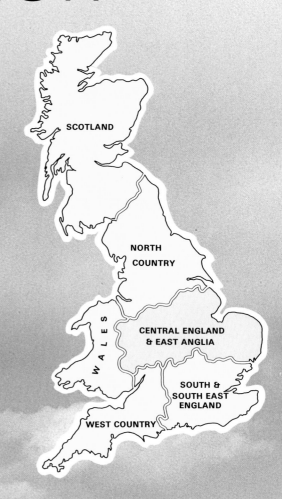

At the heart of this colourful region lies the West Midlands, cradle of the Industrial Revolution, and all around are marvellous things to discover. Here are Shakespeare's Stratford-upon-Avon, Staffordshire's porcelain, the beauty of the Peak District and the wide skies of the Fenland, where the high towers of medieval churches and old windmills rise from the low-lying landscape. The region is packed with interesting and historic towns like the beautiful stone town of Stamford and the ancient port of King's Lynn, and it offers the opportunity to wander amongst the medieval streets of Norwich, Shrewsbury and Ludlow, to experience the scholarly atmosphere of Cambridge and to marvel at the majestic towers of Lincoln's Cathedral. Here there are mighty castles too, such as Warwick and Belvoir, and magnificent houses like Chatsworth and the royal residence of Sandringham. This book reveals these treasures and more through its carefully planned motoring tours which provide the ideal way to explore this fascinating region. Each self-contained circular tour can be completed within a day and includes magnificent colour pictures to give a foretaste of what is to come.

As well as the tours the book includes 37 pages of invaluable town plans to guide you around the regions popular towns. There is also a colourful 3 miles to the inch atlas.

Touring Central England and East Anglia is just one in a series of six colourful *Regional Guides* which embrace the rich history and varied countryside of Britain. The other five guides in the series are: *Touring the West Country, Touring South and South East England, Touring Wales, Touring the North Country* and *Touring Scotland*. The six regions covered by the series are shown on the adjacent map.

ABOUT THE TOURS

The tours in this guide have been designed for clarity. Each tour occupies two pages and has a clear map accompanying the text. All the places described in the text are shown in **black** on the tour maps and are described as they occur on the road, linked in sequence by route directions. This precise wayfinding information is set in *italic*.

Castles, stately homes and other places of interest described in the tours are not necessarily open to the public or may be open only at certain times. It is therefore advisable to check the opening times of any place before planning a stop there. Properties administered by the National Trust, National Trust for Scotland and the Ancient Monument Scheme (NT, NTS and AM) are generally open most of the year, but this should be checked with the relevant organisation, as should precise opening times.

The Automobile Association's guide *Stately Homes, Museums, Castles and Gardens in Britain* is the most comprehensive annual publication of its kind and describes over 2,000 places of interest, giving details of opening times and admission prices, including many listed in this book.

Near the Staffordshire village of Gnosall the Shropshire Union Canal, which links the Mersey to the Severn, is splashed with brightly coloured boats.

HOW TO FIND THE TOURS

All the motor tours in the book are shown on the key map below and identified by the towns where they start. The tours are arranged in the book in alphabetical order by start town name. Page numbers are also given on page vii. Each tour begins at a well-known place, but it is possible to join or leave at any point if more convenient.

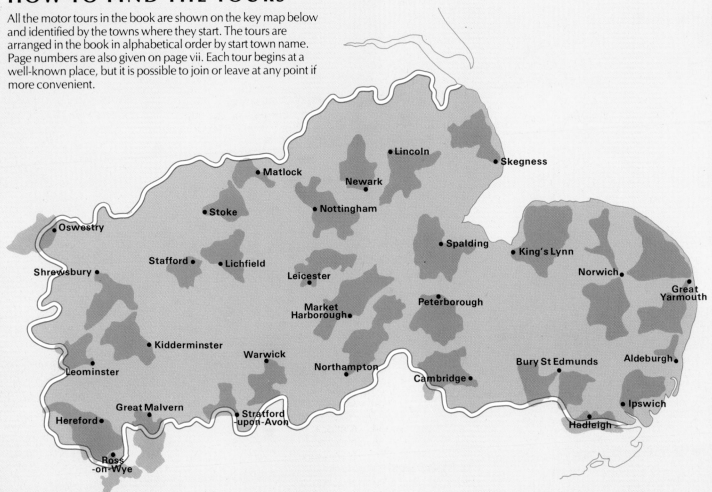

MAPS				**TEXT**	
Main Tour Route		Marshland		AM	Ancient Monument
Detour/Diversion from Main Tour Route		Memorial/Monument	m	c	circa
Motorway		Miscellaneous Places of		NT	National Trust
Motorway Access	②	Interest & Route Landmarks	▪	NTS	National Trust for Scotland
Motorway Service Area	Ⓢ	National Boundary		OACT	Open at Certain Times
Motorway and Junction Under Construction		National Trust Property	NT	PH	Public House
A-class Road	A68	National Trust for Scotland Property	NTS	RSPB	Royal Society for the
B-class Road	B700	Non-gazetteer Placenames	Thames/Astwood		Protection of Birds
Unclassified Road	unclass	Notable Religious Site	✝	SP	Signpost (s) (ed)
Dual Carriageway	A70	Picnic Site	Ⓟ		
Road Under Construction	= = = =	Prehistoric Site			
Airport	✈	Racecourse			
Battlefield	✕	Radio/TV Mast			
Bridge		Railway (BR) with Station			
Castle		Railway (Special) with Station			
Church as Route Landmark	✝	River & Lake			
Ferry	--Ⓥ--	Woodland Area			
Folly/Tower		Scenic Area			
Forestry Commission Land		Seaside Resort			
Gazetteer Placename	Zoo/Lydstep	Stately Home			
Industrial Site (Old & New)		Summit/Spot Height	KNOWE HILL 209 ▲		
Level Crossing	LC		KNOWE HILL 209 ▲		
Lighthouse		Viewpoint			

TOURING
CENTRAL ENGLAND AND
EAST ANGLIA

Motor Tours
Pages 2-67

ALDEBURGH, Suffolk

There is more to this small, salt-laden town with its long, straight, somewhat desolate shingle beach than at first meets the eye. The musicians Benjamin Britten and Peter Pears made their homes here and an annual music festival, founded by Benjamin Britten, takes place every June and focuses on the Maltings at Snape, just west of the town along the broad Alde estuary. One of Britten's most popular works is *Peter Grimes,* which is set against the background of Aldeburgh's Moot Hall. This is the town's most striking building, with its 2 tall Jacobean chimneys, dating back to the time of Henry VIII, and now standing defiantly facing the advancing sea. The council chamber (open to the public in summer) is on the upper floor, where visitors can see old maps, prints and objects of local interest. *Peter Grimes* was inspired by the work of the poet George Crabbe. He lived in the town during the 17th century when its fortunes had considerably declined since its earlier heyday as a port and ship-building centre: the Dutch Wars, the transition of shipbuilding to the Blackwall yard, and sea damage had taken their toll. At least half this Tudor town has now been destroyed by the encroachment of the sea.

Leave Aldeburgh on an unclassified road for Thorpeness.

THORPENESS, Suffolk

The building of Thorpeness began just 70 years ago and was deliberately planned as a resort of quiet and refinement. A large boating lake, called the Meare, was created and a number of pleasant houses were built

VILLAGES OF EASTERN SUFFOLK

The coastline from Aldeburgh to the vanished city of Dunwich is an area of haunting bleakness that is the prelude to an extremely varied tour through Suffolk's most delightful villages, past several bird sanctuaries, some splendid churches and a historic castle.

The curious House in the Clouds and the post mill at Thorpeness

between this and the sea. One of the town's most distinctive buildings is the extraordinary House in the Clouds. It looks like a mock-Tudor building, but beneath the facade is a water tower on stilts. The post windmill standing beside it was brought from Aldringham so the tower could use it as a pump.

At Thorpeness turn inland and follow the B1353 to Aldringham. Here turn right on to the B1122 for Leiston.

LEISTON, Suffolk

Leiston is distinguished by having one of the most advanced schools in the country — Summerhill. It was founded by educationalist A. S. Neill as an experiment in self-education and has proved very successful. The surrounding marshes were first drained between 1846 and 1850 by the Garretts of Leiston Iron Works. Richard Garrett created a portable steam engine and threshing machine and a bust of him can be seen in the town's Victorian church.

Leave on the B1122, SP 'Yoxford', and in 1 mile pass the remains of Leiston Abbey.

LEISTON ABBEY, Suffolk

Leiston Abbey (AM) was first founded on the Minsmere Marshes in 1182, and was moved to its present site in 1363 and then rebuilt by Robert de Ufford, Earl of Suffolk. The ruins incorporate an octagonal brick gate-turret which was added when it was converted into a diocesan retreat during Tudor times.

Continue to Theberton and ½ mile beyond the village turn right on to the B1125 for Westleton.

WESTLETON, Suffolk

Farmland and heathland surround the village of Westleton which consists of a variety of attractive buildings — redbrick and colour-washed. A shaded duck pond lies at one end of the village green where every summer a week-long fair is held featuring races and general festivities. Westleton used to have 2 windmills, but one, the smock mill, has been converted into a house and the other, a tower mill, is derelict.

At the end of the village turn right on to the unclassified Dunwich road and shortly pass the Minsmere Bird Sanctuary on Westleton Heath.

THE MINSMERE BIRD SANCTUARY, Suffolk

This is one of the Suffolk reserves where avocets — a rare black and white wading bird — breed, and the public are allowed access to some parts of the reserve as well as to several hides. The sanctuary covers 1,500 acres and the varied habitats it provides include reed beds, woodland and heathland.

Continue to Dunwich.

DUNWICH, Suffolk

Dunwich was a city about the size of Ipswich in the 12th century, but everything from those days has all gradually been washed away by savage sea storms. It was still an important port in Roman times, but the sea started its onslaught in 1326 and by the 16th century most of the city lay on the sea bed. It is said that church bells can be heard ringing out across the lonely beach. All that remains now beneath the crumbling cliffs is a scattering of cottages, an inn and a general store. However, a dramatic idea of the city's former glory and importance can be gained by studying the relics and pictures in the museum in St James' Street. North-east of this lonely and evocative place is the extensive Dunwich Forest where there is an excellent picnic site.

Leave on the Blythburgh road and pass through Dunwich Forest. In 1½ miles, at the crossroads, turn right on to the B1125. In 1 mile a detour may be taken by turning right on to the B1387 to Walberswick.

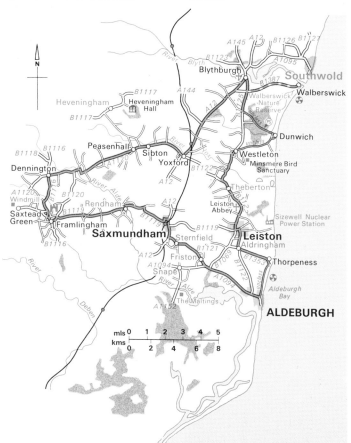

Blythburgh's church tower was crowned by a spire until 1577 when it fell through the roof, killing a man and a boy

WALBERSWICK, Suffolk
Walberswick's ruined church tower stands proudly as a landmark to those at sea. The pleasant houses around the village green have attracted artists over many years and it was a favourite spot of the artist Wilson Steer earlier this century. Just across the estuary (crossed by ferry) is the smart little town of Southwold (see page 13) with brick and colour-washed Georgian houses.
A national nature reserve, overlooking the Blythe estuary, is home to an interesting variety of waders and rare birds.

The main tour keeps forward on the B1125 into Blythburgh.

Aldeburgh is famous for its 'long-shore' herring and the best sprats in England are caught here in November and December

BLYTHBURGH, Suffolk
The collapse of the fishing trade along the east coast contributed to Blythburgh's decline from a prosperous town to the village it is today. The huge and magnificent church rising up above the marshes is the only reminder of the town's importance in the 15th century when there was a mint here, a gaol, crowded quays and 2 annual fairs. It is a light and spacious building with a great wooden roof decorated with carved angels and painted flowers. Another notable feature of the church is the bench-ends depicting the 7 deadly sins, and a wooden clock with a quarter jack.

At Blythburgh turn left on to the A12 Ipswich road for Yoxford.

YOXFORD, Suffolk
Locally known as 'The garden of Suffolk', because it is surrounded by the parkland of 3 country houses (not open), Yoxford is packed with attractive timbered houses featuring balconies and bow-windows. Cockfield Hall was originally a magnificent Tudor house built during Henry VIII's reign; it was altered in the 19th century, but is still most impressive and has a thatched Victorian lodge in the village.

Turn right on to the A1120, SP 'Stowmarket', for Sibton.

SIBTON, Suffolk
Sibton stands at the junction of 2 Roman roads in the Minsmere valley. It is a pretty place, with a group of cottages and small 18th-century bridges cross the Drain, a ditch that drains the farmland along its length. Romantic, overgrown ruins of Sibton Abbey, the only Cistercian house in Suffolk, lie in the woods near the village. It was founded in 1150 but was never prosperous and fell into neglect after the Dissolution.

Continue to Peasenhall.

PEASENHALL, Suffolk
Trickling through the village is a little stream that brings an air of serene tranquility to the cluster of houses on its banks; the stream is actually part of the Drain. Peasenhall's claim to fame is that the Suffolk seed drill was originally manufactured here. The Wool Hall has been discovered and restored only recently. About 4 miles to the north of the village stands Heveningham Hall (see page 13), a lovely Palladian house set in magnificent grounds landscaped by Capability Brown.

Remain on the A1120 for Dennington.

DENNINGTON, Suffolk
Treasures which fill the 14th-century church at Dennington include an extremely rare altar canopy, some beautiful screens and, on a bench-end on the south side, a curious carving of a giant with a webbed foot.

At the church branch left on to the B1116 for Framlingham.

FRAMLINGHAM, Suffolk
The Earls of Norfolk used to own the impressive castle in this lively market town. The castle (AM) was destroyed in 1639, but before that it was the home of Mary Tudor during her attempts to gain the throne. The ruins of the original castle are extensive and are an unusual example of the 12th-century style, using square towers rather than round ones. Next door to the castle is the church with its memorials to the Norfolk family and one of the most splendid wooden church roofs in Suffolk. The rest of the old town consists of many attractive cottages, and historic buildings, centred on the market square. Saxted Green lies 2 miles to the east of Framlingham and is the site of a famous windmill (AM). It is a very good example of an 18th-century post mill — the oldest type of windmill — where the body carrying the sails and machinery rotates on an upright post.

Leave Framlingham on the B1119, SP 'Saxmundham'. In 4 miles pass through Rendham, then in another 2¾ miles reach the outskirts of Saxmundham. Here, turn left then right, and at the T-junction turn right on to the A12 for the town centre.

SAXMUNDHAM, Suffolk
One of the more modern towns in this part of Suffolk, its origins actually go back to the 13th century when there was a market here occupying 7 acres. However, most of the existing buildings in the main street are 19th century.

Continue on the Ipswich road for 1 mile and turn left on to the B1121, SP 'Aldeburgh'. Pass through Sternfield and Friston, then later join the A1094 for the return to Aldeburgh.

EAST ANGLIAN HEARTLANDS

The last king of East Anglia ruled from Bury St Edmunds in the 9th century. Today the town is an important market centre for east Suffolk, a focal point for farming communities made rich by a flourishing wool trade in medieval times.

Once a rich and splendid monastery, the abbey at Bury St Edmunds is now an extensive ruin.

BURY ST EDMUNDS, Suffolk

Edmund, the last king of the East Angles, was killed by the Danes c869 and was subsequently hailed by his people as a martyr. In 903 his body was moved from its resting place at Hoxne to Bury, then known as *Beodricsworth*, which became an important religious centre and place of pilgrimage. The abbey that grew here prospered until it was burned by the townsfolk in 1465. Its rebuilding resulted in one of the architectural glories of England, but it became too powerful and, like many of its contemporaries, was broken at the Dissolution. Today its former splendour can be judged by extensive ruins that form a focal point for a country park. Two gates still stand, and the precincts are made splendid by the Cathedral Church of St James. A large graveyard separates this fine building from 15th-century St Mary's Church, which is known for its magnificent hammerbeam roof and the grave of Mary Tudor. Mary's life is illustrated in a window given by Queen Victoria. Bury St Edmunds itself is an attractive market town which retains its 11th-century street plan and many fine old buildings. Moyse's Hall dates from the 12th century and contains a museum, and the lovely Guildhall and Cupola House are both of 15th-century origin. Excellent Georgian shop fronts are preserved in some streets, and the Town Hall of 1771 was designed by Robert Adam. Also from this period are a brick-built Unitarian chapel with an exceptionally well-preserved interior, and the Angel Corner (NT) is a Queen Anne house, now containing a collection of clocks and watches. The Theatre Royal (NT) build in 1819 is a rare example of a Georgian playhouse. The 18th-century Angel Hotel was the scene of Mr Pickwick's meeting with Sam Weller in Charles Dickens' *Pickwick Papers*.

Some 2½ miles south west of the town, off the A143, is Ickworth House.

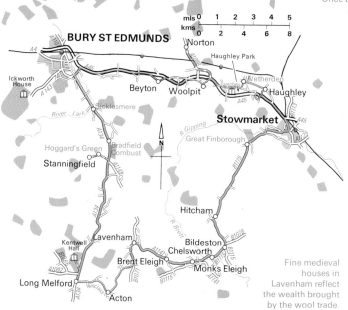

Fine medieval houses in Lavenham reflect the wealth brought by the wool trade.

ICKWORTH HOUSE, Suffolk

Started by Frederick Harvey, 4th Earl of Bristol and the Bishop of Derry, this 18th-century house (NT) is one of the most remarkable in England and an apt memorial to its builder's eccentricity. The Earl Bishop intended to fill it with works of art collected during his extensive travels, but in Rome he was imprisoned by Napoleonic troops and his enormous collection confiscated. He died in 1803, with only half his dream actually realized in bricks and mortar. Visitors today can see the full glory of the strange elliptical rotunda that grew from plans by the Italian architect Asprucci. Inside the house is a fine collection of 18th-century and French furniture. Part of the 2,000-acre grounds (NT) were landscaped by Capability Brown.

Leave Bury St Edmunds on the A134 'Sudbury' road. Drive through the villages of Sicklesmere and Bradfield Combust, and ¾ mile beyond the latter pass an unclassified right turn leading through Hoggards Green to the village of Stanningfield. This offers a pleasant detour from the main route.

STANNINGFIELD, Suffolk

Stanningfield Church has two fine Norman doorways, one within a timbered porch, and the 13th-century chancel preserves notable features. West of the village is Elizabethan Coldham Hall, which has a dovecote of the same period.

Continue on the A134 and approach Long Melford with the grounds of Kentwell Hall to the right.

KENTWELL HALL, Suffolk

Access to this mellow Elizabethan manor (open) is through a 300-year-old avenue of lime trees and over a moat. The combination of water, tree-shaded grass, and old brick forms a tranquil beauty that is a rarity in the 20th century.

LONG MELFORD, Suffolk

Perhaps the stateliest village in Suffolk, Long Melford has an impressive main street lined by fine old buildings and dominated by a magnificent church. The latter dates from 15th-century reconstruction and occupies the site of a Roman temple. Its many windows give the interior an airiness accentuated by soaring columns and slender pillars. The Lady Chapel of 1496 can almost be considered as separate from the main building, though attached in mortar if not in style to the east end. The well-proportioned tower is a sensitive addition dating from 1903. Interesting monuments include a carved 15th-century piece in the Clopton Chantry and a number of contemporary brasses that illustrate clothing and hairstyles of the period. Leading down towards the village from the church is a triangular green fringed by the 18th-century wall of the Congregational churchyard, the 15th-century Bull Hotel and 16th-century Trinity Hospital. The latter was founded by Sir William Cordell and greatly restored in the 19th century. Dominating the village is Melford Hall (NT), one of the finest Elizabethan manors in England. It occupies three sides of a lovely old courtyard and carries a splendid array of turrets.

Drive to the Bull Inn and turn left on to the unclassified 'Lavenham' road. In 1¼ miles continue forward to Acton.

ACTON, Suffolk

Inside Acton Church is an excellent brass, the most famous military memorial of its type in the country. It was raised to Sir Robert de Bures *c*1302 and depicts a knight in chain mail holding a shield. A notable sculpture of a reclining man with his wife at his feet carries the date 1722 and has been attributed to Thomas Green of Camberwell.

From Acton turn left with SP 'Lavenham'. In 2¼ miles join the B1071 and continue to Lavenham.

LAVENHAM, Suffolk

Easily one of the most outstanding villages in East Anglia, Lavenham has hardly changed in appearance since its heyday as an important wool town in the 14th and 15th centuries. Its dozens of immaculately preserved buildings include timber-framed houses, the Guildhall (NT), and the Wool Hall. Slightly apart from the village is the local church, a superb building that is considered a complete work of art in itself. It carries a 141ft tower resplendent with shiny knapped flint, and was built with money donated by a family of clothiers. Other reflections of prosperous times are 15th-century Little Hall, the old Town Cross (AM), and The Priory. An 18th-century hand-operated fire engine is preserved in the village.

Leave Lavenham on the A1141 'Hadleigh' road. After 2 miles turn left on to an unclassified road and enter Brent Eleigh.

One of the many superb old buildings preserved in Long Melford is Elizabethan Melford Hall.

BRENT ELEIGH, Suffolk

Fine wall paintings have been discovered in the 14th-century Church of St Mary here, and Jacobean woodwork is much in evidence on the pulpit, south door, and box pews. Elizabethan Brent Eleigh Hall has modern additions by architect Sir Edwin Lutyens.

Return to the A1141 and turn left for Monks Eleigh.

MONKS ELEIGH, Suffolk

This pleasant little village has a good church with a notable tower and a carved pulpit. An attractive weatherboarded mill and Georgian millhouse stand near by.

Drive to the end of the village and bear left on to the B1115 'Stowmarket' road. Continue to Chelsworth.

CHELSWORTH, Suffolk

An attractive double hump-backed bridge spans the small River Brett here, and the village features many lovely timber-framed houses.

Stay on the B1115 and turn left for Bildeston.

Moated Kentwell Hall dates from the 16th century and stands in lovely grounds about 1 mile north of Long Melford.

BILDESTON, Suffolk

Many notable half-timbered cottages survive here, and the village church is reached by a footpath across pleasant farming country.

From Bildeston continue on the B1115 to Hitcham.

HITCHAM, Suffolk

A 15th-century hammerbeam roof can be seen in Hitcham Church, which is comfortable rather than outstanding and forms a natural focus for this delightful village. Many of the local cottages are half timbered.

Continue on the B1115 and drive through Great Finborough to reach Stowmarket.

STOWMARKET, Suffolk

Poet John Milton visited this busy Gipping Valley market town many times to see his tutor Thomas Young, who lived at the vicarage. Most of the buildings are of fairly recent date, like the good Georgian and Victorian houses round the market square. Inside the town church, which displays a variety of styles, are an old organ and a rare wigstand. A large open-air museum relating to East Anglian Life has an attractive riverside setting here, with frequent demonstrations from craftsmen.

Leave the town on the A1302 'Bury St Edmunds' road. In ¾ mile join the A45, and after another 1¾ miles branch left on to an unclassified road. Continue to the village of Haughley.

HAUGHLEY, Suffolk

A Norman castle that once stood here has entirely vanished, but its mound remains as a monument to the village's previous importance. There are 30 18th-century leather buckets in the church porch, possibly a hangover from early fire precautions, and the nave has a good roof. New Bell's Farm is an experimental station of the Soil Association.

In Haughley turn left and continue to Wetherden. In the latter village turn left again, then in a further ½ mile turn right and pass the grounds of Haughley Park on the left.

HAUGHLEY PARK, Suffolk

Characteristic stepped gables and elegant octagonal chimneys are dominant features of this lovely old house, built in 1620 and restored in recent years. It stands in beautiful grounds and is open to the public on Tuesdays May to September.

After 1¼ miles rejoin the A45. In ½ mile branch left, then turn left on to an unclassified road. A short detour can be made from the main route to passing over the A45 to join the A1088 'Thetford' road and driving for 2½ miles.

NORTON, Suffolk

Excellent examples of old woodcarving, including misericords and a notable font, can be seen inside the local church. Nearby is the partly 18th-century Rectory and The Norton Bird Gardens set in 4 acres of gardens with a variety of species.

On the main route, continue to Woolpit.

WOOLPIT, Suffolk

At one time wolves were brought here to be destroyed and buried, hence the name. A local legend tells of the Green Children, a boy and girl who suddenly appeared in some obscure period of village history and were remarkable for their distinctive colour. The story goes on to say that they claimed to be from underground St Martin's Land, a place of perpetual twilight, and that the boy died but the girl married and had a family. The local church boasts a rare brass-eagle lectern and double-hammerbeam roof.

Leave Woolpit on the unclassified 'Bury St Edmunds' road and in ¾ mile rejoin the A45. In 1¼ miles turn left for Beyton.

BEYTON, Suffolk

Good Norman features of Beyton Church include a pleasing round tower and an attractively simple doorway.

After village rejoin the A45 for the return to Bury St Edmunds.

BURY ST EDMUNDS, Suffolk

'Shrine of a King, cradle of the Law' runs the city motto, which refers to the 2 great events of the city's history. St Edmund was buried here 33 years after his death in 869 at the hands of the Danes. The monastery where he lay was given abbey status in 1032 by King Crut, eager to please his new subjects. The 'Law' in the motto refers to an event in 1214 when King John's barons swore on the high altar of the abbey church to force the king to accept the Magna Carta. The best preserved remains of the abbey are 2 gatehouses, one 12th-century, the other 14th-century. Two churches stand at the edge of the abbey precincts, St Mary's, a 15th-century church with a fine hammerbeam roof, and St James', built a little later. The rest of the town follows the rectangular plan set out by Bishop Baldwin in the 11th century, but the houses are essentially Georgian, or appear so; Bury kept up with fashion, often not by rebuilding, but by adding new façades in the latest style to the fronts of existing buildings. Angel Hill is a fine example, it is a square surrounded by some of Bury's best houses — including Angel Corner (OACT), a Queen Anne Mansion which houses one of the largest collections of clocks and watches in Britain. The oldest Norman house in East Anglia is claimed to be Moyse's Hall (OACT), c1180, in the Butter Market. It is now a museum displaying Bronze-Age weapons, medieval relics and other items of Suffolk archaeology and natural history.

Leave on the A143, SP 'Sudbury', then 'Haverhill'. At Horringer is the entrance to Ickworth.

ICKWORTH, Suffolk

The centre of this most unusual house (NT) is a great rotunda with 2 arms curving away which end in square blocks, each the size of a substantial country house. The interior of the rotunda is lit by a glass dome 100ft above the floor, and the odd-shaped rooms, hung with paintings by Titian, Velasquez, Hogarth, Reynolds and Gainsborough, are furnished with fine 18th-century English and French furniture. Earl-Bishop Frederick Hervey designed the house to hold a collection of choice artefacts (now at Ickworth), collected on his European tours but sadly he died abroad before the house was finished. Capability Brown landscaped the surrounding parkland which features majestic oak and cedar trees.

Continue on the A143 and pass the edge of Chedburgh. In 3 miles, at the Plumbers Arms PH, turn right, SP 'Lidgate'. In ¾ mile bear left then turn right on to the B1063 Newmarket Road, and continue to Lidgate.

HORSES AND KINGS

From Bury St Edmunds, shrine of a martyred king, to Newmarket, the headquarters of horse racing in Britain since the 17th century — but the glamour of the sport of kings soon gives way to the continuity of tradition — lands and buildings owned by the same families for centuries.

LIDGATE, Suffolk

Suffolk House (not open), brick-gabled and timber-fronted, was the birth-place of the poet John Lydgate, who was born c1370 and lived as a Benedictine monk at Bury. He imitated Chaucer in his work and although he became a court poet, he died in poverty. In the mainly 14th-century church there is a brass of a cleric, said to be Lydgate.

In 1¼ miles keep forward on to the B1085 Kentford road to Dalham.

DALHAM, Suffolk

Thatched cottages set back from the road in their own gardens line both banks of the River Kennet, and woods climb an escarpment to the church at the north end of the village. Paintings inside depict the building of the steeple in 1625 There is a monument of Sir Marten Stukeville and his 2 wives: Stukeville was probably with Sir Francis Drake on his last fateful voyage.

Turn left across the bridge, SP 'Moulton', and ascend past a windmill. At Moulton turn left, beyond the post office, on to the Newmarket road. Gradually ascend Warren Hill, passing several racing stables on either side of the road. There are good views of Newmarket and the surrounding country on the descent into the town. At the bottom turn right, then at the clock tower turn left to enter Newmarket.

NEWMARKET, Suffolk

Newmarket, the home of English horse racing. James I often came here, hunting and tilting, and organised the first recorded horse race in 1619. The High Street, which follows the ancient road, has Jubilee Clock tower at one end, and at the other the Cooper Memorial Fountain. In between are many fine houses and hotels, including the headquarters of the Jockey Club formed in 1750. Next door is the National Horseracing Museum telling the story of horseracing development in this country. The racecourse itself has been painted by many great artists — the wide downland, high elevation and magnificent views creating a memorable setting, enhanced by the massive Anglo-Saxon earthwork known as Devil's Dyke.

Leave Newmarket on the A1304, and in ¾ mile turn left on to the B1061, SP 'Haverhill'. Shortly bear right, then go over a level crossing into Cambridgeshire. In 1 mile cross the Devil's Dyke, marked by a line of trees. Continue to Dullingham then in 1 mile turn left and pass through Burrough Green. Continue to Great Bradley.

Ickworth's central feature, the great rotunda, was built in the 1790s

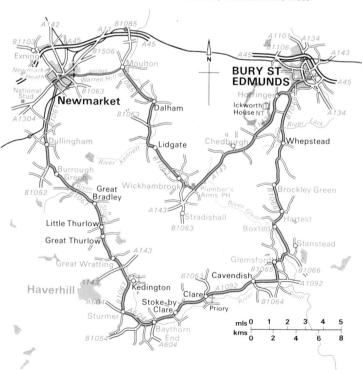

GT BRADLEY, Suffolk

The church at Great Bradley — a village set in meadowland beside the River Stour — is reputed to have the best brick porch in Suffolk: its bricks made by the 'King's own brickmaker' in early Tudor times. The tower, built in the early 14th century, retains one of its original bells and also has a fire-place, which may have been used in the preparation of the holy wafers used in communion.

Continue on the B1061 to Little and Great Thurlow.

The best of Britain's horses compete on the famous Newmarket turf, the centre of the English horse racing world

Cavendish, once the ancestral village of the Dukes of Devonshire

LITTLE & GT THURLOW, Suffolk

The 2 villages are so close together as to be almost one. Great Thurlow has a fine Georgian Hall and a Perpendicular church, originally Norman, in which there is a sanctuary chair where criminals could claim safe refuge. Little Thurlow has a past dominated by the Soames family, who built the almshouses and grammar school in the 1600s.

Continue to Great Wratting, then at the main road turn right, then left, on to the B1061 and shortly skirt Kedington.

KEDINGTON, Suffolk

Kedington possesses one of the foremost churches in Suffolk. Stepping on to the uneven brick floor, seeing the ancient pews and monuments that have not changed in centuries, is like stepping back in time. There are separate little pews for boys and girls, and another angled so that the overseers could keep an eye on their charges, a triple-decker pulpit, and the Barnardister pew. The Barnardister family was one of Suffolk's most important and oldest families, stretching back for 27 generations in an unbroken line.

Continue on the B1061 and at Sturmer turn left on to the A604. Follow the River Stour round to Baythorn End, then turn left on to the A1092 Clare road and recross the river into Suffolk to reach Stoke-by-Clare.

STOKE-BY-CLARE, Suffolk

Strung out along the road in the Stour valley, is Stoke-By-Clare, with houses of the 15th-19th centuries, some of which are timber-framed or plastered and decorated with chevrons or fish-scale patterns. Near the church stands a tall Tudor dovecot, resembling a gatehouse, which belonged to a college of priests who were transferred from a priory in Clare in 1124. A Queen Anne house, now a private school, has the remains of the old priory built into it. In 1948 wall-paintings were revealed in the church; they are thought to be some of the last executed before the Reformation.

Continue to Clare.

CLARE, Suffolk

Clare is an ancient little market town on the River Stour with a history centred upon its Norman castle of which only the 53ft-high motte and some masonry remains. Lady Elizabeth Clare, who founded Clare College, Cambridge, in the 14th century, lived here occasionally, and in those days the castle was large enough to house her 250-strong retinue and several hundred horses. The Augustinians founded their first priory in England here in 1248, and there are extensive remains still visible near the river. The Prior's house was turned into a dwelling house after the Dissolution and is complete. Among the many old houses in the town is the Ancient House, c1473. This timber-framed building is renowned for the fine plaster-work, or pargetting, on its exterior walls. Also of interest is the Swan Inn, which has a remarkable carved bracket of a swan with a crown round its neck.

Leave on the A1092, SP 'Sudbury' and continue to Cavendish.

CAVENDISH, Suffolk

Cavendish is one of Suffolk's show-pieces. A noble church rises above half-timbered thatched cottages around a village green. By the pond is the Old Rectory, a 16th-century building which was used by Sue Ryder as a home for concentration-camp victims. St Mary's Church dates from the 13th and 14th centuries and has within it 2 lecterns; one is a brass 16th-century eagle, the other is a wooden lectern with 2 17th-century books chained to it.

In 1 mile turn left on to the B1065 for Glemsford. Follow SP 'Bury St Edmunds' through the village and ¾ mile beyond the church turn left on to the B1066, following the attractive Glem valley to Boxted. Beyond the village the road becomes more winding and hilly and passes through Hartest and Brockley to Whepstead.

WHEPSTEAD, Suffolk

Set in splendid rolling country, Whepstead possesses the only church dedicated to St Petronilla, and its fair share of Suffolk manor houses (not open); Plumpton Hall, where 2 of Cromwell's brothers-in-law lived; Doveden (pronounced Duffin) Hall, moated with Tudor chimneys, and Manston Hall, red-brick, half-timbered and now a farmhouse.

3½ miles beyond Whepstead turn right on to the A143 for the return to Bury St Edmunds.

CAMBRIDGE, Cambs

This famous and attractive university town started life as a small Celtic settlement on the marshy banks of the Cam. In 1209 a split in the Oxford community resulted in a migration of students and scholars to Cambridge, and the establishment of a university that was to rival its unwilling parent in wealth and prestige. Traces of the first foundation – which was Peterhouse in 1284 – are largely disguised by later work, but 14th-century Clare College occupies buildings that were part of a 12th-century nunnery. Most of the other colleges show similar mixtures. King's College, founded by Henry VI in 1441, has an outstanding chapel that overlooks the Cam and is famous for some of the finest gothic fan vaulting in Europe. Corpus Christi is unique in having been founded by two town guilds, and lovely half-timbered Queens' of 1346 is by far the most picturesque. Much more can be learned about the university and its superb buildings, and the interested visitor is advised to invest in a guide booklet. The town itself is a delightful collection of old streets and houses alongside the river. Peaceful lawns and meadows slope down to the water's edge as grassy quays for summer punters, in marked contrast to the busy activity of the excellent shopping areas in the middle of town. Not surprisingly the city has several good museums. Extensive art and archaeological collections are housed in the Fitzwilliam, the Scott Polar Research Institute has many relics relating to famous expeditions, and the Sedgwick displays fossils from many different parts of the world. Cambridge and County Folk Museum is packed with domestic and agricultural bygones.

Leave Cambridge on the A1303 'Bedford' road and drive for 2½ miles to reach Madingley Postmill.

BETWEEN THE OUSE AND THE CAM

West of Cambridge and the willow-shaded Cam a countryside of orchards and pasture stretches flatly to low Fenland horizons. Here and there the skyline is interrupted by a windmill or church tower, the roofs of an ancient riverside town, or the bushy crown of an occasional copse.

Trinity College Bridge in Cambridge leads to the famous 'Backs'.

MADINGLEY POSTMILL, Cambs

The body of this restored windmill pivots on a central post so that the sails can be turned into the wind. Originally from Huntingdonshire, this interesting industrial relic was moved to its present site in 1936.

Continue for ¼ mile to reach the American Cemetery.

AMERICAN CEMETERY & CHAPEL, Cambs

The War Memorial Chapel that stands here is a striking example of modern architecture. Inside is a 540-square-foot map showing Atlantic sea and air routes used by American forces during World War II.

Continue and at roundabout take 4th exit on to an unclassified road to reach Madingley.

MADINGLEY, Cambs

Just outside this attractive village is Madingley Hall, a fine Elizabethan house that stands in a wooded park and serves as a hostel for university students. Both Edward VII and George VI lived here when they were undergraduates at Cambridge.

Continue to the A604 and turn left. Proceed for 4 miles, turn right on to an unclassified road, and drive to Swavesey.

SWAVESEY, Cambs

Attractively situated close to fenland, this long, narrow village has a good 14th-century church with notable window tracery. Inside the building are bench-ends with animal carvings.

Proceed to Over.

OVER, Cambs

This pretty fenland village stands in orchard country to the east of the River Ouse, a popular venue for boating and angling. Its pleasant church contains a bell that was cast some 600 years ago.

Drive to Willingham.

WILLINGHAM, Cambs

The local windmill and the impressive tower of Willingham's 14th-century church are prominent landmarks in the flat farmlands that surround this village. The church nave has a notable 15th-century hammerbeam roof adorned with over 50 carved angels.

Turn left on to the B1050 and reach the River Ouse. Follow the river and turn left on to the A1123 to enter the village of Earith. Continue through Needingworth, and after 1½ miles turn left on to the A1096 to enter St Ives.

ST IVES, Cambs

In 1110 King Henry I granted St Ives the right to hold a fair. The town grew up around its fairground and its annual market became established as one of the largest in England. The River Ouse runs through the town and is spanned here by a narrow 6-arched bridge (AM) that dates from the 15th century. The Norris Museum situated in the Broadway contains a comprehensive collection of Huntingdonshire history.

Follow the A1096 south and cross the river. After ¼ mile turn right on to an unclassified road and continue to Hemingford Grey.

HEMINGFORD GREY, Cambs

A moated mansion in this lovely village dates back to the 12th century and is thought to be the oldest inhabited dwelling in England. The 12th-century church is picturesquely sited in a bend of the River Ouse.

Turn left and shortly right, proceed to Hemingford Abbots, and follow SP 'Huntingdon' to join the A604. Drive for 1 mile and branch left. Meet a roundabout and turn right on to an unclassified road to reach Godmanchester.

GODMANCHESTER, Cambs

The site of this ancient town was once occupied by a Roman military station. Nowadays it is a treasure-house of varied architectural styles. Island Hall is a mid-18th-century mansion set in a tranquil riverside setting (open).

Turn right on to the B1043, crossing a 14th-century bridge (AM), and enter Huntingdon.

HUNTINGDON, Cambs

Both Oliver Cromwell and the diarist Samuel Pepys were born here and attended the town's former grammar school. Parts of the building date back to Norman times, and today it houses a museum of Cromwellian relics.

Leave Huntingdon on the A141 'Kettering' road and drive to Hinchingbrooke House.

King's College Chapel, a medieval masterpiece, is one of the principal glories of Cambridge.

HINCHINGBROOKE HOUSE, Cambs

Now restored and in use as a school, this Tudor and later mansion (open) has been home to the Cromwells and the Earls of Sandwich. It incorporates parts of a medieval nunnery.

Continue on the A141 'Kettering' road to Brampton.

BRAMPTON, Cambs

Pepys House in Brampton is a lovely old gabled cottage that was the home of the diarist's parents, and was owned by him from 1664 to 1680. The stalls in the local church display excellent carving.

Leave Brampton and in 2 miles join the A1 for the outskirts of Buckden

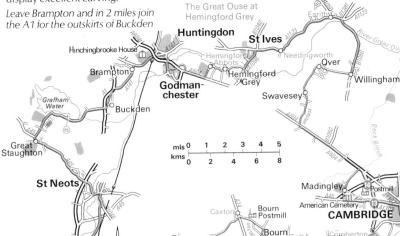

The Great Ouse at Hemingford Grey.

Britain's oldest surviving postmill at Bourn resembles those seen in illuminated manuscripts.

BUCKDEN, Cambs

Considerable remains of Buckden Palace, a former residence of the bishops of Lincoln, comprise a fine Tudor tower and an inner gatehouse of c1490 (open). The buildings are well restored and in use as a school. The local church is known for its notable spire and carvings.

Continue to a roundabout on the A1 and take the B661 'Kimbolton' road to reach Grafham Water.

GRAFHAM WATER, Cambs

This 2½-square-mile reservoir supplies drinking water for 1½ million people and is a valuable leisure amenity offering long bankside walks and facilities for boating and trout fishing. Several picnic sites have been laid out around the edge.

Continue to Great Staughton.

GREAT STAUGHTON, Cambs

Opposite 14th-century and later Great Staughton Church, which has a fine tower and contains good monuments, is a mansion with a pair of picturesque timber-framed barns. The village cross dates from the 17th century and features a sundial.

A rare medieval chapel survives in the centre of the 15th-century bridge over the Great Ouse at St Ives.

At Great Staughton turn left on to the A45 and continue for 4 miles, crossing the A1. Cross the River Ouse and enter St Neots on the B1428.

ST NEOTS, Cambs

The great charm of this ancient market town is its compactness. Interesting old inns can be found in many of its secretive back streets, and attractive buildings cluster round three sides of the Ouse-side market square.

Leave St Neots by turning right on to the B1043 crossing the A45 and after 3 miles join the A1. Turn left on to the B1042 and drive through Sandy.

SANDY, Beds

Low wooded hills that rise to the east of this large River Ivel village make a pleasant change from the flat countryside crossed by much of the tour. About 1 mile east is the 100-acre Lodge Nature Reserve, which is the HQ of the Royal Society for the Protection of Birds. A nature trail offers public access.

Continue along the B1042 and pass a TV mast to the left before reaching Potton. At Potton take the B1040 'St Ives' road through Gamlingay to Waresley, then drive forward on to an unclassified road for Great Gransden. Turn right, then shortly left into the village. Follow SP to Caxton and turn right then left for 'Bourn' to reach Bourn Postmill.

BOURN POSTMILL, Cambs

Although the working parts of this remarkable windmill have been replaced from time to time, the base and outer structure date back at least to 1636. It is claimed to be the oldest example in England.

Continue for 1 mile, meet a T-junction and turn right to reach Bourn.

BOURN, Cambs

Red-brick Bourn Hall has Jacobean origins but has been restored. Between it and the attractive little Bourn Brook is a church with a fine 13th-century tower.

Drive through Bourn and join the B1046. Continue through Toft and Comberton to reach Barton, and turn left on to the A603. Proceed for 1 mile, at roundabout take 3rd exit on to the unclassified 'Trumpington' road, and continue to Grantchester.

GRANTCHESTER, Cambs

Rupert Brooke immortalized this beautiful village of thatched and lime-washed cottages in his poem *The Old Vicarage, Grantchester*. He lived here for a while after leaving King's College in nearby Cambridge, and wrote of the village as 'the lovely hamlet'.

Cross the Cam and continue to Trumpington.

TRUMPINGTON, Cambs

Inside the elaborate local church is England's second oldest memorial brass. It is dated 1289 and was raised to Sir Roger de Trumpington, whose local associations are obvious in the name. Other features of the village include a 16th-century inn and two 18th-century halls.

Join the A1309 and return to Cambridge.

THE MALVERN HILLS AND THE VALE OF GLOUCESTER

The stark outlines of the Malvern Hills, an ancient natural rampart, are never far from view as the tour follows the pleasant valley of the River Leadon and skirts the fringe of the Royal Forest of Dean, before turning northwards to run through the Vale of Gloucester and the broad valley of the Severn.

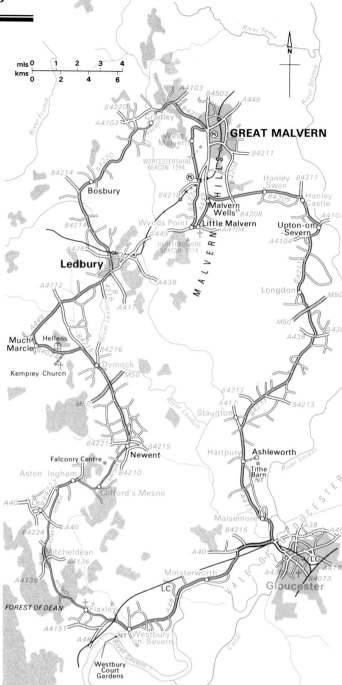

GT MALVERN, Herefs & Worcs

The distinctive character of this busy holiday centre was established in the Victorian and Edwardian periods when people came to take the waters and promenade in the Winter Gardens. Great rambling houses looking out across the town towards Worcester cling precariously to the steep slope of the dramatic Malvern Hills. The town itself clusters around the ancient priory church, a magnificent building which contains exquisite 15th- and 16th-century stained glass and beautiful tiles from the same period. Above the main street of the town by the Mount Pleasant Hotel, a steep flight of steps leads up to St Anne's Well, the source of the pure water for which visitors flocked to Malvern. Among many distinguished residents, the most famous was the composer Sir Edward Elgar, in whose memory an annual festival is held. George Bernard Shaw was a frequent visitor, and several of his plays received their world premiere at the festival.

Herefordshire Beacon, a summit of the Malvern range, is where Owain Glyndwr rallied his forces in 1405

THE MALVERN HILLS, Herefs & Worcs

The Malvern Hills rise abruptly from the broad, flat valley of the River Severn, an impressive 9-mile range of wild, upland country, from where 14 counties can be seen on a clear day. The Worcestershire Beacon at the northern end is the highest (1,395ft) point and the entire length of the ridge can be walked to the Herefordshire Beacon (1,114ft) at the south. The banks of a great Iron-Age fort, known as the British Camp, crown this hill, which Elgar used as the setting for *Caractacus*.

Leave Great Malvern on the B4219, SP 'Worcester' then 'Hereford'. In 2 miles turn left on to the A4103 and in 1 mile turn left on to an unclassified road for Cradley. Beyond the village turn right, SP 'Bromyard', and later turn left on to the B4220, SP 'Ledbury', and continue to Bosbury.

BOSBURY, Herefs & Worcs

Bosbury stands on the banks of the River Leadon, in the centre of a fertile hop and fruit growing region. The village has a charming street of black and white houses around an imposing Norman church with a detached tower. Inside the church, 2 remarkable 16th-century monuments to members of the Harcourt family face each other in baroque splendour.

¾ mile beyond Bosbury turn left on to the B4214, and continue past hop fields to Ledbury.

LEDBURY, Herefs & Worcs

An unspoilt town with a wealth of 16th- and 17th-century black and white buildings, Ledbury is set in a lovely corner of the English countryside where rich green meadows are watered by slow-moving streams. The main street, lined with old houses, leads to the market place where the 17th-century market house, timbered in a herringbone pattern, stands on pillars of oak. Here the Feathers Hotel rubs shoulders with the medieval chapel of St Katherine's Hospital, and a narrow cobbled lane where the houses project over the street takes the visitor straight back to Elizabethan England. At the end of the lane, St Michael's Church displays the grandeur of a small cathedral. Inside is a formidable collection of monuments of every period from the medieval to the 19th-century. Elizabeth Barrett Browning's stern father, Edward Moulton Barrett, lies in the north aisle.

At the crossroads in Ledbury turn right on to the A449, SP 'Ross', and continue to Much Marcle.

MUCH MARCLE, Herefs & Worcs

Cider-making has been a local industry around Much Marcle for nearly 400 years and in the 19th century a local firm was one of the first to build a cider factory. There are 2 manor houses in this attractive black and white village: Homme House (not open) and Hellens, a lovely old brick house (OACT) whose ancestry goes back to Norman times, although the present building is mostly 16th century. The church contains some exquisitely sculptured tombs, including a rare 14th-century oak figure of a man carved from a single block of wood.

Turn left on to the B4024, SP 'Newent'. After 1½ miles a detour can be taken to Kempley Church by turning right on to an unclassified road.

KEMPLEY CHURCH, Glos

The village, whose inhabitants once attended services in Kempley Church, has moved away to Kempley Green, leaving the old vicarage and 17th-century farmhouse isolated beside the Norman Church of St Mary. This small building is unique in England for the series of frescoes in the chancel painted between 1130 and 1140. The centre-piece shows Christ seated on a rainbow, surrounded by sun, moon, stars and the emblems of the Evangelists. Other figures include the Virgin Mary, St Peter and the Apostles.

The main tour continues on the B4024. In 1 mile, turn right on to the B4215 for Dymock, pleasantly situated in the Leadon valley. In 3½ miles turn right, then left, into Newent.

NEWENT, Glos

This small, essentially Georgian town lies in the heart of an intensely rural part of Gloucestershire. The crooked main street has some well-kept 18th-century houses and a few older, timber-framed buildings, including a market house standing on posts, whose one large upper room is approached by outside stairs.

In the town turn right on to an unclassified road , SP 'Cliffords Mesne'. After 1¼ miles pass the Falconry Centre.

FALCONRY CENTRE, Glos

The ancient art of falconry can be studied at this fascinating centre (OACT) which specialises in birds of prey. There is an interesting museum with many photographs and displays about birds of prey; a wide variety of birds in aviaries; a falcon flying ground and a Hawk Walk where hawks are kept.

Continue through Cliffords Mesne SP 'Ashton Ingham', and in ¾ mile keep left to join the B4222, SP 'Ross', to Aston Ingham. In 1 mile keep forward, SP 'Mitcheldean'. In 1½ miles cross the main road, then in another 1½ miles join the B4224 into Mitcheldean which lies at the northern edge of the Forest of Dean.

THE FOREST OF DEAN, Glos

The Forest of Dean is one of the most ancient royal forests in Britain. For centuries this was an important industrial area, as a vast coalfield underlies the woodland, and iron ore has been worked here since Roman times. Weapons for the Crusades were forged here, and in Tudor times trees were felled to provide timber for warships. These days the Forest has been made more accessible by nature trails, picnic sites and way-marked routes.

At the far end of Mitcheldean go over the crossroads, SP 'Flaxley and Westbury', to follow a pleasant byroad, passing Flaxley. In 1½ miles turn left on to the A48, SP 'Gloucester', and at Westbury-on-Severn pass Westbury Court Gardens.

WESTBURY COURT GARDENS, Glos

Very few of the formal water gardens, modelled in the 17th-century after the Dutch style, survived the 'landscaping' craze of the 18th-century. However, Westbury Court Gardens (NT) lay forlorn and derelict for years, its hedges overgrown, its canals silted up, and its lawns covered with weeds and so remains as one of the best examples of its time. Ten years of devoted work and replanting have restored its elegant design, and the charming colonnaded pavilion has been rebuilt. Plants that are known from records to have flourished there originally have been replanted, including old roses, quince and morello cherry trees.

Continue on the A48, following the River Severn before reaching Minsterworth, a good viewpoint for the famous Severn Bore tidal wave. In 2 miles, at the roundabout, join the A40. There are distant views of Gloucester, with its cathedral, before the tour turns left on to the A417, SP 'Ledbury'. Follow the River Severn through Maisemore to Hartpury, where there is a fine, old tithe barn near the church. A detour can be taken by turning right to Ashleworth.

ASHLEWORTH, Glos

The pretty cottages in this charming little village, tucked away down a country lane, are grouped about a green. Another lane leads to Ashleworth Quay, down by the River Severn, where a church, a manor house (not open) and a great 16th-century tithe barn (NT) make up an outstanding group of medieval limestone buildings. The barn is 125ft long and has a magnificent roof.

The main tour continues on the A417. In 1¼ miles turn right on to the B4211, SP 'Upton-on-Severn'. In 5 miles, at the T-junction, turn right then left, continuing to Longdon with views of the distant Malvern Hills to the left. In 2¼ miles turn right on to the A4104 for Upton-on-Severn.

UPTON-ON-SEVERN, Herefs & Worcs

A delightful reminder of country towns as they used to be, with old-fashioned shops, old inns and streets where it is a joy to stand and look around. Looking out over the meadows of the River Severn, the old church tower, crowned with an 8-sided cupola, is the sole remnant of the original parish church. Locally known as the 'Pepperpot' it is now a Heritage Centre showing the development of the town and the Civil War battle of Upton Bridge.

In Upton-on-Severn turn left, then keep forward on the B4211, SP 'Malvern', to Hanley Castle. Turn left again on to the B4209, SP 'Malvern Wells', to pass through Hanley Swan, and continue to Malvern Wells.

MALVERN WELLS, Herefs & Worcs

Malvern Wells is a continuation of Great Malvern, liberally sprinkled with the gracious villas of a bygone age. In the churchyard of St Wulstan's Church at Little Malvern where primroses and violets flower among the graves in spring, is the simple tombstone to the composer Sir Edward Elgar and his wife.

At Malvern Wells turn left on to the A449, SP 'Ledbury', and 'Ross', and ascend to Wynds Point, a notable viewpoint beneath the Herefordshire Beacon. At the British Camp Hotel turn right on to the B4232, SP 'West Malvern', along Jubilee Drive. In 2¼ miles turn right, then left, and skirt the Worcestershire Beacon to West Malvern. Continue on the B4232 for the return to Great Malvern.

GREAT YARMOUTH AND HER HINTERLAND

Something for everyone; traditional seaside entertainment is to be had at lively Yarmouth, with its pier, arcades and illuminations. Southwold offers the homely attractions of a small fishing town (as well as fresh seafood), and for those who prefer to get away from it all, and admire unspoilt coastal scenery, there is Covehithe.

GT YARMOUTH, Norfolk

Three rivers, the Yare, the Bure and the Waverley, flow into the sea at Great Yarmouth which stands on the long spit of land separating the fresh and salt waters. For over 1,000 years Yarmouth has been a great herring fishing port, but its fleet has dwindled during this century and the tourism which began in the 18th century has overtaken it. A promenade runs along the seaward side of the town and behind there are entertainments of every kind: bowling greens, tennis courts, boating lakes, theatres, amusement arcades and piers which are brilliantly illuminated during the summer season. Although air raids in World War II devastated much of the old town, there are still remains of its medieval town walls and a part of the Rows, a complex grid-iron pattern of narrow streets which grew up within the walls. The Old Merchants House (AM) in Row 117 is a 17th-century house typical of those owned by merchants not quite rich enough to live in the great houses on the quayside. A museum of local history is sited in the Tolhouse (OACT) in Tolhouse Street, a 13th-century building said to be the oldest civic building in Britain. On South Quay the rich merchants had their houses, such as the Customs House of 1720 where John Andrews lived, the most famous of herring merchants, and the Elizabethan House (OACT), a 16th-century house which had a new façade added in the 19th-century. In one corner of the market place is the attractive Fishermen's Hospital, founded in 1702, and next to it is Sewell House (OACT) (1646), where Anna Sewell, authoress of *Black Beauty,* was born in 1820.

Leave Yarmouth on the A12. At the roundabout at the edge of Gorleston-on-Sea, take the 3rd exit, SP 'Burgh Castle'. In 2 miles turn right for the village of Burgh Castle.

BURGH CASTLE, Norfolk

The village is named after the Roman fort (AM) here, which was one of a chain the invaders built along the east coast. After the Romans left, St Fursey, an Irishman, built a monastery within the fort walls, but the site was later used again as a castle by the

Normans. In later centuries stone from the castle was used for building in the village. The substantial walls and bastions, still held together by Roman mortar, give an idea of the scale of the fort, built in about AD 300.

From Burgh Castle follow the Belton road and in 1½ miles, at the T-junction, turn left, SP 'Yarmouth'. In 1 mile turn left on to the A143, then immediately right, SP 'Blendeston'. In 1½ miles turn right, SP 'Somerleyton', then after another mile turn left. Later pass (left) Somerleyton Hall.

SOMERLEYTON HALL, Suffolk

The Victorian railway entrepreneur Sir Morton Peto had this Anglo-Italian mansion (OACT) built around an old Elizabethan hall in 1844. He also had the church, school and cottages of the village built to complement it. The house stands among magnificent trees and shrubs, and of particular interest is the clipped yew maze. The oak parlour in the house has beautiful carved panelling by Grinling Gibbons, and the dining room is hung with paintings by old masters. The game trophies proudly displayed throughout the house are the victims of the sporting Crossley family, who bought the house in 1866.

At the next T-junction turn right on to the B1076 and continue to St Olaves. From here a short detour can be made by turning right on to the A143 to visit Fritton.

FRITTON, Suffolk

The church here has a Saxon tower and a chancel showing the work of Norman stone masons. There are several notable wall-paintings, and a trap door under the thatched roof of the chancel is said to have been used by smugglers when prudence required them to lie low. Near the partly-ruined St Olave's Priory (AM), is the Fritton Decoy, a long, wooded lake used to trap wildfowl.

At St Olaves the main tour turns left on to the A143. Cross the River Waveney and continue through Haddiscoe to Tofts Monks. In 2¼ miles, at the roundabout, take the A146. After 1 mile turn right on to the A145 into Beccles.

The superbly restored post mill at Holton: the mill is pivoted on a central post and turns with the wind

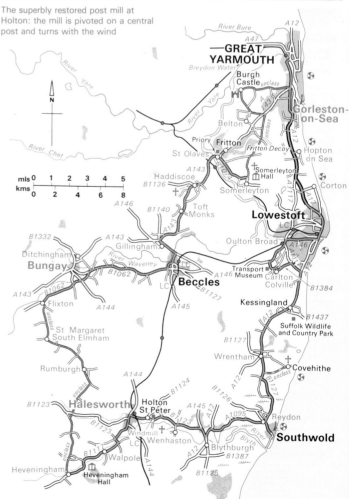

Southwold — a pleasant seaside resort with the character of a fishing port

BECCLES, Suffolk
Beccles quay on the River Waveney is an ideal centre for exploring the network of local waterways, and the boats provide a colourful scene in the summer months. The 14th-century chapel is unusual in having a separate 92ft-high bell tower, holding a peal of 10 bells.

Leave Beccles on the B1062, and follow the Waveney valley to the outskirts of Bungay (see tour 55). Here, turn left on to the B1062, SP 'Diss'. In ½ mile go over the staggered crossroads and continue to Flixton. Pass the Buck Inn and at the next road junction turn left, SP 'St Margarets', and in 1¾ miles turn left into St Margaret South Elmham. Continue to Rumburgh and in 1 mile turn right, SP ''Cookley', then in 1 mile bear right, SP 'Heveningham'. In another mile go over the staggered crossroads and continue to Heveningham. Turn left into the village and join the B1117, SP 'Halesworth', and in 1 mile pass the entrance to Heveningham Hall.

HEVENINGHAM HALL, Suffolk
In 1777 Sir Gerald Vanneck MP commissioned Sir Robert Taylor to enlarge the family's Queen Anne house, Heveningham Hall. Taylor built an impressive Palladian mansion; he screened the north front with Corinthian columns and added a wing to either side. Then James Wyatt took over, his task being to oversee the interior decoration. Biagio Rebecca, an Italian artist, was employed to do the house painting. The result is a magnificent Georgian house typical of all that is fine of the period. The grounds were landscaped by Capability Brown, and include one of Suffolk's finest 'crinkle-crankle' walls (curves in and out to give plants' protection) and a beautifully-proportioned orangery by Wyatt.

Continue through Walpole and in 2 miles join the A144 for Halesworth. At the end of the main street turn right on to the B1132, SP 'Southwold', and continue to Holton-St-Peter.

HOLTON ST PETER, Suffolk
An attractive village which takes the latter half of its name from the Church of St Peter. This has a round Norman tower, a Norman doorway, a 15th-century octagonal font and a 16th-century linenfold pulpit. Overlooking the village from a hillside is a post mill situated among pine woods.

At the edge of the village bear right, then in 3½ miles turn right on to the A145. At the next T-junction turn left on to the A12, then skirt an inland lake formed by the River Blyth before turning right on to the A1095. Continue through Reydon to Southwold.

SOUTHWOLD, Suffolk
Southwold, perched on cliffs overlooking the North Sea, has flint, brick and colour-washed cottages, a church and a market place. There are 7 spacious greens which resulted from a disastrous fire in 1659, because as the herring trade declined, there was less money for rebuilding, and the damaged areas were left as open spaces. There is, however, evidence of Dutch influence in the buildings that did arise, as can be seen in the gabled cottages in Church Street, and the museum in Bartholomew Green (OACT). The museum displays relics of the Southwold Railway (1879-1929), and illustrates local history, including an archaeological collection.

The tour returns to Reydon and turns right on to the B1127, SP 'Wrentham'. After 3 miles a byroad (right) may be taken to visit Covehithe.

COVEHITHE, Suffolk
This delightful, unspoilt village has a stretch of sandy beach that is often empty. The beach is backed by cliffs and the village dominated by the ruins of a huge 14th-15th century church. Judging by the size of the church, Covehithe must once have been a prosperous place; the church fell into disrepair in the 17th century.

Chinese ring-necked pheasants in John Gould's *Book of Birds,* which can be seen in the library of Somerleyton Hall

The River Blythe at Southwold

The main tour continues to Wrentham. Here turn right on to the A12 and continue to Kessingland.

KESSINGLAND, Suffolk
The village is mainly in 2 parts; near the coast road, from where the church's 13th-century tower has served for centuries as a landmark for sailors; and the popular beach and caravan site by the sea. Nearby is the Suffolk Wildlife and Country Park, (OACT) a small, attractive zoo with a mixed collection of animals, including lions, tigers, a walk-through aviary, monkeys, badgers and a lake full of waterfowl.

Remain on the A12 for another 2 miles, than at the roundabout take the A1117, SP 'Great Yarmouth'. At the next roundabout take the B1384. In ¾ mile turn right, SP 'Beccles', then at the T-junction turn left and shortly pass the East Anglia Transport Museum at Carlton Colville.

EAST ANGLIA TRANSPORT MUSEUM, Suffolk
The museum covers 3 acres which can be seen from a tramway and narrow-gauge railway, and exhibits include historic cars, commercial vehicles, trams, buses and trolleybuses as well as collections of curios connected with the historical development of transport.

Continue to the A146 and turn right to reach Oulton Broad. At the traffic signals turn right with the A146 and continue into Lowestoft.

LOWESTOFT, Suffolk
During the 14th century Lowestoft was an important fishing port, valuable to the nation, and although the fleets are now a shadow of their former glory, the town is a lively place, and the trawlers docking and unloading their catch to be cleaned and gutted on the quayside ready for the busy fish market, is an exciting spectacle. South Town is the tourist section, with many seaside lodgings giving it a traditional seaside atmosphere, and a long esplanade runs alongside the beach to Claremont Pier. At one end is a children's corner, a boating lake and a miniature steam railway. The northern limit of the old town is marked by the Upper Lighthouse, open at weekdays. A feature of this part of the town are the 'Scores', narrow alleys which cut steeply down from the High Street to the shore, where the fish-houses for curing herring used to stand, few of which still survive.

Leave on the A12. In 5 miles re-enter Norfolk and later skirt Gorleston-on-Sea before the return to Great Yarmouth.

HADLEIGH, Suffolk

Many fine Georgian and Victorian houses are preserved in this River Brett market town, and the High Street shows a remarkable architectural mixture of timber, brick, and plaster-faced buildings. Some of the plasterwork has been raised in decorative relief, known as pargetting, and most of the structures are excellent examples of their type. The fine 15th-century Guildhall (open) has two overhanging storeys and has been a school and an almshouse. Also of note is the imposing Deanery Tower, a remnant of the medieval palace of Archdeacon Pykenham. Features of the local 14th- to 15th-century church include a bench-end that depicts the legend of a wolf which found and guarded the decapitated head of St Edmund.

Leave Hadleigh on the A1071 'Sudbury' road. At the edge of the town turn right on to the A1141 'Kersey, Lavenham' road and follow the shallow valley of the River Brett for 1¼ miles. Meet crossroads and turn left on to an unclassified road for Kersey.

CONSTABLE LANDSCAPES

Here is the country of John Constable, who immortalized much of its rural beauty in his paintings. Here also are the ragged estuaries of the Stour and Orwell, which carve the coastline into a confusion of small bays, sheltered shingle beaches, and reed-covered marshes.

Hadleigh's superb timbered Guildhall has been well restored and extended. The ground floor originally formed almshouses.

KERSEY, Suffolk

Shakespeare mentioned the cloth once made in this beautiful old weaving centre in his plays *Measure for Measure* and *Love's Labours Lost*. Nowadays Kersey's Brett Valley position, sloping streets, and numerous half-timbered buildings make it known as one of the most picturesque places in Suffolk. The local church is a gem of 14th- and 15th-century architecture on a site mentioned in the *Domesday Book*.

Drive to the church in Kersey and follow the 'Boxford' road. Continue to Boxford.

BOXFORD, Suffolk

This quaint old village takes its name from an attractive stream that runs close to its timber-framed cottages. Its church features an unusual wooden porch that may be the earliest of its kind in the country, and contains an unusual 17th-century font with doors.

Leave Boxford on the A1071 'Sudbury' road and continue for 2¼ miles. Turn right on to the A134 and drive to Sudbury.

Wildlife of all kinds and restored Thames barges co-exist on the Orwell estuary.

SUDBURY, Suffolk

Sudbury stands on the River Stour and is famous as the birthplace of painter Thomas Gainsborough in 1727. His house at 46 Gainsborough Street is now a local arts centre and museum containing a selection of his work, and he is commemorated by a bronze statue on Market Hill. Novelist Charles Dickens referred to the town as 'Eatanswill' in *Pickwick Papers*. St Peter's Church was built in the 15th century as a chapel of ease and contains a fine painting by a local artist named Robert Cardinall. St Gregory's is much older, having been built on the foundations of an old college by the Archbishop of Canterbury c1365. In 1381 he was brutally murdered in the Peasants' Revolt, and his skull is preserved as his memorial in the vestry. Other features of the building include beautifully carved choir stalls and one of the finest 15th-century font covers in the country. Also in the town is the notable Corn Exchange, containing the Quay Theatre and Arts Centre.

Leave Sudbury on the B1508 SP 'Bures' and continue to Great Cornard.

GREAT CORNARD, Suffolk

Although almost a suburb of nearby Sudbury, the nucleus of this village is still centred on its charming church and preserves an identity entirely separate from its large neighbour.

Stay on the B1508 and drive through the Stour Valley to Bures.

BURES, Suffolk

Fine half-timbered houses and an elegant church dating from the 13th to 15th centuries are the main features of this pretty little village, which stands on the banks of the River Stour. Inside the church is a font adorned with painted shields and a private chapel containing a monument dated 1514. Chapel Barn is an ancient thatched building that was once attached to the former Earl's Colne Priory.

Drive to Bures Church and turn left on to an unclassified road SP 'Nayland'. Follow the Stour Valley for 3¾ miles to reach a right turn that can be taken as a short detour to Wissington.

WISSINGTON, Suffolk

Many people come to this attractive village to see the famous series of 13th-century wall paintings in St Mary's Church, a well preserved Norman building with later additions. Close by is an 18th-century house built by architect Sir John Soane.

On the main route, continue with the 'Nayland' road and in 1 mile meet staggered crossroads. Drive across on to the B1087 to enter Nayland at the start of Dedham Vale.

The Chapel Barn near Bures preserves several alabaster tomb chests.

NAYLAND, Suffolk

Alston Court, an attractive half-timbered courtyard house, is one of many 15th-century buildings to be seen in this River Stour village. John Constable painted the altar piece in the local church.

DEDHAM VALE, Essex

This area of outstanding natural beauty stretches from Nayland village to Flatford Mill, and is familiar to many people through the paintings of John Constable.

From Nayland continue on the B1087 to reach Stoke-by-Nayland.

STOKE-BY-NAYLAND, Suffolk

Visitors who are also lovers of John Constable's paintings will recognise the lofty 120ft tower of Stoke-by-Nayland's handsome church. Entry to the south end of the building is through magnificently carved doors, and inside are many notable monuments. Close by are the timber-framed Maltings and the Guildhall, both superb survivals from the 16th century.

Leave Stoke-by-Nayland on the B1068 'Ipswich' road and drive to Thorington Street.

THORINGTON STREET, Suffolk

Early 18th-century additions are evident in the mainly 16th-century structure of Thorington Hall (NT), a fine house that completely dominates this tiny village.

Continue on the B1068 and later cross the River Brett to enter Higham.

HIGHAM, Suffolk

Attractive St Mary's Church and 19th-century Higham Hall preside over this pleasant little village, which has a number of good timber-framed cottages.

Leave Higham on the B1068 and after 2 miles meet the A12. Turn left then in ¼ mile turn left again onto the B1070 'East Bergholt' road. Continue for 1 mile into East Bergholt.

EAST BERGHOLT, Suffolk

In 1776 the great landscape painter John Constable was born here, and speaking of the area he once said 'These scenes made me a painter.' Clustered round the 14th-century church are mellow Elizabethan cottages set amid beautiful gardens. Separated from the church but close by is a unique timber-framed belfry. Stour, home of the late Randolph Churchill, stands near by in the gardens which he created (open).

Drive to East Bergholt Church and bear right to reach Flatford Mill.

FLATFORD MILL, Suffolk

Perhaps the most famous and admired of all Constable's landscape subjects, Flatford Mill (NT) is picturesquely situated on the River Stour and serves as a field-study centre. Both it and nearby Willy Lott's Cottage (NT) attract legions of artists every summer.

Leave Flatford Mill and bear right along a one-way street. After ⅔ mile meet crossroads and turn right. Continue for ⅓ mile to meet the B1070 'Manningtree' road, then drive forward and continue for another 1⅓ miles to the A137. Turn left here SP 'Ipswich' to reach Brantham.

BRANTHAM, Suffolk

Inside Brantham Church is an altar-piece with a painting by John Constable.

Leave Brantham on the A137. Continue for 1 mile, reach the Bull Inn, and turn right on to the B1080 'Holbrook' road. Continue to Stutton.

STUTTON, Suffolk

Architecture from many periods survives in the church, and there are a number of notable private houses in the neighbourhood. Among these is Stutton Hall (not open), which dates from 1553.

Drive forward for 1 mile and pass through the grounds of the Royal Hospital School.

ROYAL HOSPITAL SCHOOL, Suffolk

An impressive tower with a white stone pinnacle that can be seen for miles around marks the location of the Royal Hospital School, which was founded in 1694 for the sons of sea-men. The present group of buildings was occupied when the school moved from Greenwich in the early part of this century.

From the school continue for ⅓ mile and turn right on to an unclassified road for Harkstead.

Dark-framed and pastel-tinted weavers' houses line Kersey's pretty main-street, which runs down to a small ford.

HARKSTEAD, Suffolk

Notable features of this solitary 14th-century church are its contemporary tower and fine Easter Sepulchre. The building as a whole is an interesting example of medieval architecture.

Continue on the winding 'Shotley' road and drive through Erwarton.

ERWARTON, Suffolk

Red-brick almshouses are a striking feature of this pretty village, which also has an Elizabethan hall with a fine gateway.

Leave Erwarton and pass the gatehouse of Erwarton Hall. Continue to Shotley and turn right on to the B1456 for Shotley Gate.

SHOTLEY GATE, Suffolk

Views of the busy shipping traffic into Harwich and Felixstowe can be enjoyed from this promontory. Close by is the former naval training centre HMS Ganges.

Return along the B1456 'Ipswich' road, pass through Chelmondiston, and reach Woolverstone.

The scene at Flatford Mill has changed little from the days when it was the subject of Constable's famous pictures.

WOOLVERSTONE, Suffolk

Imposing Woolverstone Hall, built in the 18th century by William Berners, is beautifully situated overlooking the attractive Orwell estuary. It now houses a school.

Continue along the B1456 beside the River Orwell, then later turn right on to the A137 and drive to Ipswich.

IPSWICH, Suffolk

Modern commercial development has made this major port and agricultural centre into the largest town in Suffolk. In spite of this it has managed to preserve a number of historic buildings.

Leave Ipswich with SP 'Colchester', then join the A1071 'Sudbury' road. Cross the River Gipping and proceed to Hintlesham

HINTLESHAM, Suffolk

The Great Hall was recently owned by the the internationally famous chef Robert Carrier, but is now a Hotel. The building itself has an Elizabethan core behind a fine Georgian acade and features a drawing room with an exceptional filigreed plaster ceiling. Inside the local church are notable monuments to the Timperley family.

Leave Hintlesham on the A1071 and return to Hadleigh.

HEREFORD, Herefs & Worcs

Once the capital of Saxon West Mercia, this ancient town is at the centre of a rich agricultural district and is especially noted for the production of cider. There has been a cathedral in the city since the 7th century, but the present building dates mainly from the 12th and shows a variety of later alterations. It is dedicated to St Mary and to St Ethelbert, a king of East Anglia who was murdered near Hereford in AD 794. His tomb later became a famous shrine. Other notable relics in the cathedral are the 14th-century *Mappa Mundi* (Map of the World), King Stephen's 800-year-old chair, the best library of chained books in the country, and many monuments and tombs. Cloisters leading to the ancient Bishop's Palace contain a rare 12th-century timbered hall, and the College of Vicars Choral dates from the 15th century. There is another chained library in All Saints Church. The 11th-century St Peter's Church is the oldest in Hereford. A wealth of half-timbered buildings is preserved here, including the outstanding early-15th-century Old House, now a museum. In Widemarsh Street is the St John Coningsby Museum, which incorporates a 12th-century chapel and hall with 17th-century almshouses. Preserved main-line steam locomotives are maintained at the Bulmers Railway Centre. The lovely Wye flows under the ancient Wye Bridge, past the cathedral grounds and castle ruins. Also to be seen are the Museum and Art Gallery, the Churchill Gardens Museum in a fine Regency house, the Cider Museum with a reconstruction of a cider factory, and the Waterworks Museum containing a collection of pumping engines. There are also some remains of the medieval city walls.

Leave Hereford on the A438 SP 'Brecon'. After 5 miles reach The Weir on the left.

THE WEIR, Herefs & Worcs

Fine views of the Wye and the Black Mountains can be enjoyed from this steeply sloping riverside garden (NT, open). The house (not open) dates from the 18th century.

Continue to Letton, with occasional views of the Wye, and 1¾ miles beyond the village turn left and pass through Willersley and Winforton. Proceed to Whitney-on-Wye.

Follow the Wye to enter the Welsh county of Powys. Continue, with views of the Black Mountains to the left, to reach the outskirts of Clyro.

CLYRO, Powys

Francis Kilvert the diarist was curate of this quiet little village between 1865 and 1872. His notes and records paint a highly detailed picture of life in the Radnorshire hills during the 19th century, and have been the subject of a television series. The local church was rebuilt in 1853 but

RIVERS OF THE SOUTH

After looping from its mid-Wales source the magical Wye swings in great curves down to Hay, Ross, and the cathedral city of Hereford. West of the Wye the River Dore flows gently through its fertile valley to join the Monnow, a Wye tributary overlooked by ruined border fortresses.

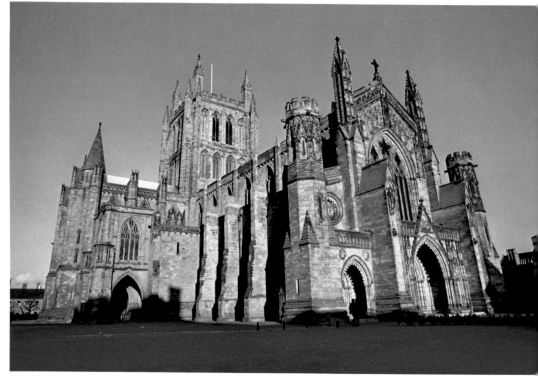

Hereford Cathedral's massive sandstone tower was designed and built at the beginning of the 14th century.

retains some of its original 13th-century structure. There are slight remains of a Norman castle, and to the east, of a Roman fort.

Turn left on to the B4351, shortly cross the Wye, then turn right into Hay-on-Wye.

HAY-ON-WYE, Powys

Book lovers are in their element here, for Hay has more than its fair share of book shops. Narrow streets winding through the old town are full of fascinating small shops, and on market day are alive with bustling activity. William de Braose, one of the most ruthless of the Marcher Lords, built a castle here to replace one burned down by King John. Folk hero Owain Glyndwr destroyed the later castle during the 15th century, but a fine gateway, the keep, and parts of the wall remain. Alongside the ruins is a Jacobean house.

At the Blue Boar Inn turn left on the B4348 'Peterchurch' road and re-enter England. After 2¼ miles turn right SP 'Ross' and continue to the edge of Dorstone.

Winding its way from its mountain source, the River Wye sweeps in great loops into the rolling farm and pasture lands at How Caple.

DORSTONE,
Herefs & Worcs

Thomas de Brito, one of the four knights who murdered Thomas à Becket in Canterbury Cathedral, founded the local church. Although largely rebuilt in 1889 it retains a 13th-century tower arch. A lane from Dorstone leads 1 mile north to Arthur's Stone, a prehistoric tomb (AM) dating from *c* 2000 BC. The view from here is magnificent.

Continue and in ¼ mile at crossroads turn right. Drive along the Golden Valley to Peterchurch.

PETERCHURCH, Herefs & Worcs
Situated in the heart of the lush Golden Valley, Peterchurch has a large and exceptionally well-preserved Norman church. A wooden panel representing a fish with a chain round its neck hangs over the south door. Wellbrook Manor (not open) is one of the best examples of a 14th-century hall-house in the country.

After 2 miles turn right on to the B4347 SP 'Pontrilas', still following the River Dore; later enter Abbey Dore.

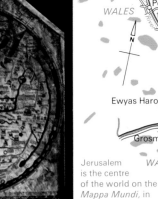

ABBEY DORE, Herefs & Worcs
The meadows and orchards of the Golden Valley surround this little village, which is famous for its parish church. In 1174 an abbey was founded here, but after the Dissolution of the Monasteries its buildings were neglected. In 1633 Lord Scudamore commissioned the brilliant craftsman John Abel to rebuild the church. Much of the original fabric was restored; additions by Abel included the fine wooden screen. Court Gardens (open) across the river have 4 acres of walled and river gardens and exotic plants.
Continue to Ewyas Harold.

EWYAS HAROLD, Herefs & Worcs
An important Norman castle stood here during the 13th century, but only the mound has survived to the present day. The church, partly rebuilt in 1868, retains its impressive 13th-century tower.
Bear left over a river bridge. After ¾ mile cross the A465 and the River Dore, then turn right SP 'Monmouth'. After 1½ miles turn right to re-enter Wales and ascend to Grosmont.

GROSMONT, Gwent
This small old-world town, set amid beautiful scenery by the River Monnow, was a borough until 1860. Inside its massively towered church is a huge, flat-faced stone knight of ancient origin. The castle (AM) here was one of 3 erected in the vicinity to protect the border between England and Wales, the others being Skenfrith and White Castle. It is quite likely that the first on this site was built as early as

c 1070, but it was largely rebuilt during the reign of Henry III. Owain Glyndwr, the Welsh partisan, took the castle in 1410 but was ousted by Harry Monmouth (who was later to become King Henry V). This was Glyndwr's last recorded battle.

Continue through pleasant hill country and after 4¼ miles turn left on to the B4521 SP 'Ross'. Reach the edge of Skenfrith.

The craggy ruins of Skenfrith Castle stand near the River Monnow.

Jerusalem is the centre of the world on the *Mappa Mundi*, in Hereford Cathedral.

SKENFRITH, Gwent
Remains of 13th-century Skenfrith Castle (AM, NT), one of a trio built to defend the English border, include a central keep enclosed by a four-sided curtain wall and a moat. In its western range is a flight of stone steps leading down to a central room which contains a fireplace with beautifully carved capitals. The local church also dates from the 13th century and has an impressive partially-timbered tower.
Cross the River Monnow, re-enter England, and after 1¾ miles at Broad Oak crossroads turn right on to an unclassified road SP 'Welsh Newton'. After 1¼ miles reach the entrance to Pembridge Castle.

PEMBRIDGE CASTLE. Herefs & Worcs
Dating originally from the 13th

century, this castle (not open) has a 16th-century chapel and a 17th-century hall. Some of the structure was restored during this century, and the buildings are partly used by a local farmer.

Continue and in 1 mile reach the A466, and turn right into Welsh Newton. Take the next turning left on to an unclassified road SP 'Llangarren' and after 1¾ miles turn right to enter Llangrove. Continue and descend into Whitchurch.

WHITCHURCH, Herefs & Worcs
Roman remains were found on the outskirts of this village in the 19th century. The Church of St Dubricius is set beside the River Wye and contains a Norman font. Nearby are the Jubilee Maze and Museum of Mazes.

Follow SP 'Ross' to join the A40 and continue through Pencraig, with occasional views of the Wye. Later reach Wilton.

WILTON, Herefs & Worcs
The splendid bridge and nearby buildings here are described in tour from Ross-on-Wye.
At the roundabout take 3rd exit B4260 into Ross.

Ross-on-Wye is dominated by its 13th-century church.

Prehistoric Arthur's Stone is situated near Dorstone.

ROSS ON WYE, Herefs & Worcs
A handsome market hall standing in the centre of this town is just one of many attractive buildings preserved here. Overlooking all is the fine 13th-century church.

Follow SP 'Ledbury' and after 1 mile at roundabout take 2nd exit on to the A449. At the next roundabout take 1st exit SP 'Worcester'. After 1¾ miles branch left to join the B4224 SP 'Hereford'. In ¼ mile turn left and proceed to Fownhope.

FOWNHOPE, Herefs & Worcs
Wooded hills, leafy lanes with grassy verges, and old timbered buildings exist in a magical combination in and around this picturesque Wye-side village. The church has a Norman tower and preserves a contemporary tympanum which depicts the Virgin and Child.

Continue to Mordiford

MORDIFORD, Herefs & Worcs
Parts of the beautiful bridge that spans the Lugg here date from the 14th century. Near by, making a delightful group, are the partly-Norman church and a Georgian rectory. The Palladian mansion of Sufton Court to the north is open occasionally.

Keep left and cross the River Lugg and continue through Hampton Bishop to re-enter Hereford.

FARMLANDS OF SUFFOLK

This corner of rural Suffolk is the England of the romantics, an ideal of pastoral beauty hauntingly captured in the paintings of John Constable. It is a place of rolling meadows and tiny rustic villages, where life moves at an easy pace and the air of timelessness can almost be touched.

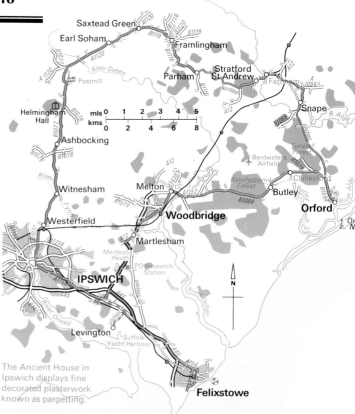

The Ancient House in Ipswich displays fine decorated plasterwork known as pargetting.

This rare old mill on the river Deben at Woodbridge is operated by the rise and fall of water between tides. Records of East Anglian mills worked in this way date back as far as the 12th century.

IPSWICH, Suffolk
Centuries of development have made this major port the largest and one of the most successful towns in Suffolk. It is the main centre of employment in the eastern part of the county, and despite continued expansion has managed to keep many relics of its eventful past intact. A red-brick gateway bearing royal arms survives from the unfinished Cardinal College of St Mary, which was founded by Cardinal Wolsey – a native of the town – in the 16th century. The Ancient or Sparrowe's House of 1567 stands in the Buttermarket and is noted for its exterior decoration of intricate patterns and features carved in plaster, an outstanding example of the East Anglian art of pargetting. Original oak panelling and heavy carved beams can be seen by visitors to the bookshop which it now houses. Close by are the Great White Horse Hotel, which features in Charles Dickens' *Pickwick Papers*, and many old streets lined with well-preserved timber-framed houses. Christchurch Mansion (open) was built by a Tudor merchant and is isolated in an oasis of parkland near the centre of town. It contains fine collections of furniture and paintings. Exhibits relating to local history and wildlife can be seen in the Ipswich Museum of Archaeology and Natural History, which stands in the High Street. The number of good

churches in the town reflects its former importance and prosperity. Among the best are: St Margaret's, with a fine hammerbeam roof; St Peter's, with an impressive black Tournai font; and St Mary-le-Tower, which boasts a lovely pulpit carved by Grinling Gibbons. A remarkable 16th-century Unitarian Meeting House stands in Friar Street.

Leave Ipswich on the A1156 with SP 'Felixstowe' and in 5 miles reach an unclassified right turn leading to Levington. A short detour can be taken to Levington from here.

LEVINGTON, Suffolk
This attractive small village stands on the banks of the Orwell and is the base for the Suffolk Yacht Harbour. Its church dates from the 16th century.

On the main route, continue along the A45 and after 5 miles follow SP 'Town Centre' to enter Felixstowe.

FELIXSTOWE, Suffolk
Towards the end of the 19th century this sheltered spot on the Suffolk coast was developed as a seaside resort. It attracted fashionable society, including the German Kaiser, and acquired a 2-mile length of promenade bordered by delightful flower displays and beautifully tended lawns. Long before this a 16th-century stronghold which became the Landguard Fort (AM) was defending the sea approach to

Harwich. A later period of insecurity this time generated by Napoleon's hold on Europe, resulted in the building of a Martello tower c1810. Felixstowe Dock is an important container port. A modern leisure centre offers all year round entertainment.
Leave Felixstowe on the A45 'Ipswich' road and in 7 miles turn right on to the A12 SP 'Woodbridge' and 'Gt Yarmouth'. After 4 miles reach a roundabout and go forward, passing the Post Office Research Station on Martlesham Heath. In ¾ mile turn right on to the A12 to reach Martlesham.

MARTLESHAM, Suffolk
Martlesham village is picturesquely sited on a creek of the River Deben and features a church with an unusual 7-sided wagon roof. The local Red Lion Inn displays a curious sign that was taken from a Dutch ship in 1672.
Continue on the A12 to the end of Martlesham, drive under a railway bridge, then turn right on to the B1438 to reach Woodbridge.

WOODBRIDGE, Suffolk
Attractive houses of major historical interest surround the old market square round which this port has grown. Many date from the 16th century, and the entire group is centred on the superb Shire Hall, which features work from the 16th to 19th centuries and picturesque Dutch-style gables. Multi-period Woodbridge Church carries a tall, flint-flushwork tower and contains a seven sacrament font. One old mill, a rare example which depends on the tide, is open. The port's status as a busy centre of ocean trade declined a long time ago, but today it is a popular sailing centre with a fine riverside park at Kyson Hill (NT).

From Woodbridge continue on the B1438 to Melton.

MELTON, Suffolk

A small colour-washed brick building known as Friar's Dene was once the village gaol. Melton Church has a handsome tower with an attractive broach spire.

From Melton turn right on to the A1152 SP 'Orford'. Cross the railway line and the River Deben, then bear left and in ¾ mile keep forward on to the B1084. After a short distance enter part of Rendlesham Forest, which contains a picnic site, and continue to Butley.

BUTLEY, Suffolk

An Augustinian priory founded here in 1171 has vanished but its superb 14th-century gatehouse has survived as one of the finest medieval buildings of its kind in Suffolk. Particularly notable are the heraldic designs cut into its stonework.

Leave Butley, remaining on the B1084, then skirt part of Tunstall Forest and pass through Chillesford. In 1¾ miles meet crossroads and turn right to reach Orford.

The finely-preserved postmill at Saxtead Green is typical of many in Suffolk.

ORFORD, Suffolk

In 1165 Henry II built a moat-encircled castle with an 18-sided keep here in an attempt to establish Norman power over the peoples of East Anglia. Today the building (AM) that developed from these early beginnings contains a collection of arms and affords excellent views of the picturesque houses and fishermen's cottages below its walls. On the seaward side of the village the River Alde is separated from the sea by Orford Ness.

ORFORD NESS, Suffolk

This long strip of coastal marshland is occupied by the Orford Ness and Havergate national nature reserve, one of the few places in England where the rare avocet can be seen.

From Orford return along the B1084 and in 1¾ miles drive forward on to the unclassified 'Snape' road. Skirt another part of Tunstall Forest for nearly 4 miles and join the B1069. Pass The Maltings, cross the River Alde, and enter Snape.

Tudor Helmingham Hall's moat is spanned by two drawbridges.

SNAPE, Suffolk

The magnificent Maltings concert hall, built on the site of old maltings where barley was stored prior to export, is the yearly venue for the famous Aldeburgh Music Festival. Its situation on the banks of the River Alde adds an extra dimension to its pleasing architecture. Snape Church houses a richly carved 15th-century font, and close to the village are slight remains of an ancient Benedictine priory.

Leave Snape, continue for ¾ mile, then meet the A1094 'Ipswich' road and turn left. In 2 miles turn left on to the A12 and pass through Farnham for Stratford St Andrew.

STRATFORD ST ANDREW, Suffolk

Close to this pleasant little village is 17th-century Glemham Hall (open), an impressive red-brick mansion standing in 350 acres of beautiful parkland. Inside are panelled rooms appointed with fine paintings and Queen Anne furniture. The village church contains Norman workmanship and houses a 13th-century font.

Remain on the A12 and in 1 mile, at an entrance to Glemham Hall, turn right on to the unclassified 'Parham' road. In a further 1 mile turn right, then in a short distance turn left and continue to Parham.

PARHAM, Suffolk

Tranquilly set in the upper valley of the River Alde, this little village has a church where the village stocks and a beautiful 14th-century screen are preserved. Just to the south-east is 16th-century Moat Hall, a picturesque timber-framed house that is encircled by a moat and nowadays serves as a farm.

Leave Parham on the B1116 and continue to Framlingham.

FRAMLINGHAM, Suffolk

Framlingham's superb Norman castle (AM) was started in 1190 and represented an important advance in castle design. Fragments of the Great Hall are incorporated in picturesque 17th-century almshouses, and the towers carry distinctive Tudor chimneys. Monuments to the Howard family, who took possession in the 15th century, can be seen in the local church. The town itself is a historic market centre with many old houses and a well-known college.

From Framlingham follow the B1119 SP 'Stowmarket' to reach Saxtead Green.

Thames barges moored on the Orwell estuary near Ipswich are reminiscent of a maritime past when the elegance of sail was commonplace.

SAXTEAD GREEN, Suffolk

One of the finest postmills (AM) in Suffolk with its wooden superstructure and brick round house stands here. Stones and machinery inside are in excellent working order. It was first recorded in 1706 and substantially rebuilt at least twice during its working life. Today it stands 46ft high and carries sails with a span of almost 55ft.

Leave Saxtead Green on the A1120 'Stowmarket' road and continue to Earl Soham.

EARL SOHAM, Suffolk

Old cottages and Georgian houses face rows of allotments across a long street in this somewhat rambling village. The local church carries a 15th-century tower and contains several good monuments.

Drive to the end of Earl Soham village and turn left, then in 3 miles turn left again on to the B1077 'Ipswich' road. In 1 mile pass another fine windmill on the left, then in a further 1¼ miles reach Helmingham Hall on the right.

HELMINGHAM HALL, Suffolk

Every night the two drawbridges that span the moat to this lovely manor house are raised, though more for the sake of tradition than against rival lords or jealous monarchs. Home of the Tollemache family since the 16th century, the hall has Georgian additions with crenallations by John Nash and stands amid beautiful gardens (open) in an ancient deer park. More than 500 red and fallow deer share the estate with herds of Highland cattle. Visitors may recognise parts of the grounds from John Constable's great landscape painting *Helmingham Dell*.

Continue to Ashbocking.

ASHBOCKING, Suffolk

The medieval church in this village carries a 16th-century tower which is contemporary with Ashbocking Hall, an attractive timber-framed building near by.

Continue to Witnesham.

WITNESHAM, Suffolk

Situated near a tributary of the River Deben, this peaceful little village has an Elizabethan hall and a good church. The hall includes a few Victorian additions and the church, which contains an 8-sided font, has an excellent hammerbeam roof.

Continue on the B1077 to Westerfield.

WESTERFIELD, Suffolk

Westerfield Hall is a 17th-century building with attractive Dutch gables. The local church dates from c1300 and features a nave window in which pieces of a Norman doorway have been re-used. The roof in both the chancel and nave is of hammerbeam construction.

Leave Westerfield and drive through built-up areas to re-enter Ipswich.

KIDDERMINSTER, Herefs & Worcs

Carpets were the foundation of Kidderminster's prosperity, and the carpet-weaving industry that was introduced here in 1735 continues to be a major concern. The town's architecture is homely rather than distinguished, although handsome St Mary's Church and the cluster of Georgian buildings in Church Street have much to offer the eye.

Leave Kidderminster on the A456 'Leominster' road and shortly reach the West Midlands Safari Park.

WEST MIDLANDS SAFARI PARK, Herefs & Worcs

Giraffes, elephants, and many other exotic beasts can be seen in the 200 acres of this interesting wildlife park. Other attractions include a pets' corner for the children, a 'boat safari', bird gardens, and a complete dolphinarium.

Cross the River Severn via Telford's bridge and enter Bewdley.

BEWDLEY, Herefs & Worcs

Telford's fine bridge spanning the Severn at Bewdley was built in 1795. Severnside is a beautiful street lined with 17th- and 18th-century houses. An elegant parade of Georgian and earlier buildings line both sides of Load Street, which is eventually closed off by a large Georgian house and 18th -century St Anne's Church. Bewdley's more distant history is represented by several excellent half-timbered buildings. Past industries of the town are demonstrated at the museum housed in 18th-century buildings called The Shambles, and

ANCIENT TOWNS

From Kidderminster this tour visits the handsome Georgian streets of Bewdley, the purpose-built canal town of Stourport, and delightful Ludlow – an ancient gem in the English landscape. Scattered between are villages, each one unique in its character.

a craft centre in Lax Lane specialises in brassrubbing. Overlooking the town is Tickenhill House, and period mansion refaced in 1738 and incorporating a royal palace.

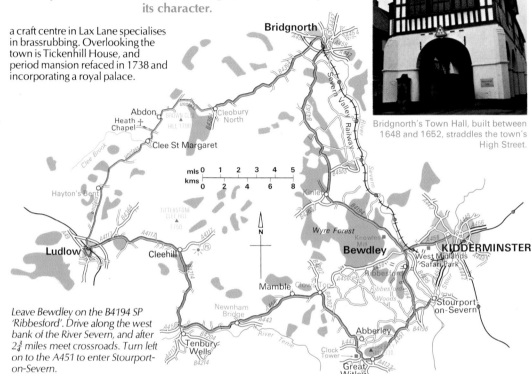

Bridgnorth's Town Hall, built between 1648 and 1652, straddles the town's High Street.

Leave Bewdley on the B4194 SP 'Ribbesford'. Drive along the west bank of the River Severn, and after 2¾ miles meet crossroads. Turn left on to the A451 to enter Stourport-on-Severn.

STOURPORT-ON-SEVERN, Herefs & Worcs

After the opening of the Staffordshire and Worcestershire Canal, built by the engineer James Brindley in 1766, Stourport became a major canal port. It has survived to the present day as the only example of a purpose-built canal town in England.

Return along the A451 SP 'Great Witley' and recross the River Severn. After 4½ miles reach Great Witley.

GREAT WITLEY, Herefs & Worcs

Entry into Great Witley's Chapel of St Michael transports the visitor from the English countryside to some remote part of Italy. Rich rococo decoration completely alien to rural Britain assaults the eye – not unpleasantly – from skilfully-patterned walls and painted ceiling panels. Close to the chapel, which was consecrated in 1735, is the ruined shell of 17th-century and later Witley Court.

At the end of the village turn right on to the A443. SP 'Ludlow'. After 1 mile branch right on to the B4202 SP 'Cleobury Mortimer'. Shortly reach the edge of Abberley.

Winter holds the canal basin at Stourport-on-Severn in an icy grip. A Georgian warehouse stands in the background.

ABBERLEY, Herefs & Worcs

Overlooked by 930ft Abberley Hill, this peaceful little village is centred on the ruins of a Norman church that was replaced by a handsome Victorian successor. The clock tower of Abberley Hall is visible for miles.

Continue, and gradually ascend to Clows Top for good all-round views. Meet crossroads and turn left on to the A456 SP 'Leominster'. Descend with distant views into Mamble.

MAMBLE, Herefs & Worcs

Mamble's church dates almost entirely from the beginning of the 13th century and carries an unusual timber bell turret.

Continue to Newnham Bridge and turn right then follow the Teme Valley to the edge of Tenbury Wells.

TENBURY WELLS, Herefs & Worcs

Mineral springs discovered here in 1839 brought instant fame as a spa town to Tenbury, and the Pump Room and Baths from this period can still be seen. 'Taking the waters' has long since ceased to be fashionable, and nowadays the town fulfils a quiet rôle as a little market centre for the surrounding countryside. Half-timbered buildings make a pleasant contrast with two fine churches dating from the 19th century.

Take 2nd main turning on to the B4214 SP 'Cleehill' and proceed through hilly country to Cleehill.

CLEEHILL, Salop

Just east of Cleehill on the A4117 is an AA viewpoint which affords superb views to the east and south. North is 1,750ft Titterstone Clee Hill, whose bare slopes rise to a summit crowned by the vast 'golf ball' of a satellite tracking station.

Turn left on to the A4117 and descend then cross the bypass into Ludlow.

LUDLOW, Salop   SO57

Ludlow is a latterday Camelot on the banks of the Corve and Teme, among the gentle Shropshire hills. High above the town's roof tops soars the 135ft tower of the parish church, while on the ground the lovely River Teme adds its own enchantment to the picture-book quality of Ludlow Castle. The church, mainly of 15th-century date, is the largest in the county and preserves contemporary choir stalls. The ashes of poet A E Housman are kept here. Near by are the beautiful black-and-white Reader's House (open on application), and the 17th-century Feathers Hotel. These are possibly the best of many half-timbered buildings preserved in the town. Georgian architecture testifies to the continued popularity of Ludlow and is epitomized in the elegant Butter Cross, which now houses a museum. Broad Street, lined with many fine dwellings from the same period, extends from the Butter Cross to Ludlow's sole surviving medieval gate, the Broad Gate. The town's earliest structure is, of course, the castle. From as early as 1085 this occupied a strategic position in the contentious England/Wales border country known as the Marcher Lands. The town was actually planned round the castle in the 12th century. John Milton's 'Comus' was given its first performance here in 1634. Ludford Bridge (AM) spans the Teme and is of medieval origin.

To leave Ludlow return along the A4117 'Kidderminster' road and pass under a railway bridge. Immediately turn left into unclassified Fishmore Road. After 1 mile branch right SP 'Hayton's Bent'. Ascend, with views to Corve Dale, Wenlock Edge, and the Clee Hills, and follow SP 'Clee St Margaret' to reach that village.

CLEE ST MARGARET, Salop

Remotely set in the Clee Hills by the Clee Brook, this little village is built mainly of stone and is centred on a church with a Norman nave.

Cross a ford and turn left SP 'Abdon'. After ½ mile meet crossroads; a detour (SP 'Bouldon') may be taken left from here across pleasantly rural Shropshire countryside to visit Heath Chapel.

Scenes such as this, of the steam-operated Severn Valley Railway, were once commonplace throughout Britain.

HEATH CHAPEL, Salop

This simple, barn-like building stands on its own in a field and is a perfect example of Norman ecclesiastical architecture. It contains a Norman font and various furnishings dating from the 17th century.

Continue on the main route to Abdon.

ABDON, Salop

Bracken-covered slopes rise from this village to Abdon Burf, a tract of rough country that culminates in the dominating eminence of 1,790ft Brown Clee Hill. Excellent views across to Wenlock Edge are afforded by this high region.

The impressive remains of Ludlow's castle are reflected in the waters of the River Teme near 15th-century Dinham Bridge.

Turn right SP 'Ditton Priors' and after 1 mile turn left then in ¾ mile bear right SP 'Cleobury North'. Skirt the north side of Brown Clee Hill, and after 1½ miles turn left and descend to a T-junction. Turn right and continue for ½ mile, then turn left on to the B4364 SP 'Bridgnorth'. Enter Cleobury North.

CLEOBURY NORTH, Salop   SO68

Wooded Burwarton Park adds much to the charm of this village, which boasts a large and picturesque Norman church that was carefully restored by architect Sir Gilbert Scott in the 19th century.

Continue on the B4364 to the

outskirts of Bridgnorth, then turn right on to the A458 to enter the town.

BRIDGNORTH, Salop

Shropshire has more than its fair share of lovely old towns, and Bridgnorth vies with the best of them. It is divided into two parts — Upper Town and Lower Town — by a steep ridge which is negotiated by a twisty road, several flights of steps, and a funicular railway with a breathtaking gradient of 1 in 2. In Lower Town is Bishop Percy's House, a fine half-timbered building of 1580 which is possibly the oldest structure in Bridgnorth. Upper Town is on the site of the original settlement and though much of it burned down during the Civil War the High Street is still straddled by its picturesque town hall (AM). The half-timbered upper storey of this building was made from a barn after the old town hall became a battle casualty. Many fine inns can be found in the High Street as it leads to the ancient North Gate, and at the other end are the elegant Georgian houses of East Castle Street. A precariously leaning tower (AM) is all that remains of Bridgnorth Castle. Nearby St Mary Magdalene's Church was built by engineer and architect Thomas Telford in 1794, and St Leonard's Church stands at the heart of a charming mixture of buildings dotted among grassy verges. The Hermitage (AM) is one of several local caves inhabited until fairly recent times. The station and engine shed at the northern terminus of the Severn Valley Railway provide much interest. East of the town on the Stourbridge road the Midland Motor Museum has over 90 exhibits.

THE SEVERN VALLEY RAILWAY, Salop

Steam locomotives operate between Bridgnorth and Kidderminster over one of Britain's best preserved railways, following the Severn Valley and providing a mobile viewpoint through the beautiful countryside of the area. Trains run most months in the year.

Leave Bridgnorth on the B4364 'Cleobury Mortimer' road and drive to Kinlet. Turn left on to the B4363 SP 'Bewdley', then shortly meet a T-junction and turn left on to the B4194. Continue through Wyre Forest.

WYRE FOREST, Salop, Herefs & Worcs

This one-time royal hunting forest covers an extensive area of mixed heath, scrub, and woodland. During the spring its many wild cherry trees make a picture of white blossom, and in summer the forest is a great attraction to walkers and picnickers. Knowles Mill, a National Trust property set in an orchard, stands close by off the B4194.

Enter Bewdley and turn left for the return to Kidderminster.

SALTINGS ON THE WASH

Along the sweeping coastline of the Wash are wide sandy bays backed by wild salt marshes populated by wildlife suited to the open surroundings. Here and there the flint tower of a medieval village church breaks the skyline, providing a landmark for travellers on both land and sea.

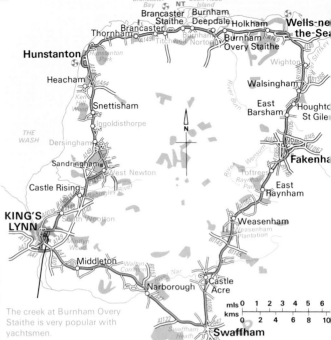

The creek at Burnham Overy Staithe is very popular with yachtsmen.

KING'S LYNN, Norfolk

Two markets were founded here in Norman times, medieval merchants came here to build warehouses on the River Ouse, and 20th-century industry has continued the town's long history of commercial significance. Everywhere are survivals from periods that the settlement has grown through, and its medieval buildings are some of the finest in the country. Traces of the ancient walls show how the town has expanded since the troubled times in which they were built, and the superb Hanseatic Warehouse of 1428 recalls full-sailed barques laden with exotic goods. To complement the two market places are two guildhalls, both of which date from the early 15th century. The biggest of these (NT) is the largest medieval guildhall extant and is now used as a theatre. The other contains old town regalia, including a 14th-century vessel known as King John's Cup. Both the last-mentioned building and the much more recent Town Hall of 1895 display a striking flint-chequerwork design. The superb Custom House, perhaps the most outstanding building in the town, was built by architect Henry Bell while he held office as mayor in 1683. Many other of the town's old buildings have ancient roots but have been changed over the centuries. Clifton House dates originally from the 14th century but has later additions; Hampton Court shows period work from the 14th to 18th centuries; and Dutch-gabled Thoresby College of c1500 now reflects the tastes of the 17th century. The huge parish church contains two outstanding memorial brasses that are the biggest and most famous in England. Red Mount Chapel of c1485 is an octagonal building with beautiful fan vaulting.

Leave King's Lynn by the A47 'Swaffham' road and continue to Middleton.

MIDDLETON, Norfolk

Major Everard-Hutton, one of the famous Six Hundred who fought at Balaclava, is commemorated by a memorial in the local church. Some 3 miles north west is Middleton Tower, a splendid red-brick gatehouse of mainly 19th-century date.

Pass Walton Common, then cross the River Nar to enter Narborough.

NARBOROUGH, Norfolk

Several fine brasses and a standing effigy can be seen in the local church.

Continue, and later pass Swaffham Heath to reach Swaffham.

Dutch influence is evident in King's Lynn's charming Custom House.

SWAFFHAM, Norfolk

Legend tells of the 'Pedlar of Swaffham', who travelled to London to throw himself into the Thames but was dissuaded by a man he met on London Bridge. This stranger related a dream in which he found treasure in a remote village garden – a garden that the pedlar recognised as his own. He hastened home to find two pots of gold; an image of the pedlar is now incorporated in the town sign. The triangular market place has a domed rotunda built by the Earl of Oxford in 1783 as a market cross. Features of the local church include a splendid angel-carved double-hammerbeam roof and a fine 16th-century west tower.

Leave Swaffham on the A1065 'Cromer' road. In 2¾ miles turn left on to an unclassified road for Castle Acre.

CASTLE ACRE, Norfolk

This aptly-named village lies within the outer bailey of an 11th-century castle, of which only the earthworks and a 13th-century gateway remain. Impressive ruins of an 11th-century Cluniac priory, including fine Norman arcading (AM) and a Tudor gatehouse, can be seen near by.

Continue through the village and turn right SP 'Newton'. Rejoin the A1065 'Cromer' road and drive to Weasenham.

WEASENHAM, Norfolk

Prehistoric barrows in all shapes and sizes, including bell, bowl, disc, and saucer types, can be seen in the countryside round Weasenham Plantation.

Continue to East Raynham.

EAST RAYNHAM, Norfolk

Raynham Hall, a magnificent 17th-century building which has been ascribed partly to Inigo Jones, was once the home of the agricultural innovator nicknamed Turnip Townshend.

In 2¼ miles turn right SP 'Town Centre' for Fakenham.

FAKENHAM, Norfolk

This attractive market town dates from Saxon times and was a Royal Manor until the 17th century. Its Market Place has two old coaching inns, both showing traces of earlier work behind Georgian façades, and the parish church has a commanding 15th-century tower.

From Fakenham town centre follow SP 'King's Lynn' to join the A148. In ¼ mile turn right on to the B1105 SP 'Walsingham' and descend into East Barsham.

EAST BARSHAM, Norfolk
East Barsham is known for its brick and terracotta manor house, a splendid example of early Tudor work. Fine chimneys typical of the style rise high above the rooftops, and the approach is guarded by an imposing two-storeyed gatehouse.

Continue for 1 mile to Houghton St Giles.

HOUGHTON ST GILES, Norfolk
On the far side of the Stiffkey river, about 1 mile south west of this attractive village, is the last in a chain of wayside chapels which once lined the Walsingham Way. It is known as the Slipper Chapel because pilgrims to the shrine of Our Lady at Walsingham would remove their shoes here before completing their journey barefoot. It is now the official Roman Catholic Shrine of Our Lady.

Continue to Walsingham, also known as Little Walsingham.

The legendary Pedlar of Swaffham is commemorated by the town sign.

WALSINGHAM, Norfolk
The shrine at Walsingham, a place of paramount importance to the pilgrims of the middle ages, was founded in the 11th century. Virtually every English king from Richard I to Henry VIII came here, and the last-named had the shrine robbed when he dissolved the monasteries. In the 19th century the pilgrimages were revived, and a new Shrine of Our Lady was built for the Anglican Church in the early part of the 20th century. Remains of what was once a giant concourse of buildings date mainly from the 13th and 14th centuries, and include the superb east wall of the priory.

Continue on the B1105 'Wells' road and skirt Wighton to meet the A149. Turn left, then right, with SP 'The Beach'. Enter Wells-next-the-Sea.

WELLS-NEXT-THE-SEA, Norfolk
Old houses and the picturesque quayside make a charming group in this small resort and port. Bathing may be enjoyed in a nearby creek.

Leave the resort on the A149 'Hunstanton' road and drive to Holkham.

The Marble Hall in the Palladian mansion of Holkham exemplifies William Kent's lavish style.

HOLKHAM, Norfolk
Holkham Hall (open), a vast Palladian mansion, is one of the show-pieces of the county. The present house was rebuilt in the 18th century to plans by William Kent, who also designed much of the furniture to be seen inside. Experts consider the entrance into the wonderful alabaster hall to show Kent's genius at its peak, and all the rooms are sumptuously decorated in the fashion of the day. An impressive art collection is displayed in the house, and the library has an excellent collection of 18th-century books. The lake-watered grounds were laid out by Capability Brown in 1762.

Continue to Burnham Overy Staithe.

BURNHAM OVERY STAITHE, Norfolk
Close to this tiny village are a water mill (NT) and tower windmill (NT), both in a good state of preservation. Neither is open to the public at time of publication.

After a short distance cross the River Burn and continue to Burnham Deepdale.

BURNHAM DEEPDALE, Norfolk
Inside the local church, which carries a rare Saxon round tower, is an outstanding Norman font.

Continue to Brancaster Staithe.

BRANCASTER STAITHE, Norfolk
A boat service operates from here to Scolt Head Island, where there is a bird sanctuary (NT) and nature reserve.

Continue for ½ mile to Brancaster.

BRANCASTER, Norfolk
This one-time Roman station is now a golfing resort. A lane leads from the church to a pebble beach which, though not as attractive as its large sandy neighbour, is far safer for bathing.

Continue through Titchwell to Thornham.

THORNHAM, Norfolk
A rectangular earthwork on a slope overlooking the waters of the Wash here was excavated in 1960, revealing the remains of an iron-age village. The complex, thought to date from cAD40, measures 133 by 175ft and includes a defensive ditch cut into the soft chalk.

Drive through Old Hunstanton and ½ mile farther turn right on to an unclassified road SP 'Sea Front'. Continue into Hunstanton.

A peaceful atmosphere pervades Wells-next-the-Sea.

HUNSTANTON, Norfolk
Hunstanton is the largest seaside resort in west Norfolk and the only East Anglian coastal town to face west. Great stretches of sand are backed by cliffs of mixed chalk and sand rising 60ft above the beach.

Pass the Pier, bear right into Westgate, and in ½ mile meet a roundabout. Take the 1st exit SP 'King's Lynn', then meet the main road and turn right on to the A149 to reach the outskirts of Heacham.

HEACHAM, Norfolk
Pocahontas, the Red Indian princess who married John Rolfe at Heacham Hall in 1614, is commemorated in both the village sign and a memorial in the local church. Her son founded a line which was to include the wife of US president Woodrow Wilson.

Continue to Snettisham.

SNETTISHAM, Norfolk
One of the finest churches in Norfolk stands here. Its lofty spire can be seen for many miles across the flat local countryside, and its superb west front is reminiscent of Peterborough Cathedral. Also in the village is attractive Old Hall, an 18th-century house with Dutch gables.

Continue through Ingoldisthorpe to Dersingham. Turn left on to the B1440 SP 'Sandringham'. Ascend through wooded country and in ½ mile pass the gates of Sandringham House.

SANDRINGHAM, Norfolk
Included in this 7,000-acre estate, owned by the Royal Family, are a 19th-century house and museum (open), the farms and woodlands of 7 parishes, and a 300-acre country park. The park church is of exceptional note and contains an organ that was the last gift of King Edward VII. Many superb royal memorials enrich the interior, and the nave is roofed in English oak.

In 1 mile turn right on to the B1439 into West Newton. Continue to the main road and turn left to rejoin the A149. In 1 mile turn right on to an unclassified road for Castle Rising.

CASTLE RISING, Norfolk
The sea has long withdrawn from this one-time port, but the Norman castle (AM) built to protect it still stands. It occupies a Roman site and has a great keep in which a fascinating sequence of rooms, galleries, and minor stairs are reached by a single dramatic staircase. The local Church of St Lawrence is famous for its Norman west front, which has a fine doorway on the lower level and houses a richly carved square font on a circular shaft. Bede House or Trinity Hospital dates from the 17th century and is an almshouse charity for elderly ladies.

Continue to South Wootton, meet traffic signals, and drive over crossroads. After another 1¼ miles meet a T-junction, turn right, and return to King's Lynn.

LEICESTER, Leics

Situated on the River Soar and Grand Union Canal, this county town and university city has been a thriving centre at least since Roman times. Relics from its very early history include Roman pavements under the former Central Station and below a shop fronting St Nicholas' Church. Other traces of the occupation have been found at the Jewry Wall site, including remains of 2nd-century Roman baths and the wall itself. Various relics from ancient times to the middle ages can be seen in the Jewry Wall Museum and site. The Leicestershire Museum and Art Gallery stands in New Walk, a delightful promenade of elegant houses, mature trees, and carefully preserved Victorian lamp-posts. An ancient city gateway known as The Magazine houses the museum of the Royal Leicestershire Regiment, and the Newarke Houses Museum offers a vivid insight into social history from the 16th century to Victorian times. It is housed in an interesting old Chantry House of 1511, and its immediate neighbour dates from c1600. Wygston's House Museum of Costume is laid out in a 15th-century house, and the Leicestershire Museum of Technology preserves various items of industrial interest in the apt surroundings of Abbey Pumping Station. Among many interesting churches in Leicester is St Martin's, which stands on a Saxon site that was previously occupied by a Roman temple and now enjoys cathedral status. It was largely rebuilt in the 19th century and has a well proportioned tower and spire. Good Norman work is retained by the Church of St Mary de Castro. The city's Guildhall is a fine late 14th-century building with magnificent timbering, and the 17th-century Court House incorporates fragments of a Norman hall. There is also a Norman castle, but very little of it survives. Close to the university is a fine public park and cricket ground, and the University Botanic Gardens are of note.

Leave Leicester on the A46 'Newark' road and after 3 miles branch left on to the B667 into Thurmaston.

THE CRAGS OF CHARNWOOD

Charnwood Forest is a huge upthrusting of rock whose wind-blasted heaths dominate miles of Leicestershire's gentle farming country. Now treeless and pitted with great quarries, it is an eerie place where open moorland flows round fascinating outcrops of rock and the lines of ancient forts.

The small brook at Rearsby is spanned by a quaint medieval bridge.

THURMASTON, Leics

This large suburb of Leicester stands on the east bank of the River Soar and has a number of developing industries. In its older quarter is a fine church with distinctive 13th century nave arcades.

Continue through the town on the B667, reach a roundabout at the far end, and take the 2nd exit on to the A607 SP 'Melton'. Drive through Syston.

SYSTON, Leics

The tower buttresses of Syston Church display curious sculptures of a man and two women, possibly representations of the founder and his wives. Many of the houses in the area are brick-built structures of 18th-century date.

Continue to Rearsby.

REARSBY, Leics

Situated on a tributary of the River Wreake, this village has a good 13th- and 14th-century church with an unusual drum-shaped font. To the east of the church is an attractive 6-arched medieval bridge, and a gabled house of 1661 stands in Mill Road.

Turn right on to the B674 for Gaddesby.

GADDESBY, Leics

One of the largest and most beautiful of Leicestershire's many lovely village churches can be seen here. Its south side is richly decorated with stone carvings, and the south aisle is a showpiece. Inside is an equestrian statue of Colonel Cheney at Waterloo.

Charnwood Forest's windswept character is well appreciated from Beacon Hill.

Stay on the B674, and within 1 mile turn left on to an unclassified road to Great Dalby. Meet a T-junction and turn right into Great Dalby. Pass the village church, turn right on to the B6047, and proceed to Twyford. Turn left on to the unclassified 'Burrough' road and proceed to Burrough-on-the-Hill.

BURROUGH-ON-THE-HILL, Leics

Breached ramparts of an iron-age fort at Burrough Hill are thought to mark the site of a pre-Roman capital. The local church dates from the 13th century and has a good tower.

Continue to Somerby, meet a T-junction, and turn left SP 'Pickwell' and 'Melton'. In 2¼ miles cross the A606 and follow SP for Stapleford. To the right, on the approach to Stapleford, is Stapleford Park.

STAPLEFORD PARK, Leics

Home of Lord and Lady Gretton, this fine old house (open) has an early wing dating from 1500 and was restored in 1633. Its exterior decoration includes an exceptional collection of stone sculptures depicting scenes from history, the scriptures, and legend; inside are rooms that have been attributed to John Webb. As well as fine pictures, tapestries and furniture, the house contains the famous Thomas Balston collection of Victorian Staffordshire pottery figures (NT). In the grounds are a lake with an island bird sanctuary, a miniature steam passenger railway, and many other diversions for both children and adults.

From Stapleford proceed north and after a short distance turn left to join the B676. A short detour from the main route to the village of Saxby can be made by turning right here on to the B676.

SAXBY, Leics

An ancient Saxon cemetery has been discovered at Saxby, and the local rectory and church both date from 1789.

On the main route, continue along the B676 to Melton Mowbray.

MELTON MOWBRAY, Leics

No matter what various sections of public opinion feel about hunting it is still a thriving tradition, and nowhere is it in better health than at Melton Mowbray. Three famous packs meet here, and the district is often loud with the noise of horns, hounds, and horses. The town is internationally famous for Stilton cheese and pork pies, and its attractive situation on the River Eye makes it a popular goal for summer visitors. St Mary's is arguably the stateliest and most impressive of all the county's churches, and beautifully illustrates the early-English, decorated, and perpendicular architectural periods. Anne of Cleves House is of ancient origin. The Melton Carnegie Museum depicts the making of Stilton cheese and pork pies. Attractive parks and gardens border the river.

Leave Melton Mowbray on the A6006 'Loughborough' road, pass Asfordby, and in 3¼ miles turn left on to the B676. After 1¼ miles pass beneath the A46, which follows much of the course of the ancient Fosse Way.

FOSSE WAY

Certain stretches of this famous Romanized road are mere tracks, but much of its diagonal route across England from Axminster to Lincoln is followed by modern main roads. Excavations have shown that the courses of earlier paths were adopted by the Roman engineers who plotted the road.

Continue to Burton-on-the-Wolds, turn left on to an unclassified road, then shortly join the B675 and drive to Barrow-upon-Soar.

BARROW-UPON-SOAR, Leics

This attractive and popular village stands on the east bank of the River Soar and has a curious village sign that depicts an aquatic prehistoric reptile. Good local

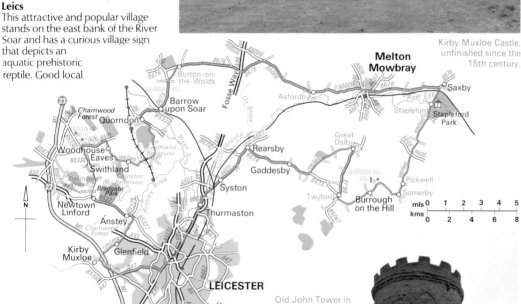

Kirby Muxloe Castle, unfinished since the 15th century.

Old John Tower in Bradgate Park is an 18th-century folly built on a 700ft hill.

buildings include an old hospital of 1694 and almshouses of 1825.

Drive to the end of Barrow-upon-Soar, at roundabout take 2nd exit then cross a river bridge. Turn right into Quorndon.

QUORNDON, Leics

Valuable Tudor relics are preserved in the 14th-century Farnham Chapel of Quorndon's fine granite church, which also has a good Norman doorway. The village gives its name to the most famous hunt in England, and has a station on the Great Central Railway. The latter runs 5 miles between Loughborough and Rothley and a 3-mile extension to Birstal is currently undergoing reconstruction.

CHARNWOOD FOREST,

Once an important hunting ground, the bracken-covered summits of Charnwood Forest thrust their bare crags of ancient rock high above the fertile wooded plains of Leicestershire. Their presence in the generally unspectacular Midlands countryside is a startling scenic contradiction, and the fascinating range of geological beds that make

up their bulk is a constant source of interest to geologists. Fine views can be enjoyed from the forest, and its sweeping barrenness gives an invigorating sense of freedom.

At Quorndon, turn left on to the A6 and drive for 200 yards, then turn right on to the unclassified 'Cropston' and 'Anstey' road to skirt Hawcliff Hill and Buddon Wood, on the edge of Charnwood Forest. After 2¼ miles meet crossroads and turn right towards Swithland. After a short distance cross the end of lovely Swithland Reservoir, a noted local beauty spot. Ascend through the village of Swithland.

SWITHLAND, Leics

An attractive village associated with the traditional industry of slate cutting, Swithland stands near the eastern edge of Charnwood Forest in pleasantly wooded surroundings. Good monuments can be seen in the local church.

Drive 1 mile beyond Swithland and turn left for Woodhouse Eaves.

WOODHOUSE EAVES, Leics

Several of the cottages in this picturesque hill village are made of rough stone taken from the slate pits at Swithland. To the west is 818ft Beacon Hill, an AA viewpoint and the site of an iron-age encampment.

Drive to the end of the village and turn left on to the B591; in 1¼ miles pass the Beacon Hill carpark and viewpoint, then in a short distance at crossroads turn left on to the B5330 and meet crossroads. Drive forward on to the unclassified road for Newtown Linford, and pass the main entrance for Bradgate Park on the approach to the village.

BRADGATE PARK, Leics

The 850 acres of untouched heath and woodland that make up this superb country park were given to the city and county of Leicester in 1928 as permanent public space. The area, which extends from Cropston Reservoir to Newtown Linford, offers excellent walks through stands of cedar and oak, and alongside the course of a tiny stream. Bradgate House, now in ruins, was completed c1510. In 1537 it was the birthplace of the unfortunate Lady Jane Grey, who was the uncrowned Queen of England for nine days before being beheaded by order of Mary Tudor. At the highest point of the park is an 18th-century folly tower known as Old John, which was erected to the memory of a retainer who was killed by a falling flagpole.

Continue into Newtown Linford.

NEWTOWN LINFORD, Leics

This village stands on the borders of Bradgate Park and has some attractive old houses, but it is a little too close to the suburbs of Leicester for comfort. Its 18th-century church features painted royal arms.

Follow the B5327 'Leicester' road to Anstey.

ANSTEY, Leics

The 5-arched packhorse bridge that spans Rothley Brook in this Charnwood village is considered one of the finest in England. It dates from the 14th or 15th century and is complemented by some fine old cottages. Anstey was the birthplace of Ned Ludd, who as an apprentice initiated the infamous Luddite riots of 1812 by wrecking machinery that had been introduced to take over his job.

Meet a roundabout and turn right, crossing Rothley Brook with the old packhorse bridge to the right. Continue for 200 yards and turn right on to the unclassified 'Glenfield' road, then after a further 1 mile meet a roundabout and keep forward to enter Glenfield.

GLENFIELD, Leics

Victorian St Peter's was built to replace the old Glenfield Church, which stands in ruins near by. Several architectural features salvaged from the interior of the older structure can be seen inside.

From Glenfield follow SP 'Kirby Muxloe' to Kirby Muxloe.

KIRBY MUXLOE, Leics

Considered an excellent example of its type, this moat-encircled fortified manor (AM) was begun by Lord Hastings in 1480 – towards the end of the Wars of the Roses. The wars ended before the house was completed, and Hastings was executed for treason.

Meet roundabout at the edge of Kirby Muxloe and turn left towards Leicester. In 1 mile meet a roundabout and turn left on to the A47 for the return to Leicester.

HEREFORD'S QUIET VALLEYS

Great Marcher fortresses like Ludlow Castle were built by the Normans to subdue the turbulent Welsh. Fierce battles have left no scars on these mild green hills and fertile valleys which epitomize the serenity and certainties of the rural way of life in one of the few remaining true pastoral regions of England.

Crowning the height of Ludlow Hill is one of England's finest Norman castles

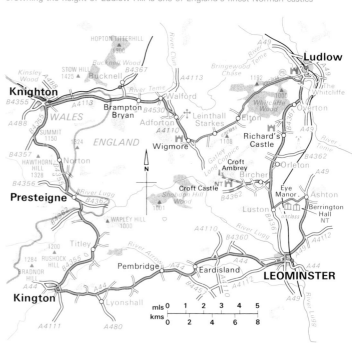

LEOMINSTER, Herefs & Worcs
Hop gardens and orchards flourish around Leominster, one of the great wool towns of England from medieval times until the 18th century. Narrow medieval streets with their tightly-packed jumble of timber-framed houses contrast with the more spacious layouts of the Georgian era, best seen in Broad Street. A grey-stone priory church of 3 naves, stands amid green lawns shaded by trees. According to tradition it was founded in the 11th century by Earl Leofric, husband of Lady Godiva. A medieval ducking stool, last used to punish a nagging wife in the early 19th century, is on view in the church. Nearby, Grange Court, a delightful brick and timber house built in 1633 by John Abel, was moved to this site in 1855. It was originally the town hall and stood at the crossroads in the centre of Leominster. In Etnam Street is a folk museum devoted to the local history of the area.

Follow the A44, SP 'Rhayader', to Eardisland.

EARDISLAND, Herefs & Worcs
The village of Eardisland presents an exquisite picture in an idyllic setting among the green meadows bordering the River Arrow. Half-timbered black and white façades stand out among the old brick and colour-washed cottages that represent a medley of traditional styles of building. Near the old bridge over the river stands a 14th-century yeoman's hall, Staick House, and the old school house and village whipping post face the 17th-century manor house (not open) in whose garden stands a tall, 4-gabled dovecot of unusually charming design.

Continue on the A44 to Pembridge.

PEMBRIDGE, Herefs & Worcs
Pretty black and white timbered houses, their upper storeys drunkenly overhanging the pavements, are the keynote of this appealing village. Behind the New Inn, in the tiny market square, the old market house is raised on 8 oak columns. In the centre of the main street, weathered stone steps lead steeply uphill to a church with an unusual detached bell tower dating from the 14th century.

In 4½ miles pass the edge of Lyonshall and continue to Kington.

KINGTON, Herefs & Worcs
Sheltered by Hergest Ridge and Rushock Hill, Kington is an ancient town famous for its sheep markets. Offa's Dyke, the old Mercian defence against the Welsh, crosses Rushock Hill to the north. West of the town, the house called Hergest Court (not open) and for generations the home of the Vaughan family, was reputedly haunted by the ghost of 'Black Vaughan' until a 17th-century exorcism was said to have transformed his evil spirit into a bluebottle.

Turn right SP 'Presteigne' to join the B4355. After 6 miles cross the border into Wales and shortly enter Presteigne.

PRESTEIGNE, Powys
Presteigne stands on the bank of the River Lugg, at this point the boundary between England and Wales, in the rich green countryside of hill and vale so characteristic of the Welsh Marches. A priest hole, where a Roman Catholic priest remained hidden from persecution for 2 years, can be seen in the 17th-century Radnorshire Arms. In the churchyard is the grave of Mary Morgan, hanged in 1805 aged 17 for the murder of her illegitimate child. Her lover, who was a party to the crime and gave her the knife with which to do it, then sat as a member of the jury that condemned her. A royal pardon was granted but, sadly, arrived too late to save her.

Pembridge — typical Hereford architecture

Continue on the B4355 and at the end of the town turn right, SP 'Knighton'. Cross the River Lugg to reach Norton then ascend past Hawthorn Hill to 1,150ft before a long descent to the edge of Knighton.

KNIGHTON, Powys
In 1971 the Offa's Dyke Path was officially opened by Lord Hunt of Everest at a ceremony held in Knighton's riverside park. The earthworks of Offa's Dyke, the ancient frontier between England and Wales, built by King Offa of Mercia in the 8th century, are clearly visible on the west of the town, and Knighton stands at about the half-way point of the walk. The central Wales railway line, one of only 2 railways surviving in mid Wales, passes through Knighton at an enchanting neo-Gothic railway station. It owes its design to the owner of the land who, when he sold it to the railway, insisted in approving the plans of all the buildings.

At the near edge of Knighton turn right on to the A4113, SP 'Ludlow', to follow the Teme valley, later recrossing the border into England.

BRAMPTON BRYAN, Herefs & Worcs

The name of the village derives from Bryan de Brampton who built a massive fortress here in the 13th century. Two great round towers, the gatehouse and hall survive, standing in the grounds of the manor house (not open). De Brampton's daughter, Margaret, married Robert Harley, and one of their descendants became a Lord Mayor of London. Harley Street, fashionable West End home of many exclusive medical practices, is named after him.

In 1½ miles at Walford turn right on to the B4530, SP 'Hereford'. In 1 mile turn right on to the A4110, and continue through Adforton to Wigmore.

WIGMORE, Herefs & Worcs

Between the manor house (not open) and the church lie the delightful half-timbered cottages of Wigmore. Little remains of the moated 14th-century castle, owned by the Mortimer family, which was dismantled during the Civil War in 1643, but near Adforton are the picturesque ruins of an Augustinian abbey founded in 1179.

Turn left on to the Ludlow road, and pass through Leinthall Starkes and Elton. After the descent through Whitcliffe Wood there is a magnificent view of Ludlow before reaching Ludford Bridge. To reach Ludlow town centre turn left on to the B4361, cross the River Teme and ascend into the town.

These splendid bow-windows, known as oriels, belong to the Angel Hotel — one of Ludlow's many memorable buildings

LUDLOW, Shrops

The tour climbs from the River Teme up the steep hillside whose summit is crowned by the mighty walls of Ludlow Castle (OACT), one of the great Marcher fortresses, constructed in 1085 by the Earl of Shrewsbury. It was to Ludlow Castle that Prince Arthur, elder son of Henry VII, brought his young Spanish bride Catharine of Aragon, and had gardens laid out for her in a series of pleasant walks. He died here and his younger brother not only ascended to the throne as Henry VIII, but also married his brother's widow. The town is a feast of old buildings, from the black and white Feathers Inn, its façade ornamented with rich carving, to the restrained elegance of Georgian town houses. Broad Street, leading up from the river to the castle, is said to contain no building later than the 15th century. Near the top, Broad Gate, the only one of the original town gates that remains, leads to the 18th-century stone Butter Cross where the town museum is housed. The great 15th-century church of St Lawrence bears a graceful spire 135ft high. The interior is famous for the exquisitely carved misericords of the choir stalls, and for its lovely east window which depicts the life and miracles of the saint in 27 separate scenes.

The main tour turns right on to the B4361, SP 'Leominster', and in 1½ miles turns right again, SP 'Presteigne', to reach Richard's Castle.

RICHARD'S CASTLE, Herefs & Worcs

A steep path leads north-west from the village through woodland to the earthworks of the ancient castle. It was built in the reign of Edward the Confessor and is one of only 2 in the county that pre-date the Norman Conquest.

Continue on the B4361, passing the edge of Orleton. The main tour continues south on the B4361, but from here a detour can be made to Croft Castle. Turn right on to the B4362, SP 'Presteigne', and in ½ mile bear right into Bircher. In 1 mile turn right for the entrance to Croft Castle and footpaths to Croft Ambrey.

CROFT CASTLE, Herefs & Worcs

Apart from a break of 173 years, from 1750 to 1923, this splendid Marcher castle (NT) has been the home of the Croft family ever since the medieval period. Walls and towers date from the 14th century, but the magnificent interior, with its superb collection of Gothic furniture, belongs to the 18th and early 19th centuries. The outstanding features of the extensive park, planted with many varieties of rare trees and shrubs, are the avenues of beech, oak and Spanish chestnut. The chestnut trees are particularly ancient — thought to be more than 350 years old. Close to the castle stands the church, with a monument to Sir Richard Croft. His finely carved armour represents the suit he wore at the Battle of Tewkesbury (1471).

Return to the B4361 and turn right to rejoin the main tour. At the edge of Luston turn left, SP 'Ashton', to reach Eye Manor.

CROFT AMBREY, Herefs & Worcs

This Iron Age fort is situated at 1,000ft on the edge of Leinthall Common. It covers an area of 24 acres and was occupied from 400 BC to 50 AD. The climb to the top is rewarded with wide views of several counties.

EYE MANOR, Herefs & Worcs

This Carolean manor house (not open) is renowned for its elaborate superbly moulded and painted plaster ceilings. The finest are those of the great parlour and the dining hall. Eye Manor originally belonged to a Barbados sugar planter and slave trader, Ferdinando Gorges.

Continue, passing in 1½ miles on the right, Berrington Hall.

BERRINGTON HALL, Herefs & Worcs

When the estate was bought by London banker and former Lord Mayor Thomas Harley, 3rd son of the 3rd Earl of Oxford, in 1775, he employed Capability Brown to create the park and choose the site for the house. Brown's son-in-law, Henry Holland, designed Berrington Hall (NT) as a neo-Classical building, completed in 1781. The style of the interior echoes the Classical theme: its outstanding features are the marble hall and the staircase hall.

At the A49 turn right, (care required), for the return alongside Berrington Park to Leominster.

Delightfully delicate 17th-century stucco work at Eye Manor

IN THE WOODLANDS OF CANNOCK CHASE

Nowadays the great chase, or hunting ground, of Cannock is a protected area of woodland famous for its superb stands of mature oak and birch. All around are the quaint black-and-white villages typical of the area, guardians of tradition.

LICHFIELD, Staffs

A city of great age and architectural distinction, Lichfield has a fine red sandstone cathedral which carries three tall spires popularly known as the Ladies of the Vale. They form a well-known local landmark easily discernible above the rooftops of the town, and the grand west front of the building carries no less than 113 statues within its arcades and panels. Before the Commonwealth this type of decoration was reasonably common, but Cromwellian troops tracking down the sin of idolatry smashed such work wherever they could. Inside the building is preserved the 7th-century manuscript book of the *St Chad Gospels*, a rare treasure indeed. Other features include beautiful windows, a sculpted group by Chantrey, and numerous good memorials. The Bishop's Palace of 1687 is a lovely old example of its type, and restored Lichfield House dates from the 16th century. An old house in the Market Square was the birthplace of Dr Johnson and now serves as a Johnsonian Museum featuring, amongst other relics, his favourite silver teapot. The Lichfield Heritage Exhibition and Treasury is housed in the ancient Guild church of St Mary's, included is an audio-visual on the Civil War and siege of Lichfield and examples of the silversmith's craft.

Leave Lichfield with SP 'Tamworth A51', passing the Barracks to the left on Whittington Heath.

WHITTINGTON BARRACKS, Staffs

The official museum of the Staffordshire Regiment can be visited at Whittington Barracks, themselves evidence of Lichfield's long association with the military.

Pass a TV mast on the right and descend past Hopwas Hays Wood to Hopwas, then continue to Tamworth.

TAMWORTH, Staffs

Tamworth's fine castle (open) displays an intriguing mixture of architectural styles ranging from the original Norman to the charming pretence of the 19th century. The 10ft-thick walls of the keep are typically Norman, but the less massive warden's lodge and beautiful banqueting hall both show the delicacy of Tudor workmanship. A frieze of 55 oak panels in the state dining room, which is in the north wing, is painted with the arms of the lords of the castle up to 1718. A museum of local history is housed in the castle. Tamworth Church has a unique square tower with a double-spiral staircase at one corner, and the red-brick Town Hall of 1701 is one of the prettiest in the country.

Follow the A513 'Burton' and 'Alrewas' road, and after 4 miles pass an unclassified left turn that can be taken as a detour from the main route to Elford village.

Tranquillity reigns today on the Trent and Mersey Canal, formerly an important route for the pottery trade.

Rich furnishings in Lichfield Cathedral include an ornate choir screen.

TRENT & MERSEY CANAL, Staffs

Designed by the great engineer Brindley to service the industrial heartlands of England, this canal was begun in the late 18th century and was the first safe means by which fragile goods could be transported from the Potteries district. Josiah Wedgwood, owner of one of the more famous Staffordshire china industries, worked in association with Brindley to produce this undoubted advantage to his interests. Just beyond Alrewas the canal actually joins the Trent by lock, and leaves the river by the same method after 250 yards.

In 1¾ miles at junction turn left on to the B5016 for Barton-under-Needwood. Continue forward SP 'Yoxall', then in 1 mile reach The Bell (PH) and turn right on to the unclassified 'Tutbury' road. In 3 miles cross a main road and continue to Tutbury.

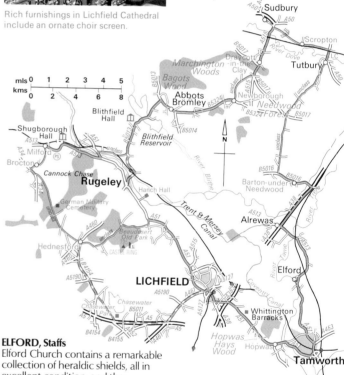

ELFORD, Staffs

Elford Church contains a remarkable collection of heraldic shields, all in excellent condition, and the evocative monument to a child who is said to have been killed after being hit on the temple by a tennis ball in 1460. Many other fine memorials can be seen here.

On the main route, continue along the A513 to Alrewas.

ALREWAS, Staffs

Famous for its River Trent eel fishing and basket-weaving industries, this charming little village of thatched black-and-white Tudor cottages is considered one of the prettiest in the county. Its 13th- and 14th-century church contains a fine font, and its situation on the Trent and Mersey Canal offers fine towpath walks.

Turn right on to the A38 SP 'Burton', and in 1 mile cross the River Trent before continuing alongside the canal.

TUTBURY, Staffs

This picturesque old town stands on the banks of the River Dove and claims to have the finest Norman church in the Midlands. The west front of the building is certainly magnificent. Mary Queen of Scots was twice imprisoned in Tutbury Castle (open), and led a thoroughly miserable existence in the cramped surroundings of a high tower that still stands. Nowadays this sad place is visited for the outstanding views it affords over Needwood Forest. Other remains of the castle, dramatically situated on an isolated outcrop of rock, include 14th-century John of Gaunt's Gateway. The most striking building in the main street of the town is the old Dog and Partridge Inn.

Drive forward into the A50 High Street and cross the River Dove. Continue over a level crossing, then turn left on to an unclassified road SP 'Scropton' and 'Sudbury'. Continue for 2 miles beyond Scropton and turn left on to the A515. A short detour from the main route to attractive Sudbury can be made by turning right here on to the A515, then left on to an unclassified road leading to the village of that name.

Tutbury Castle offers excellent views over Needwood Forest.

SUDBURY, Derbys
Built largely in the 17th century, this village is an excellent early example of unified design being applied to a community rather than being allowed to develop in its own random fashion. Sudbury Hall (NT), seat of the Vernon family, contains exceptional carving by the sculptor Grinling Gibbons. A stained glass window given by Queen Victoria can be seen in the village church.

On the main route, continue along the A515 and recross the River Dove. Reach Draycott-in-the-Clay and ascend, then in ¾ mile meet crossroads and turn right on to an unclassified road for Newborough. Continue to Newborough and turn right on to the B5324 SP 'Abbots Bromley', then cross rolling countryside and turn right on to the B5014 to enter Abbots Bromley.

ABBOTS BROMLEY, Staffs
People from all over the country come to Abbots Bromley on the Monday after September 4, when the curious and ritualistic Horn Dance is performed through the streets and surrounding country lanes. Six of the twelve dancers carry ancient reindeer antlers on their shoulders, a seventh rides a hobby horse, a fool capers along the route in multi-coloured costume, and the entourage is completed by a young girl alongside a boy carrying a bow and arrow. The dance as it is seen today is thought to commemorate the granting of hunting rights to the local people by the Abbot of Bromley in the 12th century. However, it is likely to have been derived from a pagan ceremony with roots far back in prehistoric times. Features of the town itself include many half-timbered houses and a market place with an old butter cross. The 16th-century Church House and Bagot Almshouses are of particular note.

Continue along the B5014 and in ¼ mile turn left on to the B5013 SP 'Rugeley'. In 1 mile cross the extensive Blithfield Reservoir.

BLITHFIELD RESERVOIR, Staffs
The Queen Mother opened this 4,000 million gallon reservoir in 1953, and today it has become naturalized to such an extent that it is a valuable sanctuary for wildlife. Views can be enjoyed from the road, but a permit is required to visit the banks.

Pass a viaduct to reach Blithfield Hall on the right.

BLITHFIELD HALL, Staffs
Set graciously in the peaceful Blithe Valley, this estate has been the home of the Bagot family and their ancestors for 900 years and includes a fine old house of Elizabethan origin. Additions from later periods are evident in the design of the building, and inside is a magnificent staircase in carved oak. Of particular interest is a unique collection of relics from the Stuart period. Herds of black-necked Bagot goats roam the park.

Continue along the B5013 and in 1¾ miles turn right on to the unclassified 'Stafford' road. A short detour from the main route to the village of Rugeley can be made by keeping forward along the B5013 for a further 2¼ miles.

RUGELEY, Staffs
During the 19th century this village became nationally famous as the home of notorious Dr William Palmer, who was found guilty of poisoning a bookmaker to whom he owed money. On its own this act is not sensational, but it appears that this unfortunate victim was the last in a long line of poisonings by Palmer, including many relatives and friends. The grave of the bookmaker, John Cook, can be seen in the local churchyard. The actual town is a pleasant little place that easily lives down its connexion with the Prince of Poisoners. About 4 miles south-south-east is Hanch Hall of 13th-century origin. House and gardens (open).

On the main route, continue along the unclassified 'Stafford' road and in 1½ miles meet crossroads. Turn left, then left again to join the A51, then cross the River Trent and at roundabout take 2nd exit A513 SP 'Stafford'. Follow the Trent Valley and pass the entrance to Shugborough Hall on the right before reaching Milford.

SHUGBOROUGH HALL, Staffs
Now run by Staffordshire County Council and housing the county museum, this great white mansion (NT) stands in beautiful grounds on the River Sow and contains fine collections of furniture and period bric-à-brac. Access to the gardens is by a bridge over a lovely ornamental lake, and the grounds are scattered with superb classical monuments and follies. The most notable of the latter are the Doric Temple and the Tower of the Winds.

Continue to Milford and turn left on to the unclassified 'Brocton' road. At Brocton drive forward SP 'Stafford', then meet a main road and turn left on to the A34 SP 'Cannock'. In ¼ mile turn left on to the unclassified 'Hednesford' road and climb to Cannock Chase.

CANNOCK CHASE, Staffs
Once the private hunting ground of the kings of England, the 26 square miles of wooded Cannock Chase form a designated area of outstanding natural beauty that is available for everybody to enjoy. Several pine and spruce plantations have been established in the area by the Forestry Commission, but a few of the majestic oaks that were once commonplace can still be seen in Brocton Coppice. The feather-like plumes of birches grace Black Hill, and to the west the bracken-clad forest glades give way to heather and gorse. Among many wild creatures to be seen here are deer and the rare native red squirrel. Good views are afforded by the hilltops of Seven Springs, which culminate in 795ft Castle Ring; the latter is crowned by the ramparts of a good iron-age hillfort.

Sudbury Hall is a typical example of 17th-century elegance.

Continue along the unclassified 'Hednesford' road and pass a German military cemetery on the left. Meet crossroads and ascend, then meet more crossroads and drive forward into the colliery district round Hednesford. In ½ mile drive forward, descend to crossroads, and keep forward to cross a railway bridge. Turn right on to the A460, drive under a railway bridge, and turn left on to an unclassified road SP 'Rawnsley' and 'Hazelslade'. An alternative return to Lichfield, taking in the Chasewater Park Railway at Brownhills, can be taken by continuing with the A460 and following the route indicated on the tour map. On the main route, continue along the unclassified road and after ¾ mile turn left. Drive over a level crossing and climb through thick woodland to crossroads. Turn right into Startley Lane and descend. Continue, with Castle Ring rising from Cannock Chase to the right, and meet a main road. Turn right on to the A51 for the return to Lichfield.

The Abbots Bromley Horn Dancers performing outside Blithfield Hall.

LINCOLN AND THE WITHAM VALLEY

The proud triple towers of Lincoln Cathedral can be seen for many miles across the flat lands of the Witham Valley, a fertile area of farms and fens whose threatened monotony is relieved by picturesque villages of honey-coloured stone.

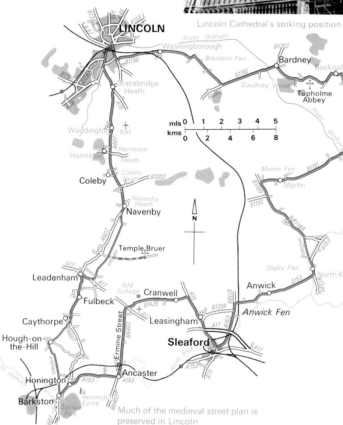

Lincoln Cathedral's striking position is emphasized by its impressive west front.

LINCOLN, Lincs

Historic Lincoln rises majestically from the north banks of the River Witham, on a slope crowned by its beautiful triple-towered cathedral. This splendid building, the third largest of its type in England, completely dominates the city and overlooks miles of countryside. Its 11th-century origins are largely hidden by extensions and additions from subsequent periods, and its many ancient treasures include the best preserved of four existing copies of *Magna Carta*. In the Library are first editions of *Paradise Lost*, *Don Quixote*, and part of Spenser's *Faerie Queen*. Amongst many other interesting churches in the city are St Benedict's and St Peter at Gowt's, both of which include a great deal of Saxon work. Newport Arch (AM), the only surviving Roman gateway to span an English street, is a relic of the ancient walled city of *Lindum Colonia*. The Close, also known as Minster Yard, contains a superb collection of buildings including a fine tithe barn of 1440 and the ancient Bishop's Palace (AM). Lincoln Castle was founded by William the Conqueror in 1068 and over the centuries has grown into the impressive structure that occupies some 6 acres of city ground today. Its main features include 14th-century Cobb Hall, which was once a place of punishment, the Observatory Tower, and a fine Norman keep. Other old buildings in

the city include the Jew's House, a fine example of 12th-century domestic architecture, and nearby Aaron's House – a product of the prosperous wool age and the oldest inhabited dwelling in England. Timber-framed 16th-century houses line the High Street as it crosses High Bridge, preserving in miniature the appearance of old London Bridge before it was destroyed in the Great Fire that razed the capital in 1666.

From Lincoln follow SP 'Sleaford A15' and ascend to Bracebridge Heath. Turn right on to the A607 SP 'Grantham' and after a short distance pass the large RAF base at Waddington on the left. Continue past Harmston Heath (on the left) and the village of Harmston in attractively wooded countryside to the right. After a short distance pass Coleby on the right, with Coleby Heath stretching away to the left.

Much of the medieval street plan is preserved in Lincoln

COLEBY, Lincs

Interesting old buildings in this pleasant village include the church and 17th-century Coleby Hall. The former is of Norman date and incorporates a Saxon tower, and the latter shares attractive grounds with the Temple of Romulus and Remus, by Sir William Chambers.

Continue on the A607 into Navenby, with Navenby Heath on the left.

NAVENBY, Lincs

Stone and pantiled houses form charming architectural groups in this pleasant little village, and the restored church rises grandly above their rooftops to complete the picture. Inside the church is a notable Easter Sepulchre decorated with carved figures.

Beyond Navenby turn left on to an unclassified road SP 'Ancaster, Sleaford'. Continue for 2¼ miles and meet crossroads. A detour from the main route can be made here by turning left and driving for 2¼ miles to Temple Bruer; access is via a road through Temple Farm.

TEMPLE BRUER, Lincs

A preceptory of the Knights Templar was founded here during the reign of Henry II, and the restored 13th-century tower (AM) of their church can still be seen. Very few of their distinctive round churches survive in the British Isles.

On the main route, continue for 1¾ miles and meet more crossroads. Turn right on to the A17 SP 'Newark' and descend into Leadenham.

LEADENHAM, Lincs

Leadenham Old Hall (not open) is a beautiful building of c1700 built entirely of golden ironstone. One of its main features is a delightful rustic doorway. The village itself is dominated by its lovely church spire and boasts a 19th-century drinking fountain beneath a hexagonal canopy.

Meet traffic lights in Leadenham and turn left on to the A607 SP 'Grantham'. Continue to Fulbeck.

FULBECK, Lincs

A delightful combination of woods and farmland surrounds this pretty village. The hall, dating from 1773, contains fine period furniture and is set in an 11-acre garden.

Proceed on the A607, passing the edge of Caythorpe.

CAYTHORPE, Lincs

The characteristically utilitarian appearance of Caythorpe's village architecture is lifted by the mellow gold of local ironstone. Notable Ivy House dates from 1684 and has projecting wings with gables. The local church features a good tower.

Drive ½ mile beyond the Caythorpe crossroads and turn right on to an unclassified road for the village of Hough-on-the-Hill.

HOUGH-ON-THE-HILL, Lincs

As its name suggests, this village occupies a lofty site that makes it an excellent viewpoint. The local church is noted for its tower, which features a curious Saxon turret containing a newel stairway.

Beyond the local church turn left SP 'Barkston, Grantham' and proceed to Barkston.

BARKSTON, Lincs

Barkston Church features a good ironstone tower. Close by is a group of almshouses that reflect a style uniformly applied to the buildings of the local Belton estate.

From Barkston turn left on to the A607, with Syston Park ahead. After ¾ mile drive forward on to the A153, skirting Honington.

North Kyme Fen typifies the Kesteven area of Lincolnshire

HONINGTON, Lincs

About ¾ mile south-east of this village is Honington Camp, one of the few major hillforts built in this part of the country. It is of iron-age date and was probably manned to defend the Ancaster Gap. During the 17th century an urn of Roman coins was found here, which seems to suggest that the inhabitants of nearby Ancaster found the camp useful. Honington Church contains some good Norman work.

Continue on the A153, passing Honington Camp, and proceed for 2¼ miles. Turn left on to the B6403 to Ancaster.

ANCASTER, Lincs

Sited on the old Roman road of Ermine Street, this village is set in pleasantly wooded countryside and stands near the site of Roman *Causennae*. Remains of this ancient camp and posting station can be seen near by, and relics excavated from the area can be seen in Grantham Museum – including mosaic flooring and an altar. Some 2 miles south of the village are quarries where the famous Ancaster stone was worked for many of Lincolnshire's beautiful churches.

Proceed along a modern road that follows the line of Ermine Street.

ERMINE STREET, Lincs

This Roman road, built about 1,900 years ago between London and Lincoln, allowed the occupying forces to reach trouble spots in eastern England with comparative ease. The name is derived from a Saxon tribe who lived near by.

Drive for 3¾ miles beyond Ancaster and turn right on to the A17, then left on to the B1429 SP 'Cranwell', passing the RAF College. Continue to Cranwell.

CRANWELL, Lincs

Traces of Saxon workmanship can be seen in Cranwell's mainly Norman church, which houses a fine old screen. West of the village is the well-known RAF college, which was founded in 1920 and includes a number of well-designed buildings.

In ¾ mile turn right on to the A15 'Sleaford' road and pass the edge of Leasingham.

LEASINGHAM, Lincs

Notable buildings in this old village include the Ancient House of 1658, the 17th-century Old Hall, and Georgian Leasingham Manor. Later additions include Leasingham Hall and Roxholme Hall, both of the 19th century. The local church has a lofty west tower crowned by a spire.

Proceed along the A15 to Sleaford.

SLEAFORD, Lincs

Charmingly situated on the banks of the peaceful River Slea, this pleasant little market town is dominated by a 12th- to 15th-century church with one of the earliest stone spires in England. The building's outstanding window tracery is arguably the best in the country. Early structures in the town include a 15th-century timber-framed vicarage and the Black Bull Inn; a carved stone at the latter is dated 1689 and 1791, and illustrates the old sport of bull baiting. Most of the town's workaday buildings date from the 19th century, including the Sessions House, and the Carre's Hospital.

Leave Sleaford on the A153 'Horncastle' road. After 2¾ miles turn right and proceed to Anwick.

Little survives to tell of the wealth and prestige that came to Bardney Abbey before its downfall and ruin.

ANWICK, Lincs

Just south of Anwick's medieval church are adjoining cottages in the romantic gothic style. One houses the post office and the other is a smithy.

Continue with Anwick Fen on the right, and drive through the village of North Kyme. Beyond North Kyme continue forward on to an unclassified road SP 'Walcot', skirting Digby Fen on the left. In 1¼ miles turn left on to the B1189; proceed for 4 miles and turn right on to the B1191 SP 'Woodhall Spa', driving through Martin and later passing Martin Fen on the left. Cross the River Witham at Kirkstead Bridge, and after another ¾ mile pass a right turn leading to Kirkstead Abbey. It is worth making the short detour to this historic place.

KIRKSTEAD ABBEY, Lincs

Scant remains of a rich Cistercian abbey founded by Hugo Brito in 1139 can be seen here, but the site is most famous for the 13th-century architectural gem of St Leonard's Chapel. This was built outside the abbey gates for lay worshippers, and has survived in a remarkably good state of preservation. Its wooden screen is thought to be the second oldest in England and includes timber work dating from 1210.

Like many of Sleaford's buildings, Carre's Hospital, in Eastgate, dates from the mid-19th century.

Continue along the main route and enter Woodhall Spa.

WOODHALL SPA, Lincs

In Victorian and earlier times this inland resort was famous for its natural springs, and a fine pump room and bathing establishment remain from this period. Nowadays the town is well known as a golfing centre, with Lincolnshire's only championship-standard course.

Continue along the B1191 to Tower on the Moor.

TOWER ON THE MOOR, Lincs

This impressive 60ft tower dominates the local countryside and is a well-known (if enigmatic) landmark. It is thought to have been built in the 15th century.

Continue along the B1191 to Horncastle.

HORNCASTLE, Lincs

Roman *Banovallum*, the 'walled place on the River Bain', stood on the site now occupied by this pleasant little market town. Remains of the ancient fort that guarded the settlement have been incorporated in the modern town library. The local church dates from the 13th century and contains the fine Dymoke Brass of 1519, plus a 17th-century chest and various other relics. A 10-day horse fair was held in Horncastle every August and is featured in George Borrow's *Romany Rye*.

Leave Horncastle on the A158 'Lincoln' road and in ½ mile turn left on to the B1190 SP 'Bardney'. Drive through Thimbleby, Horsington, and Bucknall, later passing Tupholme Abbey to the left.

TUPHOLME ABBEY, Lincs

Remains of a religious house that was founded c1160 can be seen here, including part of the refectory.

Continue along the B1190 for 1½ miles and turn left into Bardney.

BARDNEY, Lincs

Ethelred, King of Mercia, founded a Benedictine abbey here in the 7th century. It was rebuilt in Norman times by the Earl of Lincoln, and grew to become one of the country's most powerful centres of religion and education. Excavations conducted amongst the extensive ruins in 1912 uncovered many interesting relics, some of which can be seen in the local church. The town itself is a typical fenland community on the River Witham, in an agricultural area.

Leave Bardney and cross the railway and the River Witham. Continue along the B1190, with Branston Fen to the right, and shortly bear right to skirt the Lincoln Edge. In 3 miles reach the Plough Inn and bear right SP 'Lincoln', then drive through Washingborough and return to Lincoln.

INSIDE OLD RUTLAND

Tiny Rutland has vanished in name but survives in fact. The towering spires of its churches rise from typically-clustered cottages of thatch and ironstone, and some of England's richest pasture is grown where the stag and hart were hunted in ancient times.

MARKET HARBOROUGH, Leics

A market was held here as early as 1203, and over the centuries the town has grown and prospered to become the mature community that exists today. The most recent developments have been industrial, but these have not been made at the expense of many fine buildings from previous, less intrusive periods. The most famous is the former grammar school, a lovely timbered and gabled building of 1614 that stands on wooden pillars above street level. The Three Swans is the largest of many old local inns and displays one of the finest wrought-iron signs in England. The parish church dates from the 13th to 15th centuries and is known for its tower, a beautiful structure crowned by a broach spire that is visible for miles around. Every November the church bells are rung to commemorate the rescue of a merchant lost in the Welland marshes in 1500, and the ringers traditionally receive one shilling for beer. Much of the town's present prosperity is due to the Symington family, who made liberty bodices in a Victorian factory behind the church.

Leave the town on the A427 'Corby' road to reach Dingley.

Rockingham Castle's Panel Room is part of a rich collection of treasures.

DINGLEY, Northants

The most impressive feature of this small village is Dingley Hall (not open), an unforgettable building with a south gateway flanked by polygonal towers.

Continue, and in about 2½ miles pass the village of Stoke Albany to the left.

STOKE ALBANY, Northants

Features of the fine local church, which dates from the 13th century, include good doorways and windows.

Continue along the A427 beyond East Carlton, then turn left on to the B670 and proceed to Rockingham.

Market Harborough's old grammar school was founded in the 17th century and is a fine example of its type.

Naseby was the scene of a decisive Civil War battle.

ROCKINGHAM, Northants

Set on a steep hillside overlooking the River Welland, this lovely village of flint-built thatched cottages has a number of new houses that have been built of traditional materials to harmonize with the whole. The summit of the hill is occupied by Rockingham Castle, which was originally built by William the Conqueror, and affords views into 4 counties. The site of the keep is now a rose garden surrounded by yew hedges, but surviving fragments of the old structure include the moat, foundations of the Norman hall, and the twin towers of the gatehouse. King John used the castle both as a fortress and as a hunting lodge for Rockingham Forest, a vast blanket of wood and heathland that once covered much of Leicestershire. The mainly Elizabethan house that stands here today (open) contains collections of paintings and furniture.

Turn left on to the A6003 'Uppingham' road, crossing the River Welland. (To enter Rockingham village turn right here into the A6003 main street.) Continue to Caldecott and drive forward on to the B672, then in 4½ miles pass under the Welland railway viaduct.

WELLAND VIADUCT, Northants

This 82-arch railway viaduct dates from 1874 and is a notable example of 19th-century industrial

architecture. It spans the complete width of the Welland Valley and is a well-known landmark.

In 2 miles turn right, then left, to join the A6121; continue to Ketton.

KETTON, Leics

One of the largest and most attractive of old Rutland's villages, this picturesque collection of butter-coloured buildings is a noted quarrying centre. The local stone is greatly prized as a building material and has been worked at least since Roman times. St Mary's Church has an exquisite spire that rises high above the village's sepia roofs of Collyweston slate, perfectly complementing one of the finest examples of church architecture in the east Midlands. The west front of the building is an excellent example of late 12th-century work, and the rest of the structure dates almost entirely from the 13th century.

Continue along the A6121 and drive through Tinwell to Stamford.

STAMFORD, Lincs

Justly considered one of England's most beautiful towns, stone-built Stamford has a long history that can be traced back as far as the time of Danish settlement. In the 13th and 14th centuries it was important enough to have its own university, and the powerful influence of early Christianity is evident in many fine churches and other ecclesiastical buildings. All Saints' Place is the visual centre of the town and is noted for its outstanding, multi-period architecture. Browne's Hospital has been described as one of the finest medieval almshouses surviving in England, and includes a beautiful Jacobean hall and chapel. Close to the Welland are the ancient Burghley Almshouses. The George Hotel was a coaching inn in the 14th century, and among fine buildings from many periods in St George's Square is a house that has been continuously inhabited since c1350. Even older than that is the Bastion in West Street, a section of the old town wall that has been untouched for 700 years. Close to the town is Elizabethan Burghley House (open) where the well-known Burghley Horse Trials are held. The house itself is considered one of England's greatest mansions and contains many superb rooms. It boasts over 100 works of art and antique furnishings.

Follow SP 'Grantham' and then 'Oakham' to leave Stamford by the A606. Continue to Empingham.

EMPINGHAM, Leics

Dominating this large attractive village is the handsome tower and spire of St Peter's Church, a well-proportioned building with a good west front. Features of the interior include fragments of ancient glass and considerable remains of medieval colour.

Continue, and 1 mile beyond Whitwell reach Rutland Water on the left. Turn right here on to the unclassified 'Exton' and 'Cottesmore' road, entering an avenue of trees. After 1¼ miles reach a right turn that offers a pleasant detour to Exton. The main route skirts Exton Park.

EXTON, Leics

Situated in one of the largest ironstone extraction areas in Britain, this charming village of thatched limestone cottages is well worth the small diversion needed to visit it. The ruined Old Hall, probably built during the reign of Elizabeth I, was burned down in 1810; the New Hall replaced it some 40 years later. Exton's parish church is noted for its remarkable range of monumental sculpture, which illustrates the progress of this art form in England from the 14th to 18th centuries.

On the main route, drive to Cottesmore and turn left on to the B668. Continue to Burley.

This gateway forms an imposing entrance to the mansion at Burghley.

BURLEY, Leics

Burley-on-the-Hill (not open) is considered by many to be the most beautiful country house in the county. Its fine colonnades and exquisitely restrained detail, the work of Joseph Lumley between 1694 and 1705, ornament a small hill that was once an ancient earthwork. The building is best appreciated from the south, looking down a long avenue of trees to the fine lines of the front.

Descend into Oakham.

OAKHAM, Leics

Once the capital of the tiny and now defunct county of Rutland, this well-known hunting centre preserves memories of its former status in the Rutland County Museum. This is housed in the late 18th-century indoor riding school of the Rutland Fencibles. The town's church dates from the 12th to 15th century and features unusual nave capitals. It shares its churchyard with the original grammar school, which was founded in 1584. Remains of Oakham Castle include a beautiful Norman hall (open), where a unique collection of horseshoes is nailed to the wall. These were traditionally contributed to the household by members of the royalty or peerage visiting the lordship for the first time. An old butter cross with stocks has been preserved in the town.

Follow SP 'Melton Mowbray', drive over a level crossing, and turn left then left again on to an unclassified road for Braunston.

BRAUNSTON, Leics

This lovely ironstone village stands on a hillside above the valley of the little River Gwash. Inside its distinctive church are traces of a previous building dating from the 12th and 13th centuries.

From Braunston follow the 'Leicester' road, and in 4¾ miles pass 755ft Whatborough Hill to the right. Access to the summit is by a nearby track. Continue to Tilton.

TILTON, Leics

The early-English and later church in this high village is noted for its strange gargoyles.

Join the B6047 'Market Harborough' road and in 2 miles drive over a main road. After another 3 miles reach the top of an ascent and turn right on to an unclassified road SP 'Carlton, Kibworth'. Continue to Kibworth Harcourt.

KIBWORTH HARCOURT, Leics

Examples of architecture from many periods can be seen in this village. Among the most notable are the Old House of 1678, the 18th-century Congregational Church, and 19th-century Kibworth Hall. Close to the village is the imposing tower of St Wilfred's Church.

Follow SP 'Leicester' to join the A6, then take the 1st unclassified road on the left SP 'Kilby, Wistow'. Cross the Grand Union Canal at a series of locks, continue to crossroads, and turn left for Fleckney and Saddington. Drive to Saddington, turn right, and continue to Mowsley. At Mowsley turn right and right again with SP 'Leicester'. In 1 mile turn left on to the A50, and after a further 1½ miles turn right on to the B5414. Drive to North Kilworth and turn right on to the A427, then turn left with the B5414 for South Kilworth.

SOUTH KILWORTH, Leics

South Kilworth's church is mainly of 19th-century design, although Norman and 14th-century work from a previous building can be seen inside. The font is of 12th- or 13th-century date.

Beyond South Kilworth pass Stanford Reservoir on the left, then turn left on to the unclassified 'Stanford on Avon' road. Descend to Stanford on Avon, passing Stanford Hall and Stanford Park on the right.

STANFORD ON AVON, Leics

Divided between Leicestershire and Northamptonshire by the River Avon, this pleasant village has a good church with a pinnacled 15th-century tower. Stanford Hall (open) is impressively sited in open pasture and stands on the site of an earlier house. The present building dates from the reign of William and Mary, and has an imposing facade that adds a touch of grandeur to its pleasing design. Its rooms contain collections of costumes and furniture, and there is a motor museum in the stable.

In ¼ mile turn left on to the 'Cold Ashby' road and later re-cross the Grand Union Canal. In 1½ miles climb 690ft Honey Hill. Continue to Cold Ashby and turn left on to the B4036, then drive to Naseby.

NASEBY, Northants

A stone column 1½ miles north of this village marks the field where the Battle of Naseby was fought in 1645. The Cromwellian victory heralded a new era of British government and sealed the fate of King Charles I. The Naseby Battle Museum at Purlieu Farm displays layouts of the battleground and various local relics. In Naseby Churchyard is a huge copper ball that is said to have been brought back from the Siege of Boulogne in 1544.

At Naseby turn left then right on to the unclassified 'Sibbertoft' road, and in 1 mile pass the site of the Battle of Naseby on the left. Reach Sibbertoft and turn right for the 'Theddingworth' road, and after 1 mile bear right to Marston Trussell. Return to Market Harborough via Lubenham and the main A427.

PEAK DISTRICT NATIONAL PARK

Some of England's wildest and most beautiful scenery is protected and made accessible to millions of people in the 542 square miles of this national park, which is mainly divided between the counties of Derbyshire, Cheshire, and Staffordshire. The high, craggy northern region includes gritstone Kinder Scout and various other lofty peaks, but in the south are gentler limestone landscapes that have been sculpted by water and softened by valley woodlands. The undulating White Peak area has thinly-grassed pastures separated by snaking limestone walls, and the lovely River Dove flows through its deep ravine past pinnacles, buttresses, and spires of weathered stone. East are the gritstone uplands and ridges of Millstone Edge, Froggat Edge, and Stanton Moor.

MATLOCK, Derbys

This River Derwent spa town is situated on the eastern edge of the national park, in a high area of gritstone moors and ridges. During the 19th century it was a resort for people following the fashion for taking the waters, and a great hydropathy centre was built at Matlock Bank. This impressive building now houses Derbyshire County Council. Along the banks of the Derwent stretch lovely Hall Leys Gardens.

A detour can be taken from the main route to Matlock Bath by leaving Matlock on the A6 SP 'Derby' and continuing south for 1¼ miles.

MATLOCK BATH, Derbys

Regency visitors popularized the medicinal springs of Matlock Bath, and although the resort declined in Victorian times it remains one of the district's many attractive touring centres. Its Petrifying Wells are very famous and are hung with various objects left by visitors to turn to stone. Every autumn a parade of illuminated and decorated boats is staged on the River Derwent. The resort's charming setting among tree-covered hills is overlooked by the 1,000ft Heights of Abraham, which were worked for lead in Roman times. The Victorian Prospect Tower, on the crest of the heights commands excellent views. In the town is the Peak District Mining Museum, which traces the history of the Derbyshire lead industry.

On the main tour, leave Matlock on the A6 'Buxton' road and drive to Darley Dale.

DARLEY DALE, Derbys

Stone from the quarries near here has long been prized as a building and sculpting material, and can be seen to advantage in many of Britain's large towns. The village church preserves ancient stone coffins and sections of an unusually decorated Saxon cross.

Leave Darley Dale and continue on the A6 to reach Rowsley.

HILLS OF THE SOUTHERN PEAK

This part of the Peak District national park is of gentle aspect, a region of undulating limestone hills scored by the beautifully-wooded Derwent Valley and trout-rich races of the Wye. Curtains of rich foliage screen weathered outcrops, curious stone spires, and the dark mouths of caves.

ROWSLEY, Derbys

Local examples of 17th-century domestic architecture include a fine old bridge over the River Wye and the pleasant Peacock Inn of 1652. More recent survivals include two obsolete station buildings, one of which was designed by Sir Joseph Paxton in 1849.

Drive 1¼ miles beyond Rowsley and turn left on to the B5056 'Ashbourne' road. A pleasant detour from the main route to Haddon Hall can be made by keeping straight ahead on the A6 for ½ mile.

HADDON HALL, Derbys

Medieval architecture can be seen at its best in the peaceful lines of this romantic old house (open). Parts of it date from the 12th century, and although it was originally built as a fortified manor house it has never seen military action. Among its many treasures is a chapel with a Norman font and lovely 15th-century wall paintings, and a long gallery with a painted ceiling and outstanding panelling. Terraced rose gardens are a striking feature of the grounds.

On the main tour, continue along the B5056 'Ashbourne' road and in 1 mile bear right on to an unclassified road SP 'Youlgreave'. A detour to Winster and the Nine Ladies stone circle can be made by driving along the B5056 for a further 2¾ miles, then turning left on B5057 to Winster.

WINSTER, Derbys

Set in the main street of this delightful village is a stone built 17th-18th-century market house (NT).

Return and in 1¾ miles turn right on to an unclassified road, through Birchover to Stanton Moor.

STANTON MOOR, Derbys

The most remarkable of several fascinating prehistoric sites on the moor is the Nine Ladies stone circle (AM), which stands 900ft above sea level in an area that affords splendid views into the Derwent Valley.

On the main tour, continue along the unclassified 'Youlgreave' road, enter the Bradford Valley, and after ¾ mile pass the village of Alport to the left.

Dovedale is said to be the most beautiful of the Derbyshire Dales.

ALPORT, Derbys

Pleasantly sited on a tumbling tributary of the River Bradford, attractive Alport is typical of the area and preserves a number of old houses. The oldest is 16th-century Monk's Hall.

Leave Alport and continue to attractive Youlgreave.

YOULGREAVE, Derbys

Every June, on the Saturday nearest St John the Baptist's Day, the springs and wells of this charming village are dressed with flower pictures as part of an ancient Derbyshire tradition. Today the ceremony is Christian, but it is likely that the ornamentation was once intended to appease the spirits of the springs.

Leave Youlgreave on the 'Ashbourne' road for 4⅓ miles and meet the A5012. Turn right here, then turn left to join the A515 and continue to the Newhaven Hotel.

NEWHAVEN HOTEL, Derbys

This building, a black-and-white structure with 5 bays, was built by the Duke of Devonshire in the 18th century. About 2½ miles north is the outstanding prehistoric stone circle of Arbor Low (AM).

Continue along the A515 to Alsop Plantation, with lovely Dovedale to the west of the road.

ALSOP PLANTATION, Derbys

The plantation on Alsop Moor is protected by the National Trust and extends alongside the main A515, below a 1,253ft summit. Its presence is an attractive addition to the local limestone scenery.

In 1⅓ miles pass the edge of Dovedale to the right.

DOVEDALE, Derbys & Staffs

Here the lovely River Dove flows through a 2-mile ravine where spectacular limestone scenery of craggy buttresses and curiously weathered outcrops is clothed and softened by carpets of lush vegetation. Perhaps the most famous of many beauty spots in the national park, the dale (NT) is also noted for trout fishing.

In 2¾ miles turn left on to an unclassified road and continue to the village of Tissington.

TISSINGTON, Derbys

Greystone houses line two sides of the attractive triangular green on which this exceptionally beautiful village is centred; the third side is occupied by a fine Norman and later church. Features of the latter include a good Norman font, an unusual 2-decker pulpit dating from the 18th century, and various monuments. Traditional Derbyshire well-dressing ceremonies are enacted at five different wells on Ascension Day.

Leave Tissington and turn right, then drive through attractive parkland to meet the A515. Turn left and continue to Fenny Bentley.

Beautiful gardens surround romantic Haddon Hall.

MIDDLETON TOP, Derbys
An Engine House with beam engine built in 1829.

Return to main route, then descend through the attractively wooded Via Gellia for Cromford.

SOUTH WINGFIELD MANOR, Derbys
Extensive remains can be seen of a fine 15th-century manor house where Mary Queen of Scots was imprisoned in 1584. Access to ruins is through the Manor Farm.

Continue along the B5035 to Crich and branch right on to an unclassified road SP 'Holloway' for the Crich Tramway Museum.

CRICH TRANWAY MUSEUM, Derbys
Vintage tramcars from all over Britain have been restored to working order and are on display in this fascinating museum, which occupies a disused quarry. An air of authenticity is created by a period setting comprising the reconstructed façade of Derby's Georgian Assembly Rooms and a collection of Victorian Street furniture. An exhibition illustrates the history of lead mining in Derbyshire.

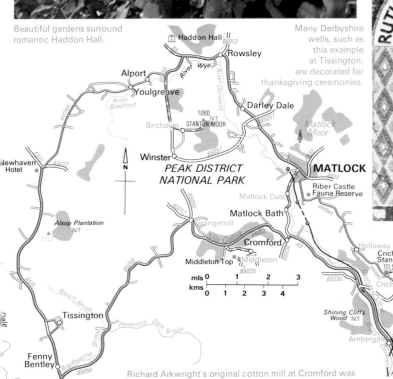

Many Derbyshire wells, such as this example at Tissington, are decorated for thanksgiving ceremonies.

Richard Arkwright's original cotton mill at Cromford was two storeys taller than the present building.

Crich Museum houses many historic trams in working order.

FENNY BENTLEY, Derbys
Features of this pleasant village include the successful amalgamation of a 15th-century manor house with the remains of an ancient tower, and a good Derbyshire church. Inside the latter is a macabre monument commemorating Thomas Beresford, his wife, 16 sons, and 5 daughters.

Leave Fenny Bentley, drive for ½ mile, and turn left on to the B5056 SP 'Bakewell'. Continue to Grangemill. At crossroads turn right on to the A5012 continue for 1¾ miles to reach a right turn B5023. A detour can be made by turning right then sharp left to Middleton. At crossroads turn right and right again for Middleton Top.

CROMFORD, Derbys
The world's first mechanized textile factory was built here by Richard Arkwright, a native of the village, in 1771 (open). The mill is gradually being restored by the Arkwright Society. One of the key figures in England's industrial revolution, he lived in Willersley Castle and built the church in which he is buried. A fine old bridge that spans the River Derwent here carries a rare 15th-century bridge chapel (AM).

Leave Cromford and turn left, then turn right on to the A6 SP 'Derby'. Pass Cromford Canal on the left, then reach Shining Cliff Wood on the right.

SHINING CLIFF WOOD, Derbys
This attractive area of woodland (NT) occupies 200 acres on the west bank of the River Derwent, and is a haven for many forms of wildlife.

Continue along the A6 to reach Ambergate and turn left on to the A610 SP 'Ripley'. Follow the Amber Valley, and after 2 miles turn left on to the B6013 SP 'Chesterfield'. In 3 miles turn left again on to the B5035 to reach South Wingfield Manor.

CRICH STAND, Derbys
High above the Crich Tramway Museum is the 940ft summit of Crich Stand, a lofty vantage point crowned by a monument to the Sherwood Foresters – the Nottingham and Derby Regiment.

Descend to Holloway. Turn right SP 'Riber' and 'Tansley', then in ½ mile meet crossroads and drive straight on. In 2 miles meet a T-junction and turn left SP 'Riber Village', and after ¼ mile keep left to reach the Riber Castle Fauna Reserve on the right.

RIBER CASTLE FAUNA RESERVE, Derbys
Near-natural surroundings are provided for comprehensive collections of European birds and animals in the 20 acres of this excellent reserve. Special features include a colony of lynx, and many breeds of domestic animals that have died out elsewhere. Picturesque ruins of 19th-century Riber Castle dominate 853ft Riber Hill.

Descend steeply through hairpin bends, turn right at the bottom, and in ¾ mile turn left on to the A615. Return to Matlock.

THROUGH THE DUKERIES

The open countryside of the Trent valley gives way to the ancient woodlands of Sherwood Forest, the traditional hunting ground of Robin Hood and his merry men. Here, a series of palatial estates known as the Dukeries were created in the 18th and 19th centuries by 4 dukes.

NEWARK-ON-TRENT, Notts
At the centre of the old market town whose ruined castle walls are reflected in the river, is the old cobbled market place surrounded by attractive buildings. Most famous is the 14th-century timbered White Hart Inn, its façade adorned by figures of angels. Nearby stands the Clinton Arms, where William Gladstone, who became Prime Minister in the late 19th century, gave his first public political speech. In the streets around the market place fine Georgian buildings lend character to the town, and opposite the castle is a remarkable Victorian extravaganza, the Ossington Coffee Palace, built by Lady Ossington to promote the cause of temperance. The castle (AM), of which only the west wall, towers and north gateway remain,

was where King John died of a surfeit of food and drink at the end of the disastrous journey during which he lost the crown jewels in the Wash. The castle, held for the king during the Civil War, proved impregnable to siege, but its commander surrendered after King Charles had given himself up to the Scots, and Cromwell's troops destroyed it. The church of St Mary Magdalen is remarkably beautiful and has a soaring 240ft slender spire.

Leave Newark on the A46, SP 'Lincoln'. In 2½ miles, at the roundabout, turn left on to the A1133, SP 'Gainsborough', and continue to Collingham.

COLLINGHAM, Notts
A plaque on the village cross records that in 1795 the River Trent burst its banks and swept through the village causing a flood 5ft deep. In the following century there was another flood almost as bad, but the Trent has since been diverted and its old course through Collingham is followed now by the River Fleet, which is no threat to this pleasant village strung out along the eastern river bank.

At the end of the village turn right on to the South Scarle road, then in ¼ mile turn left. Later, at the T-junction, turn right into South Scarle. Follow the Swinderby road, then shortly turn left, SP 'Eagle'. In ½ mile bear right and later, at the T-junction, turn right. In another ½ mile turn left, SP 'Lincoln', and ¾ mile further turn left again. Pass through Eagle and after 1½ miles turn left, SP 'Doddington', then in ¾ mile turn left again to reach Doddington.

Mighty Newark Castle was 'slighted' by Cromwell's soldiers in the Civil War

DODDINGTON, Lincs
The focal point of the village of Doddington is its lovely Elizabethan mansion (OACT), owned by the Jarvis family. Portraits by Reynolds, Lawrence and Lely decorate the walls, and the rooms contain fine period furniture, porcelain and ceramics. Among the curiosities on show is a medieval scold's bridle — a fearsome contraption put on a nagging wife to stop her talking.

Go forward on to the B1190. In 3¼ miles turn left on to the A57, and in just over ¼ mile turn left on to the Worksop road. Continue past Newton On Trent and Dunham, then in 1¾ miles turn right, SP 'East Drayton'. In 1 mile at the T-junction, turn left for East Drayton. At the church turn right and continue to Stokeham. Here, turn right then left on to the Leverton road. After 1¼ miles turn left into Treswell, then turn right for South Leverton and North Leverton.

NORTH & SOUTH LEVERTON, Notts
Dutch-gabled houses dating from the 17th and 18th centuries give these 2 villages a distinct resemblance to Holland. At North Leverton, a trim tower windmill, 3 storeys high and still in working condition, also echoes the atmosphere of the Netherlands. The mill, erected in 1813, is known as a subscription mill because all the neighbouring farmers banded together to finance it.

Continue on the unclassified road to Sturton-le-Steeple. From here a detour can be made by turning right to visit Littleborough.

LITTLEBOROUGH, Notts
As its name suggests, this is a tiny village with an even tinier Norman church. It was here that King Harold and the Saxon army crossed the Trent in 1066 on their desperate march south to Hastings to stop the Norman invasion. A drought in 1933 lowered the river level to reveal a paved ford, which has been in existence since the village was built.

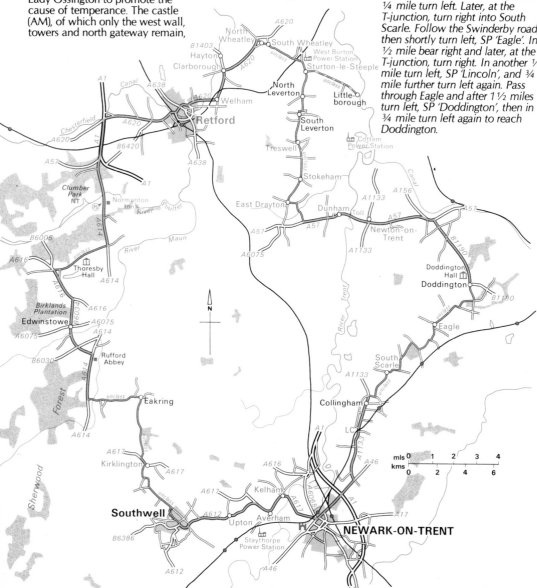

Southwell minster; unique in having pyramidal roofs to its towers

The entrance to Thoresby Hall

At Sturton-le-Steeple, follow SP 'Gainsborough', then 'Wheatley', to pass near West Burton Power Station. Beyond South Wheatley turn left into North Wheatley and at the end of the village turn left again on to the A620 and continue through Retford, SP 'Worksop'. In 3¾ miles turn left, SP 'Newark', to join the A1. Later, at the roundabout, take the A614 to enter Sherwood Forest and the area known as the Dukeries.

THE DUKERIES, Notts
The name Dukeries was given to the northern part of Sherwood Forest because, in the 18th and 19th centuries, no less than 4 dukes and several earls and marquises bought estates in the area. Most of the forest had been completely denuded of trees in the aftermath of the Civil War, and the land was desolate. It was not until the Dukes of Norfolk, Kingston, Newcastle and Portland began to establish plantations of woodland that the forest regained something of its traditional appearance. Three of the ducal estates remain: Clumber Park, Thoresby Hall and Welbeck Abbey; Rufford Abbey, an estate of the Earls of Shrewsbury is just outside the boundary of the Dukeries proper.

After 1¼ miles cross the River Poulter, with Clumber Park to the right.

CLUMBER PARK, Notts
The Duke of Newcastle created this 3,400-acre park (NT), one of the original Dukeries, in the 18th century. It was planted with noble trees, the showpiece of which is the 3-mile avenue of lime trees called the Duke's Drive. Near the ornamental lake stands an elegant 19th-century church in red and white sandstone, built by the 7th Duke as a private chapel. The imposing ducal mansion was, however, demolished in the 1930s when the estate was sold.

Continue past the Normanton Inn and in 1½ miles, at the crossroads, turn right on to the unclassified Thoresby Hall road.

THORESBY HALL, Notts
This gigantic Victorian mansion (OACT), home of the Countess Manvers, is the third stately home to stand on the 12,000-acre Dukeries park. It was designed by Anthony Salvin, who restored Windsor Castle, and is probably the largest Victorian house in England, with 29 main apartments and 78 bedrooms. The interior is lavishly decorated, and there are statues of Robin Hood and Little John in the library, carved by a Mansfield woodcarver. The estate was originally enclosed in the 17th century by the 1st Earl of Kingston. The park was laid out around beautiful ornamental lakes surrounded by avenues of chestnut trees. On the edge of the lake stands a 'model' village, built in 1807, and on the hillside above it is a folly called Budby Castle.

After 2½ miles turn left and join the A616, then in 1½ miles turn right on to the B6034 and continue to Edwinstowe.

EDWINSTOWE, Notts
This substantial colliery village is the biggest of the villages in the Dukeries area. The Birklands plantation, the oldest part of Sherwood Forest, comes right up to the edge of the village. Birklands means birch, and silver birch and oak trees are the main species in the estate. Part of Birklands is now the Sherwood Country Park and here the Major Oak stands. Named after a local historian, Major Rooke, the oak is the oldest tree in the forest, with a girth of 30ft around its hollow trunk. Although damaged by a storm in recent years, its massive branches spread a circumference of 270ft. This is said to have been Robin Hood's hideout for his outlaw band, and there is a local tale that Robin Hood and Maid Marion were married in Edwinstowe Church.

Continue on the B6034, and in 1 mile, at the traffic signals, go forward, then in ½ mile turn right on to the A614 to pass the entrance to Rufford Abbey.

RUFFORD ABBEY, Notts
A Cistercian abbey stood here from medieval times until the Dissolution of monasteries in Henry VIII's reign, when the estate was given to the Earl of Shrewsbury. It later passed into the hands of his daughter-in-law, Bess of Hardwick, who built a great mansion on the site which over the centuries has fallen in ruins. Her descendant, Sir George Savile, planted most of the oak and ash woodlands in the 18th century, and the estate is now a country park (OACT) with a lake and formal gardens.

Continue along the A614 for 1¾ miles, then turn left on to an unclassified road to Eakring.

EAKRING, Notts
Oil was first struck near this surprisingly rural village in 1939, which today stands at the centre of the Nottinghamshire oilfield. The village church contains a brass to the Revd William Mompesson who came here as vicar in 1670 from plague-ridden Eyam in Derbyshire. When he arrived in Eakring, however, his parishioners still feared the plague and at first refused to let him enter the village; a stone cross on the outskirts marks the place where he preached his sermons. Eventually all was well, and he remained in Eakring till his death in 1708.

Leave Eakring on the Kirklington road then ascend. On the descent there are good views before turning left on to the A617 for Kirklington. By the nearside of the village turn right on to the Southwell road. After 2½ miles turn right for Southwell town centre.

SOUTHWELL, Notts
The glory of Southwell is its great minster, a 12th- and 13th-century building with a Romanesque nave and transept. In the octagonal chapter house are exquisite carvings of foliage — oak, hawthorn and vine leaves. Vicar's Court, in the precinct, is a delightful group of 17th-century houses with hipped roofs. King Charles I spent his last night as a free man at the Saracen's Head, an old coaching inn in the town.

Leave Southwell on the A612 Newark road, and continue through Upton to Kelham then cross the Trent and return to Newark.

NORTHAMPTON, Northants
One of the largest market towns in England, Northampton is the administrative centre of its county and is noted for its high number of fine churches. Among the finest is Holy Sepulchre, a rare round church that was founded in 1110 and has been variously adapted through the ages. Inside is a 6ft-tall brass which dates from the 17th century and is one of the largest in England. Other old buildings include 17th-century Haselrigg House, the 16th-century Welsh House. Abington Park has landscaped surroundings, and a 15th- to 18th-century house containing a museum. The Northamptonshire Record office is housed in Delapre Abbey, a 19th-century building on the site of a Cluniac nunnery. The main industry of the town used to be shoe manufacturing whose history is displayed in the Museum of Leathercraft. One of the Eleanor Crosses erected by Edward I, can be seen on the town's southern outskirts.

Leave Northampton on the A4500 'Wellingborough' road and drive to Ecton.

ECTON, Northants
Features of this village include a 13th- and 14th-century church, a gothic-revival hall, and an elegant 17th-century manor house.

From Ecton drive for 1¼ miles and turn right on to the B573. Enter Earls Barton.

EARLS BARTON, Northants
The magnificent Saxon church tower here was built about 1,000 years ago and may once have been incorporated in the defences of a nearby Norman castle.

Continue through Great Doddington and in 1¼ miles meet traffic signals. Continue forward to Wellingborough.

WELLINGBOROUGH, Northants
Situated at the junction of the rivers Ise and Nene, this old market centre is now a rapidly developing town serving numerous light industries.

The Welland Valley near Harringworth is dominated by a stupendous railway viaduct.

NORTHAMPTONSHIRE RIVERLANDS

Between the meanderings of the Welland and Nene are forests and farms, water meadows loud with the calls of wildfowl, and villages of stone and thatch clustered round elegant church spires. Much of the countryside was once held by squires, and many of their sturdy farms survive.

Follow SP 'Peterborough' to join the A510, and continue to Finedon.

Fotheringhay's church is an imposing survival of a much larger structure.

FINEDON, Northants
Curiously decorated ironstone houses and cottages gather beneath the graceful 133ft spire of an ironstone church in this large village. The church dates from the 14th century, but most of the houses were built by the village squire in Victorian times.

Proceed for 3¾ miles and turn right on to the A604. In 3½ miles cross the River Nene into Thrapston.

THRAPSTON, Northants
The device from which the American Stars and Stripes were derived can be seen on a tablet to Sir John Washington in the village church. A nephew of Washington emigrated to America and was the great-grandfather of the first US president.

Return across the River Nene and turn right on to the A6116 to reach Islip.

ISLIP, Northants
Brasses re-created by the Reverend H Macklin, author of a standard book on this type of memorial, can be seen in Islip Church.

Proceed to Lowick.

LOWICK, Northants
Lowick's notable church has a 15th-century tower and 14th-century windows featuring 16 beautiful figures worked in stained glass.

Drive through Sudborough and on approaching Brigstock turn right on to a narrow unclassified road SP 'Lyveden'. Proceed for 2¼ miles; ½ mile to the right of the road is Lyveden New Bield.

LYVEDEN NEW BIELD, Northants
When Sir Thomas Tresham's family became involved in the Gunpowder Plot he had to stop building this ambitious house, which was begun in 1600 and still remains as a shell (NT). Its plan was meant to symbolize the Passion of Christ.

Continue for 2¼ miles and turn right on to the A427 to enter Oundle.

OUNDLE, Northants
Set in pleasant countryside by the River Nene, this stone-built town is a place of narrow streets and alleys between rows of old houses broken by the occasional tiny cottage or inn. Its well-known public school was founded in the 16th century by William Laxton, a grocer who was born here and eventually became Lord Mayor of London. Latham's Hospital dates from 1611. The Norman and later St Peters' has a magnificent 280-foot spire.

Leave Oundle and follow the 'Peterborough' road for 1¼ miles, then turn left on to an unclassified road SP 'Fotheringhay' and pass Cotterstock village on the left.

COTTERSTOCK, Northants
The poet John Dryden wrote his *Fables* in an attic room of 17th-century Cotterstock Hall while staying with his cousin, who owned it. Beautiful gardens lead from the house to the banks of the River Nene. In the village are a fine church, a 14th-century rectory, and an 18th-century mill with later mill cottages.

Drive through Tansor and continue to Fotheringhay.

FOTHERINGHAY, Northants
A mound here once carried the grim castle in which Mary Queen of Scots was imprisoned before her execution in 1587. Nowadays the mellow old cottages and willow-hung banks of the Nene create a tranquillity in which such macabre associations become difficult to believe. The imposing church was a gift from Edward IV.

Take the 'King's Cliffe' road and pass through Woodnewton to reach Apethorpe.

APETHORPE, Northants
Stone-built Apethorpe boasts a very large Tudor and later hall, and an imposing 13th- and 17th-century village church, now a museum.

Proceed to King's Cliffe.

KING'S CLIFFE, Northants
Features of this beautiful little village include 17th-century almshouses, a church with a Norman tower and 13th-century spire, and lovely surroundings.

Turn right to follow the 'Stamford' road and later turn left on to the A47. In $\frac{3}{4}$ mile turn right on to an unclassified road and drive to Collyweston.

COLLYWESTON, Northants
Stone roofing slates have been quarried here for many years. The church has a Saxon chancel wall, and a Dovecote dates from the 16th century.

Turn left on to the A43; and at roundabout take 3rd exit then shortly left into Duddington.

DUDDINGTON, Northants
Thatched cottages and a medieval 4-arched bridge across the River Welland help to make this one of the prettiest villages in the area. The picture is completed by a 17th-century watermill and mansion.

Drive through Duddington to rejoin the A43. In $\frac{3}{4}$ mile turn right on to the unclassified 'Wakerley' and 'Harringworth' road. Drive past extensive ironstone workings to reach Harringworth.

HARRINGWORTH, Northants
A spectacular feature of this village is the 82-arch brick-built railway viaduct that spans the Welland Valley here. This magnificent feat of engineering was built between 1874 and 1879.

Proceed south to Gretton.

GRETTON, Northants
Stocks and a whipping post still stand on the green in this attractive hilltop village, and fine views extend into the Welland Valley. A few 17th-century houses and a church with Norman origins are reminders of its long history.

Drive along the 'Weldon' road for $1\frac{1}{2}$ miles and turn left. In $\frac{3}{4}$ mile a detour may be made from the main route by turning left; this leads to Kirby Hall in $\frac{3}{4}$ miles and Deene Park in $2\frac{1}{4}$ miles.

Duddington's famous watermill was built in 1664

KIRBY HALL, Northants
This magnificent old house (AM) was begun in 1572 and bought by Sir Christopher Hatton, a favourite of Queen Elizabeth I. In the 17th century its appearance was completely changed by the architect Inigo Jones.

DEENE PARK, Northants
A little farther along the detour route from Kirby Hall is the 16th-century mansion of Deene Park (open), which stands in a lake-watered estate known for its rare trees.

Proceed along the main tour route to Weldon.

WELDON, Northants
The fine lantern tower carried by Weldon Church was once an invaluable landmark for travellers in thickly-wooded Rockingham Forest. An old lock-up once used for petty criminals stands on the green.

On entering Weldon turn right into Chapel Road then right at T-junction. At roundabout take 1st exit A43 for Geddington. Meet crossroads and turn left on to an unclassified road to enter the village.

Edward I erected this cross at Geddington in 1290, as a memorial to Queen Eleanor.

GEDDINGTON, Northants
One of the three surviving Eleanor Crosses stands in the main square of this lovely stone and thatch village, a reminder of the grief experienced by Edward I at the loss of his queen some 7 centuries ago. Of later date is the medieval bridge that spans the River Ise here, and $\frac{3}{4}$ mile south is 15th-century Boughton House (open), a monastery enlarged to its present magnificent proportions in the 16th and 17th centuries. Inside are art collections and sumptuous old furnishings, while all around are beautifully planned and tended gardens.

Return to the crossroads and drive forward on to the unclassified 'Newton' and 'Rushton' road. After Newton turn right then left under a railway. Continue to Rushton.

RUSHTON, Northants
Triangular Lodge (AM), a famous curiosity in the grounds of 15th-century Rushton Hall, is far more than a mere folly. Its peculiar design, in which the number three is depicted time and again, is a devout symbolization of the Trinity, disguised to fool religious persecutors during a time of repression. The village is a cluster of golden ironstone houses on the banks of the River Ise.

In Rushton turn right SP 'Desborough'; at Desborough turn left on to the A6 to reach Rothwell.

It is thought that Inigo Jones may have been responsible for the ornamental garden gateway of Kirby Hall.

ROTHWELL, Northants
Inside the mainly 13th-century church of this old industrial town is a charnel containing thousands of bones. The centre of Rothwell is graced by the elegant 16th-century Market House (AM).

Turn right on to the B576 and proceed to Lamport.

LAMPORT, Northants
Mainly 17th- and 18th-century Lamport Hall (open) is set in an attractive park featuring an early alpine rock garden. Inside the house are paintings by Van Dyck and other artists, and an excellent collection of china and furniture.

In Lamport turn left on to the A508 and drive to Brixworth.

BRIXWORTH, Northants
Local Roman buildings were cannibalised to provide materials for a fine church raised here in the 7th century. The skill of the Saxon builders has been well proved, because today the church survives as one of the finest of its type.

Pass the Red Lion (PH) and turn left on to the unclassified 'Sywell' road. Later cross the Pitsford Reservoir into Holcot, meet crossroads, and turn right SP 'Northampton' to reach Moulton. In Moulton turn left and shortly right onto the A43 to return to Northampton.

NORWICH, Norfolk

Once an important centre of the worsted trade, this county town stands on the River Wensum and boasts a cathedral with one of the finest interiors in the country. It dates from Norman times and contains the oldest bishop's throne still used in England. Other major features include a fine presbytery, a beautiful cloister, and a magnificent nave roof featuring many of the 800 roof bosses to be found in the cathedral. Access to the building is by two fine gates, the Erpingham of 1420 and St Ethelbert's of 1272 (both AM). Close to a former water gate on the river are Pull's Ferry and the Barge Inn, two reminders of the city's antiquity, and amongst the many other fine old buildings are no less than 30 parish churches. The largest and finest of these is St Peter Mancroft, which carries a notable tower, but all the others have particular details that make them worth a visit. St Andrew's dates from the 15th century and displays a remarkable series of carved shields, and St Michael-at-Coslany has fine flintwork in the Thorpe Chapel. Norwich Castle (open) was started c1130, but its Norman origins have been heavily disguised by 19th-century refacing. Survivals from the medieval city and later are many. Flint-faced Bridewell is a 14th-century merchant's house that now contains a museum; the Cow Tower (AM) dates from the same period and formed part of a defensive system along the river bank. Slightly later is the St Peter Hungate Church, a 15th-century building which carries a fine hammerbeam roof and now houses a museum. In the 1920s a chapel was converted to house the well-known Maddermarket Theatre. The most famous of the city's many picturesque streets is Elm Hill, a cobbled road lined with old colour-washed shops and houses, while the most outstanding of its lay buildings are the 15th-century Suckling House and chequered-flint Guildhall. In 1978 the supermarket magnet Sir Robert Sainsbury presented the University the Sainsbury Centre for Visual Arts, which is housed in an outstanding modern building. The colourful open-air market has been a weekday occurrence since Norman times.
Leave Norwich on the A47 'Yarmouth' road and pass through Thorpe St Andrew to Blofield.

BLOFIELD, Norfolk

Blofield Church, an impressive building that forms a landmark visible for miles round the village, is noted for its tall west tower. Inside is an 8-sided font ornamented with various scenes in relief.
Continue to Acle.

ACLE, Norfolk

This well-known touring centre is within easy reach of the lovely Norfolk Broads and is a good base from which to explore the area. Its unusual church has a picturesque thatched roof and a round tower

AMONG THE NORFOLK BROADS

Close to the great cathedral city of Norwich are marshlands, meres, and lakes in a landscape dotted with the stark shapes of old wind pumps. Hidden canals link vast acreages of water drained from the local countryside, offering ideal highways by which to explore the broadlands.

Norwich Castle rises high above the city from a landscaped hilltop.

that dates from the 12th century. East of the village, on the tour route, are several windpumps that have survived from the days when many such machines were built to pump excess water from the reclaimed marshlands.
Continue along the A47 to Great Yarmouth.

GREAT YARMOUTH, Norfolk

Holiday amenities in this important oil and fishing port include 5 miles of seafront fringed by excellent sands and backed by colourful gardens. Its situation on Breydon Water, the combined estuaries of the Bure, Waveney and Yare, gives it an

Ormesby, one of Broadland's loveliest stretches of water.

aspect that suits both the holidaymakers and the busy maritime traffic that uses its harbour. The town is very old and has managed to retain many historic features. Most of these can be seen in the South Quay area, where there are remains of the town walls and the notable Custom House. Leading from the town wall to the quay are the Rows, a number of narrow lanes where the 300-year-old Merchant's House (AM) can be seen. Close by is the 14th-century Greyfriar's Cloister (AM). The Elizabethan House Museum has a largely 16th-century interior disguised by a Georgian

façade. Exhibits include furniture from that and later periods, and a fascinating collection of Victorian toys. The 13th-century building that houses the Tollhouse Museum is one of the oldest in Great Yarmouth and incorporates ancient dungeons. Close to England's largest parish church is Anna Sewell House, a 17th-century building that was the birthplace of the authoress of *Black Beauty*. The House of Wax museum features various historical figures and scenes , and the Maritime Museum of East Anglia illustrates life saving and marine oil exploration. Near Wellington Pier in an acre of landscaped garden is the quaint Merrivale Model Village.
Leave Great Yarmouth on the A149 SP 'Caister'. In 2 miles meet a roundabout and drive forward to enter Caister.

CAISTER-ON-SEA, Norfolk

Remains of town walls and a gateway (AM) survive from the time when this popular little resort was a Roman settlement. Much more recent is the 15th-century castle (open), whose remains now house a museum of veteran and vintage cars.
From the town centre turn left on to the A1064 'Acle' road and pass the remains of Caister Roman Town on the right. Meet a roundabout and take the 2nd exit. In ¾ mile turn right on to an unclassified road SP 'Great Ormesby', and in 1 mile turn left on to the A149 to enter Ormesby St Margaret – at the edge of the Broads country.

THE BROADS, Norfolk

More than 30 large and very beautiful sheets of water, often linked by navigable channels, are contained in a triangular area between Norwich, Lowestoft, and Sea Palling. These, together with many rivers, lakes, and canals, provide some 200 miles of water for cruising and sailing. The essential character of the Broads can only be properly appreciated from a boat, and there are hire firms and tour operators in such centres as Wroxham, Horning and Potter Heigham. Angling permits are available from tackle shops in these and other towns.
A short and very pleasant detour from the main route can be made by staying on the A149 and continuing to Ormesby Broad.

ORMESBY BROAD, Norfolk

The main road between Ormesby St Margaret and Rollesby crosses this vast expanse of water and offers some of the best broadland views available to the motorist.
On the main route, drive to the war memorial in Ormesby St Margaret and turn right on to an unclassified road alongside the green, SP 'Scratby'. Meet a T-junction and turn right SP 'Hemsby'. At Hemsby, drive to the end of the village and turn left on to the B1159 SP 'Mundesley'. Continue along a winding road to Winterton.

WINTERTON-ON-SEA, Norfolk

Much of the countryside round this little fishing village is included in a 260-acre nature reserve.

Continue to West Somerton.

WEST SOMERTON, Norfolk

Situated at the weedy eastern end of Martham Broad, this quiet village is an excellent angling base and a good place to see how the marshes were drained. A maze of streams and man-made ditches still carries excess water into the main broads, and two windpumps that were used to pump from one level to another can be seen near by.

Continue with SP 'Cromer' to Horsey Mere.

Horsey Church is noted for its thatched roof and unusual stained-glass windows.

HORSEY MERE, Norfolk

Access to this important breeding ground for marshland plants and animals is restricted to naturalists and permit holders. The mere's drainage windmill (NT) was built in 1912 and has been well restored.

Continue to Horsey.

HORSEY, Norfolk

Despite frequent incursions of the sea since it was built, the thatched village church has retained its Norman round tower.

Continue to Sea Palling, then in 1¾ miles turn left B1151 to Stalham.

STALHAM, Norfolk

Two miles south east of Stalham is the Sutton windmill, the tallest windmill in the country built in 1789 it has nine floors plus a cap floor, and a museum.

Return to B1159 turn left and continue to Lessingham, then Happisburgh.

HAPPISBURGH, Norfolk

Offshore shipping is warned away from the treacherous Haisboro' Sands by a lighthouse, but the same drifts provide sun and sea bathers with a superb dune-backed beach. The name of this pretty little fishing village is pronounced Hazeborough.

In 1¾ miles meet crossroads and turn right for Walcott. Continue to Bacton.

BACTON, Norfolk

Easy access to the broad local beach of shingly sand and pebbles is via a high sea wall. The village itself is an attractive little place that grew up alongside Broomholm Priory, a 12th-century foundation that claimed to possess a piece of the True Cross and became a great centre of pilgrimage. Remains of the priory, which was mentioned by Chaucer, include the gatehouse, north transept, chapter house, and refectory.

Drive past a windmill to Mundesley.

West Somerton was the haunt of smuggling gangs in the 18th century.

The best way to appreciate the Norfolk Broads is by boat.

MUNDESLEY, Norfolk

This quiet resort has a gently shelving sand beach backed by cliffs. It is associated with the poet William Cowper.

Continue to Trimingham.

TRIMINGHAM, Norfolk

Some of the highest cliffs in Norfolk overlook a good bathing beach here. A painted screen can be seen in the local church.

Continue to Overstrand.

OVERSTRAND, Norfolk

Pleasant cliff walks lead from here to the nearby resort of Cromer, and safe bathing can be enjoyed from the local sands. The 14th-century Church of St Martin was built after the old parish church fell into the sea.

Continue to Cromer.

CROMER, Norfolk

Although a bustling resort mainly occupied with the needs of holidaymakers, Cromer still has a small fishing fleet and has the reputation for supplying the best crabs in England. Its sandy beach is backed by lofty cliffs, and its many amenities include a zoo and boating pool. The 15th-century parish church carries one of the tallest towers in Norfolk. Close to Cromer is Felbrigg Hall (NT), a fine house that dates from the 17th century.

Leave Cromer on the A149 'Norwich' road and in 2¼ miles bear left SP 'North Walsham'. Continue to Thorpe Market and North Walsham.

NORTH WALSHAM, Norfolk

Homely buildings and winding little lanes make this beautiful market town well worth a pause in any journey. Its fine church is given an air of gothic mystery by a ruined tower that fell in 1724. Inside are a painted screen, a tall 15th-century font cover, and various monuments. The local grammar school was founded in the early 17th century.

Follow SP 'Norwich' on the B1150. Pass Westwick Park and drive beneath an arched gateway which spans the road; continue to Coltishall.

COLTISHALL, Norfolk

This shooting and angling centre is situated on the River Bure and enjoys a genteelly relaxed atmosphere imparted by many 18th-century buildings.

Cross the River Bure to Horstead.

HORSTEAD, Norfolk

Horstead Church carries a slender west tower that dates from the 13th century. The delightful village mill stands opposite the miller's house.

Drive through wooded countryside and return to Norwich.

NORWICH AND THE WAVENEY VALLEY

South of the fine old cathedral city of Norwich lies an area of lovely wooded countryside that stretches down to the Suffolk border, where the River Waveney meanders through a tranquil valley of great beauty.

NORWICH, Norfolk

East Anglia's capital city is full of curious old streets and alleys, antique and curio shops, with interesting buildings at almost every turn. Elm Hill, a narrow cobbled lane, pretty, and crowded with ancient shops and courtyards, is the best known of all the old streets, but there are many more around the market place. Every day, except Sunday, there is a large bustling market beside the old Guildhall, built in the 15th century of local knapped flints. Not far away on St Andrew's Street, Strangers' Hall museum is a fascinatingly-preserved medieval merchant's house, its rooms furnished in the style of different periods. Nearby, in a little alley off Bedford Street stands the Bridewell Museum of local crafts, and near to it is a Dickensian-looking mustard shop and small museum run by Colmans, who still manufacture mustard in Norwich. The castle, a square Norman keep raised high on a mound overlooking the centre, is now the city museum and art gallery, with a fine collection of pictures by John Crome and John Sell Cotman, leaders of the Norwich School of painters who flourished in the last century. Undoubtedly the finest sight in Norwich, however, is the beautiful Norman cathedral, whose slender spire rises above the water meadows of the River Wensum. Work on the cathedral began in 1069 and continued for over 50 years. There are 2 medieval gates to the precincts, the Ethelbert and the Erpingham; just inside the latter stands Norwich School, founded in 1316, at which Horatio Nelson was a pupil for a short time. The lovely walled cathedral Close, bordered by elegant 18th-century houses, stretches down to the river where a charming 16th-century house known as Pull's Ferry (not open) is portrayed in many local paintings and postcards. Apart from the great Norman cathedral, Norwich has a Roman Catholic cathedral and 32 medieval churches; once there were even more and it was said that the city had a church for every week of the year, but a pub for every day.

Leave Norwich on the A11, SP 'Thetford'. In 9 miles turn right, SP 'Town Centre', into Wymondham.

WYMONDHAM, Norfolk

This small country town, pronounced Windham, is a delightful jumble of old cottages, traditional shops, timbered inns and 18th-century houses. At the centre of the old streets is an ornate half-timbered Butter Cross, raised on wooden pillars. The spectacular abbey church, with 2 great towers at each end, was once shared by the monks of the priory (now ruined) and the townspeople. As a result of a quarrel with the town, the monks built a wall to isolate their part of the church and so the townsfolk built the great square west tower for themselves. The monks' part of the church was later destroyed, leaving only the tower.

Leave Wymondham on the B1135, and continue to Kimberley, then turn left on to the B1108 for Hingham.

HINGHAM, Norfolk

The large number of elegant redbrick Georgian houses in this attractive village show that it was once a thriving market town. Hingham was the birthplace of one Samuel Lincoln, who emigrated to America in 1637 and there raised a family whose most famous descendant, 2 centuries later, was Abraham Lincoln, who became president of the United States. The bust of Lincoln in the imposing village church was presented by the people of Hingham, Massachusetts, the New World town in which Samuel Lincoln had settled.

Continue on the B1108 and later pass Scoulton Mere (right) before reaching Scoulton. 1½ miles beyond the village turn left on to the B1077, SP 'Attleborough'. In 2 miles, at the T-junction, turn left. The B1077 leads through Great Ellingham to Attleborough.

ATTLEBOROUGH, Norfolk

Although not a particularly attractive town, there is a fine church with a famous and beautiful 15th-century rood screen. The countryside round here is celebrated for the rearing of fine turkeys and ducks and until recently there was a vast annual turkey fair at Attleborough.

Leave Attleborough on the B1077 Diss road and continue to Old Buckenham.

OLD BUCKENHAM, Norfolk

The village green is so enormous that the groups of cottages round the edges have remained as separate little hamlets, each with its own delightful name — Hog's Snout, Puddledock and Loss Wroo are just a few examples.

1½ miles beyond the village turn left on to the B1113 to visit New Buckenham.

NEW BUCKENHAM, Norfolk

'New' is a relative term, for this charming village is at least 8 centuries old and preserves a street plan laid out in medieval times. Its pretty cottages lead up to a village green, near which stands a 17th-century market house supported on wooden posts. The one at the centre served in bygone days as a whipping post. A little way outside the village is the castle mound with the ruins of the castle built in 1145.

Return along the B1113 and follow the Stowmarket road to Banham.

BANHAM, Norfolk

The village of Banham is exceptionally pretty with elm trees round its green. Nearby, Banham Zoo and Monkey Sanctuary is famous for its colony of woolly monkeys, one of only 6 in the whole of Europe. Woolly monkeys came originally from the rain forests of the Amazon Basin in South America, and are a delicate breed, difficult to rear in our climate. Many other species of monkeys from Africa and Asia can be seen here too, as well as other types of animals and birds of prey. Also within the zoo grounds is Lord Cranworth's motor museum. Racing cars, motorcycles and children's pedal cars dating from the 1920s to the 1960s are all displayed in an imaginative setting.

Continue on the B1113 to Kenninghall, and at the end of the village turn left for North Lopham. In 1 mile, at South Lopham, turn left on to the A1066. Later (right) are Bressingham Gardens.

Colman's Mustard Shop in Bridewell Alley, Norwich, has a small museum

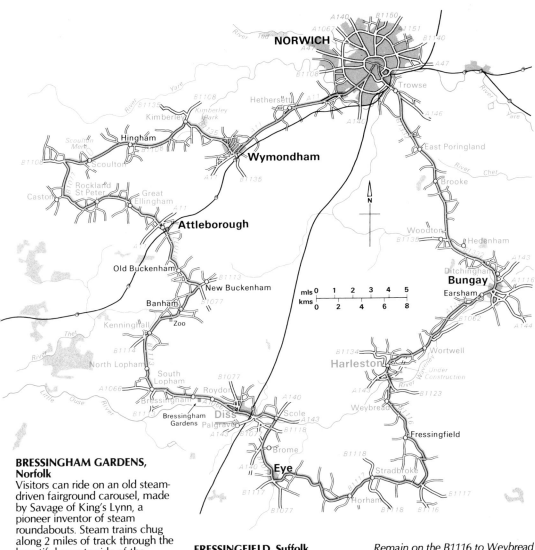

EARSHAM, Norfolk

In 1965 naturalist Philip Wayre set up an Otter Trust (OACT) on the banks of the Waveney at Earsham, and now it has the largest collection of otters in the world. As well as British otters, European, North American and Asian otters are bred here in semi-natural conditions. There are also large lakes with a variety of waterfowl and a pleasant walk can be taken alongside the river.

Continue on the A143 to Bungay.

BUNGAY, Suffolk

Bungay is a fascinating place, with a history that goes back long before the Norman Conquest. There was a massive castle here in Norman times, and in a part of the ruins, traces of an old mining gallery can be seen. This is thought to date from the days of Henry II, when the lord of the castle, Hugh Bigod, defied the king, and an attempt was made to undermine the castle walls by tunnelling. The castle in fact survived many years after this, only to be demolished by local entrepreneurs looking for good building stone. Bungay has many fine buildings, including an outstanding 17th-century Butter Cross, built to keep the butter cool on market days, surmounted by the figure of Justice. Printing and leather-working have been the town's major industries since the 18th century.

Follow SP 'Norwich' to join the B1332. Continue through Brooke and Poringland and in 3 miles, at the traffic signals, turn left on to the A146 for the return to Norwich.

The delightful village green at Banham, overlooked by church and Guildhall

BRESSINGHAM GARDENS, Norfolk

Visitors can ride on an old steam-driven fairground carousel, made by Savage of King's Lynn, a pioneer inventor of steam roundabouts. Steam trains chug along 2 miles of track through the beautiful countryside of the Waveney valley, and the 6 acres of gardens specialising in alpine plants and hardy perennials, are a delightful spectacle at all seasons of the year.

Remain on the A1066 and beyond Roydon bear right to reach Diss. Leave on the A1066 and at the end of the town join the A143 for Scole. Here, turn right on to the A140, SP 'Ipswich'. Cross the River Waveney into Suffolk then in 1½ miles turn left on to the B1077 for Eye.

EYE, Suffolk

The church at Eye, with its wonderful tower of superb Suffolk flushwork, rising over 100ft, is the pride of this enchanting little place, but its appealing streets are packed with interesting old buildings of all periods. The timber-framed Guildhall dates from the 16th century and there are a number of fine houses in the streets leading up to the ruins of the Norman castle.

At Eye branch left, then left again on to the B1117. Follow a winding road to Horham, where the road bears left and continues to Stradbrooke. In 2¾ miles turn left on to the B1116, SP 'Harleston', and later pass through Fressingfield.

FRESSINGFIELD, Suffolk

This attractive village, deep in the Suffolk countryside, is a mecca for gourmets who come from all over the country to dine at the Fox and Goose Inn, a charming timber-framed building, once the Guildhall of the village.

Remain on the B1116 to Weybread and later cross the River Waveney back into Norfolk. On reaching the main road turn right and enter Harleston. Continue on the A143 Yarmouth road, which follows the Waveney valley through Wortwell to Earsham.

GREAT HOUSES OF NORFOLK

From Norwich, the beating heart of Norfolk, the tour meanders to the peaceful seaside resorts of Cromer and Sheringham, through a landscape of broad fields and slumbering villages overlorded by churches of medieval splendour and great manor houses.

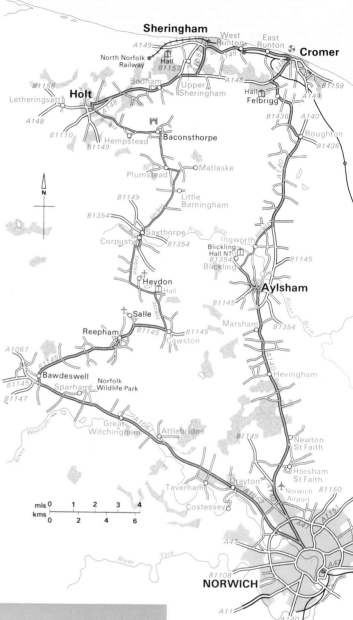

NORWICH, Norfolk

Onetime centre of the worsted trade, Norwich is now a county borough, port, industrial centre and cathedral city. The charm of Norwich lies in its combination of antiquity and modernity and the history that has made it one of Britain's most flourishing cities. See page 40 or 42.

Leave Norwich on the A140, SP 'Cromer', and beyond the Airport continue to the edge of Marsham. In 1 mile, at the roundabout, go forward on to the B1145 into Aylsham.

AYLSHAM, Norfolk

This is a charming little market town with many old buildings, brick-built and Dutch-gabled. Wherries — light flat-bottomed rowing boats — sailing up the Bure, now no longer so navigable, brought wealth in the Middle Ages to this town noted for its worsted cloth and linen. John of Gaunt is said to have held the manor at Blickling, and to have founded the church in 1380. The church has altered little since his day, and contains a fine font and, of particular interest, a copy of the Breeches Bible of 1611; so called for the passage in Genesis which reads 'they sewed fig leaves together and made themselves breeches'. The famous landscape gardener Humphry Repton (1752-1818) is buried in the churchyard.

In Aylsham turn left, SP 'Saxthorpe', on to the B1354. In 1½ miles (right) is Blickling Hall.

BLICKLING HALL, Norfolk

Yew hedges (15ft across) planted in the late 17th century line velvet lawns either side of the driveway which sweeps up to the pleasingly symmetrical Jacobean front of Blickling Hall (NT). Between 2 tall turrets a Dutch-gabled roofline culminates in a central domed turret, beneath which mullioned windows complete the picture of a perfect English country house. The house was begun in 1616 within a dry moat on the side of an old hall in which Anne Boleyn was born. The Jacobean exterior hides a Georgian interior; much was remodelled by the 2nd Earl of Buckinghamshire during the 18th century, although the long gallery still keeps its splendid plaster moulded ceiling of the 1620s.

Return along the B1354 for ½ miles then turn left, SP 'Cromer'. In 1 mile turn left and cross the River Bure into Ingworth and in 1½ miles turn left on to the A140. At Roughton turn left on to the B1436 which leads to Felbrigg.

FELBRIGG, Norfolk

The Felbrigg estate lies on top of a ridge, now divorced from the village of Felbrigg which may have been moved as a result of the plague and re-established in its present position to avoid further

infection. The Jacobean entrance front of Felbrigg Hall (NT) was built in the 1620s, and in 1665 a new brick wing was added to the south. Then in the 18th century William Windham II had the house refurbished in contemporary style, after the completion of his Grand Tour of Europe, creating a new dining room, staircase and a Gothic library. The glorious plaster ceiling in the dining room was left untouched and dates from 1687.

½ mile beyond the entrance to Felbrigg Hall turn right on to the A148 for Cromer.

The garden at Blickling Hall has a long history, but the main flower beds and lawns seen here date from the 1930s

CROMER, Norfolk

The splendid Perpendicular church tower, 160ft high, of this ancient fishing village served as a lighthouse before the construction of a purpose-built one. The old village survives in the midst of a Victorian seaside resort born of the railway age. The impressive seafront is backed by high cliffs topped by hotels which are reached by steep stone steps. The crabs along this coast are the best in England and Cromer crab is renowned. It is the chief catch here, and the boats used are a special small double-ended broad-beamed variety — a version of the Shetland boats which came down this coast after herring. There is no harbour here, and the boats are launched and landed from the beach.

Traditional gardens in Heydon

Leave on the A149, SP 'Sheringham', and pass through East and West Runton to Sheringham.

SHERINGHAM, Norfolk

Sheringham, like Cromer, was also established as a resort during the railway age, and the old flint village is still discernible within the Victorian brick town. Crab is also the main catch here, but when the weather is bad the fishermen collect the pebbles from the beach which are then ground down to make glazes for the local pottery. Sheringham Hall (open by appointment) is a Regency building in a beautiful park (OACT), both the work of Humphry Repton. The highlight of the estate is perhaps the mile-long rhododendron drive which was planted in the 19th century. Sheringham Station is the headquarters of the North Norfolk Railway and steam-hauled trains operate. There is also rolling stock and a museum.

Leave on the A1082, SP 'Holt'. Climb through wooded country then turn right on to the A148, SP 'King's Lynn', and continue to Holt.

HOLT, Norfolk

The town of Holt has a well-kept appearance and there is nothing to offend the eye. Here and there among the smartly painted walls

the flintwork shows itself to advantage, indicating that this stone is the main building material of the area. Most famous of its buildings is Gresham's School, founded by Sir John Gresham who was born here in 1519. Gresham became Lord Mayor of London and also founded the Royal Exchange there.

From the town centre follow the unclassified Baconsthorpe road and continue to Baconsthorpe.

BACONSTHORPE, Norfolk

Baconsthorpe Castle (AM) stands sadly forgotten among muddy Norfolk farmland which now has greater importance than the castle itself. It was a fortified manor house built by Sir Henry Heydon in 1486. The gatehouse stands well preserved, as do the curtain walls, the remains of a 17th-century dwelling hall and an 18th-century Gothic mansion, built in front of the castle largely from stone taken from the original building.

Follow SP 'North Walsham' to Plumstead. ½ mile beyond the village, at the crossroads, turn right on to the Saxthorpe road. In 3¼ miles keep forward on to the B1149 into Saxthorpe. Cross the River Bure and turn right, SP 'Heydon', then immediately turn left at the Dukes Head Inn. In 2 miles, at the T-junction, turn left. In ½ mile, at the crossroads, turn left again into Heydon.

HEYDON, Norfolk

This is an extremely pretty village of pleasant houses centred around a charming village green. Heydon Hall (open by appointment) begun in 1581 but much enlarged since, is the home of the Bulwer family, of whom Lord Lytton, author of *The Last Days of Pompeii* was a member. The house has an E-shaped 3-storey front and the grounds include an ice-house and a lookout tower.

Return to the crossroads and turn left, SP 'Cawston'. In 1 mile turn right and continue to the edge of Cawston. Turn right on to the B1145 Bawdeswell road, and in 1½ miles pass the turning on the right leading to Salle.

SALLE, Norfolk

The tiny village of Salle is the unlikely site of a cathedral-like church full of rich treasures, totally out of proportion to the almost non-existent parish which it serves. It was built by 3 immensely wealthy local families; the Briggs, the Fountaynes, and the Boleyns. Anne Boleyn (wife of Henry VIII) is said to be buried here, but it is more likely her remains lie in the Tower of London where she was beheaded. Over the west door are 2 lovely feathered angels carrying censers. Within is an unusual font on which the symbols of the 7 sacraments are carved.

Continue along the B1145 into Reepham.

REEPHAM, Norfolk

This little 18th-century town has outdone other similar East Anglia towns with 2 parish churches sharing the same churchyard, because Reepham has 3. Hackford parish church burnt down in 1543, and only a ruined wall remains, but the other 2 are still standing. St Mary's is the parish church of Reepham and contains an especially delicate altar-tomb to Sir Roger de Kerdiston, who died in 1337. Nearby St Michael's has an excellent Jacobean pulpit.

Cromer's Victorian seafront. The tower of the old village church soaring above the 19th-century town was used as a lighthouse in days gone by

At the crossroads turn right with the B1145 for Bawdeswell.

BAWDESWELL, Norfolk

This village lies on an ancient route once used by pilgrims on their way from Norwich to the shrine of Our Lady of Walsingham. A timber-framed house in the village street, called Chaucer House, recalls that the reeve in Chaucer's *Canterbury Tales* came 'from Norfolk, near a place called Bawdeswell.'

At the end of the village turn left on to the A1067, SP 'Norwich'. In 2¼ miles pass, (left), the Norfolk Wildlife Park.

NORFOLK WILDLIFE PARK, Norfolk

The well-known naturalist Philip Wayre opened the Norfolk Wildlife Park and Pheasant Trust in 1961, which was originally his private collection. It boasts the largest collection of European animals in the world, but the zoo breeds more animals than it takes from the wild, and where possible returns animals bred in captivity to their natural habitat to boost the native population. The zoo has a remarkable breeding record, and is dedicated to the conservation of endangered species. Animals which are kept here range from the European beaver to the European bison, stone curlews to European eagle owls. This 50-acre site is also the home of the Pheasant Trust. This was started in 1959 to begin the captive breeding of endangered species of wild pheasants in order that natural populations could be restocked, a policy carried out with outstanding success.

Follow the A1067 through the Wensum valley and pass through Great Witchingham (Lenwade) before the return to Norwich.

NOTTINGHAM, Notts

The growth of this ancient city was influenced by the Saxons, Danes, and Normans, but it was the industrial revolution that made it a thriving commercial centre famous for fine lace. Early prosperity was aided by the natural highway provided by the River Trent, a strategic advantage that may have prompted William the Conqueror to build a strong castle here soon after his invasion of Britain. It was destroyed in the reign of Stephen, rebuilt by Henry II, and throughout the turmoil of the Wars of the Roses remained loyal to the cause of the Yorkists. When the Tudors came to the throne it fell into a slow decline and was reduced to ruins by the time it was bought by the Duke of Newcastle in 1651. The duke converted the soundest parts of the building into a house, but this was gutted by Reform Bill rioters in 1831. Nowadays the castle is the property of the Corporation and houses a museum and art gallery. Among several good churches in Nottingham is St Mary's, a splendid example of 15th-century architecture with excellent windows and a glorious Madonna and Child painted by Bartolommeo. Other notable buildings include the 18th-century Shire Hall, the partly-medieval Trip to Jerusalem Inn, and a wealth of Georgian domestic architecture. The city's natural history museum is in Wollaton Hall, a 16th-century building that stands close to the university campus.

Leave the city with SP 'Loughborough A60' and cross the River Trent. A pleasant detour from the main route to Holme Pierrepont can be made by turning left on to the A6011.

HOLME PIERREPONT, Notts

This early Tudor hall (open) was built to a medieval design c1500 and contains a fine collection of 17th-century English oak furniture. Its grounds include a formal courtyard garden of Victorian date, a country park, and a national and international competition and training centre for water sports.

On the main route, continue along the A60 and pass Ruddington and Bradmore to reach Bunny.

Victorian Belvoir Castle dominates the surrounding landscape.

THE FORESTS OF SHERWOOD

Away from the industry of the coalfields is a picturesque countryside of forests, farms, and villages thick with legends of Robin Hood and his outlaw band. Great oaks grow in Sherwood, and fertile countryside follows the meandering course of the River Trent.

BUNNY, Notts

A great deal of this village was designed in the 17th century by Thomas Parkyns, who did as much as he could to improve the living conditions of his tenants by rebuilding farms and providing four charming almshouses. He lived at Bunny Hall, and his great love for sporting combat earned him the title The Wrestling Baron. This passionate interest is evident in his book *The Cornish Hugg*, and his self-designed graveyard monument shows him in an aggressive stance at the start of a bout. The local church dates from the 14th century and contains several good monuments.

Beyond Bunny turn right on to an unclassified road SP 'Gotham, East Leake' and skirt wooded Bunny Hill. Reach a railway bridge and after another ½ mile turn left. Continue to East Leake, meet a T-junction, and turn right for East Leake Church.

EAST LEAKE, Notts

Inside the partly Norman church at East Leake is an unusual vamping horn, a type of trumpet that was once used during choir services to 'vamp up' or encourage the singers.

Return to the centre of East Leake and keep straight on to Costock. Cross a main road, continue through Wysall to Keyworth, then turn right and drive to Widmerpool.

WIDMERPOOL, Notts

Some of the county's loveliest woodland scenery makes a perfect setting for this charming little village. The picturesquely ruined church has a 19th-century body with a 14th-century tower and contains an exquisite marble sculpture.

On the nearside of Widmerpool turn left SP 'Kinoulton', and in 1¼ miles cross two main roads. The 2nd of these follows the old Fosse Way.

FOSSE WAY

Much of this ancient Romanized track is followed by modern main roads, though parts are still foot and bridle paths.

In a short distance descend and keep forward into Kinoulton.

KINOULTON, Notts

Glorious views over the rich Vale of Belvoir and mature woodlands known as the Borders can be enjoyed from this high village, which claims to have one of the best cricket grounds in the county. The local church, built in brick by the Earl of Gainsborough c1793, stands opposite a forge.

Meet a T-junction and turn right to Hickling, then drive forward along a winding road for Nether Broughton. Continue with SP 'Melton' to turn left on to the A606, and in 1¼ miles climb Broughton Hill at the northern end of the Leicestershire Wolds. Meet crossroads, turn left on to the unclassified 'Eastwell' road, then in ¾ mile keep forward and meet a T-junction. Turn left SP 'Eastwell', and after 4 miles meet crossroads and turn left again, SP 'Harby'. After a short distance descend 524ft Harby Hill, and continue to Harby. Turn right SP 'Bottesford', and in 4 miles pass a right turn leading to Belvoir Castle. A worthwhile detour can be made from the main route to this historic building.

BELVOIR CASTLE, Leics

Nowadays the superb site overlooking the Vale of Belvoir is occupied by a 19th-century 'castle' by architect James Wyatt, but originally this windy ridge was guarded by a strong medieval fortress that was occupied by the Manners family in the 16th century. This original castle was built in the late 11th century by Robert de Todeni. His coffin is on display in the present castle. The old castle was twice remodelled and finally much of it was destroyed by fire in the 19th century. Its rebuilding and refurbishment were supervised by Sir John Thoroton, friend and chaplain to the Manners family. The present structure (open) is renowned for its pictures, superb Gobelin Tapestries, and a regimental museum of the 17th/21st Lancers. The attractive grounds of the castle contain a number of interesting features including several statues, a mausoleum and a temple.

Continue to Bottesford.

BOTTESFORD, Leics

The church in this village is one of the best in the county and contains an outstanding collection of monuments. Old stocks and a whipping post are preserved near the remains of an old cross, and attractive Fleming's Bridge dates from the 17th century.

In Bottesford turn left on to the A52 and continue to Bingham.

Bottesford still retains its old stocks and whipping post.

BINGHAM, Notts

The most notable building in this village is the church, which boasts a fine tower capped by a spire. Some of its windows date from the 14th and 15th centuries.

Meet traffic signals and turn right on to the B687 SP 'Newark'. In 1 mile meet a roundabout and take the 2nd exit on to the A6097, then after a further 1 mile pass East Bridgford on the right.

EAST BRIDGFORD, Notts

Several good Georgian cottages and houses can be seen in this village, which occupies an attractively wooded site above the River Trent.

Descend and cross the River Trent, then meet a roundabout and take the 2nd exit to skirt Lowdham. In 1¼ miles turn left on to the unclassified 'Woodborough' road. Continue to Woodborough.

WOODBOROUGH, Notts

The broad upper windows in the terraced cottages of this village were once filled by the frames of stocking knitters, for whom the terraces were originally built. Inside the attractive 14th-century church is later monumental sculpture and carving.

Drive to the end of Woodborough, turn left to reach high ground, and in 1½ miles turn right on to the B684. After another 1½ miles turn right on to the A614, then in 3½ miles turn left on to the unclassified 'Kirkby-in-Ashfield' road to enter Sherwood Forest.

SHERWOOD FOREST, Notts

All that remains of the 100,000-acre wood and pasture land that surrounded Nottingham in the 13th century are a few tracts between that city and the Dukeries District. The area is inextricably meshed with the legend of Robin Hood, the philanthropic outlaw who is popularly thought to have been born in Locksley c1160. Tradition has it that Robin of Locksley was the true Earl of Huntingdon, and the legend is perpetuated by many local

Magnificent old oak trees still survive in Sherwood Forest, part of which is now a country park.

references. An old oak known as Robin Hood's Larder stands within the boundaries of Sherwood, but the oldest tree in the forest is claimed to be Green Dale Oak, which stands south of Welbeck Abbey and is also said to be the largest in the district. Part of the area has been preserved as the Burntstump Country Park.

In 1¼ miles turn right SP 'Blidworth', and after a further ½ mile turn left on to the B6020 SP 'Sutton-in-Ashfield', passing through the edge of Blidworth.

BLIDWORTH, Notts

Tradition has it that this colliery village was the home of Friar Tuck and Maid Marian, characters that add the essential ingredients of humour and romance to the Robin Hood legend. The fellow outlaw and friend of Robin, Will Scarlet, is said to be buried in the local churchyard.

In 2½ miles meet crossroads and turn left on to the A60 to pass the entrance of Newstead Abbey on the right.

The superb lake provides a perfect setting for Newstead Abbey.

NEWSTEAD ABBEY, Notts

An abbey founded here in the 12th century was converted into a house in 1550 and later was to be the ancestral home of the poet Lord Byron. In 1931 the house (open) was given to the city of Nottingham, and today it provides a fitting setting for

relics of the poet, and of the explorer Dr Livingstone – who stayed here in 1864. Surviving features of the religious foundation include the west front of the priory church, the cloisters, and the Chapter House.

Continue along the A60 and in ½ mile turn right on to the B683. Continue to Papplewick.

PAPPLEWICK, Notts

Papplewick Pumping Station is a fine Victorian building situated in a landscaped park. It contains two Boulton and Watt beam engines and is open most Sundays. On seven weekdays during the year, the boilers are steamed with engines working.

Turn right on to the B6011 SP 'Linby'; continue to Linby.

LINBY, Notts

The combination of red-roofed stone cottages with two crosses and a small stream flowing on each side of the main street makes this one of the county's prettiest villages. East of Linby is Castle Mill, which was rebuilt and castellated in the 18th century by the then Lord Treasurer.

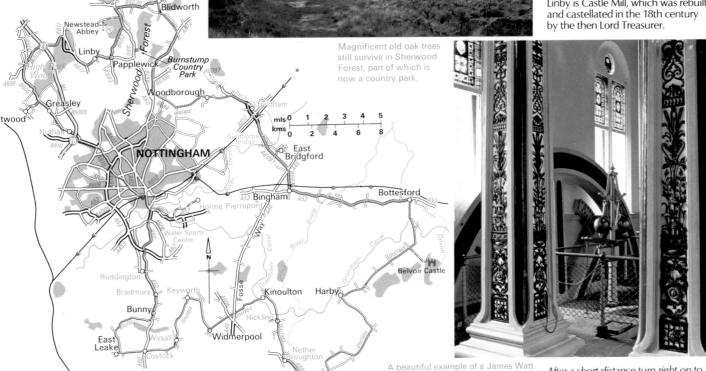

A beautiful example of a James Watt beam engine is preserved at Papplewick.

After a short distance turn right on to the A611. Gradually ascend, skirting the southern part of Sherwood Forest, and after 1½ miles turn left on to the A608. Ascend, cross the M1 motorway, then after another 1½ miles join the B600 SP 'Nottingham' and continue through wooded country. In 2¼ miles pass an unclassified right turn offering a detour to Eastwood.

EASTWOOD, Notts

The house in which D H Lawrence was born in 1885 in this old mining town, has been restored and furnished to depict working class life in Victorian times (open). The sharp contrast between pithead and countryside are reflected in many of his novels.

On the main route, continue along the B600 to Greasley.

GREASLEY, Notts

Handsome Greasley Church has a tall 15th-century tower that serves as a landmark for many miles around.

Drive into a built-up area, then meet a T-junction in Nuthall and turn left. After a short distance meet a roundabout and go forward on to the A610 for the return to Nottingham.

OSWESTRY, Shrops

Sometimes in England, sometimes in Wales, Oswestry was for centuries a battleground between the 2 countries, until the Act of Union in 1535 permanently established the border to the west of the town. Three times ravaged by fire, and by plague in 1559, when nearly a third of the inhabitants perished, few of Oswestry's medieval buildings have survived. Among those which have, Llwyd Mansion, a black and white timbered building in the centre of the town, bears the double-headed eagle of the Holy Roman Empire on one wall. The crest was granted to the Lloyd family in recognition of its services during the Crusades. Other noteworthy ancient buildings include the row of cottages near the church which originally housed Oswestry Grammar School. This was founded in 1407 and is thought to be the oldest secular foundation in the country. In Morda Road, the Croeswylan Stone, or Cross of Weeping, marks the place to which the market was shifted during the plague. Oswestry supported the Royalist cause in the Civil War, but Cromwell's forces took the town and destroyed the castle, of which only a grassy mound and a few fragments of masonry survive. King Oswald's Well sprang up, according to legend, on the spot where an eagle dropped one of the limbs of King Oswald of Northumbria, slain at the Battle of Maserfield by King Penda of Mercia in 642. The parish church is dedicated to Oswald, and Oswestry is a corruption of his name.

Leave Oswestry on the A483 Wrexham road, and in 1 mile pass (left) Old Oswestry.

THE WELSH MARCHES AND THE BERWYN MOUNTAINS

The turbulent history of the borderlands between England and Wales resulted in a series of magnificent Norman castles. The tour leads from the Border town of Oswestry, to Chirk, through the delightful woodlands of the Ceiriog valley, across the foothills of the wild Berwyn Mountains and along the Cain and Vynrwy valleys.

The coat of arms decorating the wrought iron gates of Chirk Castle belongs to the Myddleton family, who have lived in the castle since 1595

OLD OSWESTRY, Shrops

On a ridge a little to the north of Oswestry lie the remains of a massive Iron-Age hill fort, known in English as Old Oswestry and in Welsh as Yr Hen Dinas, 'the old fort'. It dates from about 250BC, when the first lines of defence, 2 great banks and ditches, were constructed. At a later date a third bank was added and the whole site was enclosed by a formidable double rampart. The fort was inhabited for more than 300 years, until the Romans destroyed it in AD75.

Continue on the A483 and at Gobowen turn left at the roundabout on to the A5, SP 'Llangollen'. In 2 miles descend into the Ceiriog valley where the Chirk Aqueduct can be seen ahead. Cross the river into Wales and ascend to the edge of Chirk.

CHIRK, Clwyd

Chirk is an attractive small town with streets of pleasant houses shaded by trees. A short footpath leads west from Chirk to the stone arched aqueduct built by Thomas Telford between 1796 and 1801. Its 10 great arches carry the Shropshire Union Canal high over the Cairiog valley. Alongside runs the railway viaduct, built in 1848.

A detour can be taken by keeping forward with the A5, then take the next turning left on to an unclassified road to Chirk Castle.

CHIRK CASTLE, Clwyd

The Welsh name of the castle, Castell y waun, meaning 'meadow castle' aptly describes its beautiful setting. Built by Edward I in 1310, Chirk (NT) is a fine example of a border stronghold — a rectangular stone fortress with massive, round drum towers at the 4 corners. In 1595 it became the home of Sir Thomas Myddelton, later Lord Mayor of London. His son held the castle for Parliament during the Civil War, and relics of that period can be seen in the courtyard. Later, the family supported Charles II, and the magnificent long gallery contains portraits and furniture dating from the Restoration. There is a beautifully decorated and furnished suite of 18th-century rooms, whose elegance is echoed by the graceful wrought iron gates at the entrance to the park. These, with their delicate tracery of foliage, were the work of Robert and John Davies, 2 brothers who lived near Wrexham. Through the park runs a part of Offa's Dyke, which for many centuries after King Offa's death in AD796, marked the boundary between England and Wales. There is a walk to Llangollen from here.

The main tour turns left at the edge of Chirk on to the B4500, SP 'Glyn Ceiriog'. Follow the Ceiriog valley, through Pontfadog, to Glyn Ceiriog.

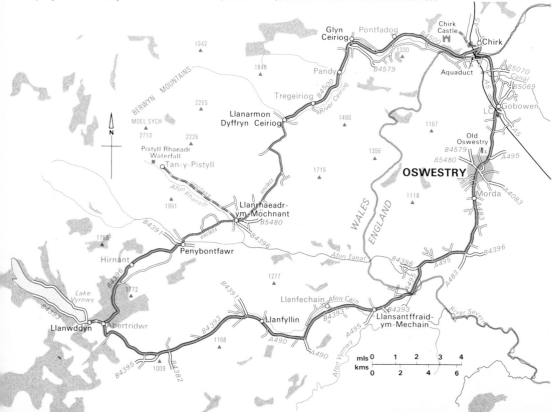

The dramatic waterfall of Pistyll Rhaeadr is the highest in Wales

GLYN CEIRIOG, Clwyd

Llansantffraid Glyn Ceiriog, to give the village its full name, stands on the swift-flowing River Ceiriog and is the main centre for exploring the lovely Ceiriog valley. Quarrying was once a major industry and in the Village Institute there are relics of the narrow-gauge tramway that ran from the quarries to the canal at Chirk.

Continue on the Llanarmon road for the gradual climb through the narrowing valley, passing the villages of Pandy and Tregeiriog and approaching the foothills of the Berwyn Mountains, to Llanarmon Dyffryn Ceiriog.

LLANARMON DYFFRYN CEIRIOG, Clwyd

Situated at the head of the Ceiriog valley, Llanarmon, a secluded village hidden in the foothills of the Berwyn Mountains, makes an excellent centre for walkers and for riding holidays. Penybryn, just above the village, was the birthplace of the great lyric poet John Ceiriog Hughes (1832-87). A farm labourer, who later became stationmaster at Glyn Ceiriog, Hughes wrote in Welsh but is, paradoxically, best remembered among the English for the translation of one of his less accomplished poems, *God Bless the Prince of Wales*.

Go forward over the crossroads, SP 'Llanrhaeadr', and climb out of the valley. In 1¾ miles, at the top, turn left and descend following a hilly, narrow byroad to Llanrhaeadr-ym-mochnant.

LLANRHAEADR-YM-MOCHNANT, Clwyd

This large market village has grown up around a tiny square where the 17th-century inn and the solid, square tower of the parish church make a pleasant group. The village was the birthplace in 1540 of William Morgan, later Bishop of St Asaph, who made the first translation of the Bible into Welsh, thus helping to preserve the language from extinction. It was published in 1588 by permission of Elizabeth I, who revoked a decree of Henry VIII which had officially banned Welsh.

A detour can be taken by turning right in the village to Tany-y-pistyll and the remarkable Pistyll Rhaeadr waterfall.

PISTYLL RHAEADR, Clwyd

The falls of Pistyll Rhaeadr, rightly considered to be one of the Seven Wonders of Wales (see Llangollen tour), cascade down a tree-covered gorge high up in the Rhaeadr valley. The water falls for 200ft, then pours through a natural rock arch to tumble down a further 100ft in a series of leaps and rocky pools.

The main tour continues through the village. Cross the river bridge and by the Three Tuns PH, go forward for Penybontfawr.

PENYBONTFAWR, Powys

Its picturesque setting amid the Berwyn Mountains is the charm of this small village on the Afon Tanat. As with many hill villages, church, vicarage, school and terraced houses were all built in the 19th century and only the outlying farms date from an earlier period. To the north-east of the village rises the bleak summit of the 3,713ft-high Moel Sych.

At the T-junction turn right then left on to the B4396, SP 'Lake Vyrnwy', and follow a winding narrow road to Llanwddyn.

LLANWDDYN, Powys

This is a new, model village, built in the 1880s when the Afon Vyrnwy valley was drowned to form Lake Vyrnwy. The old village, which lies at the bottom of the lake, originally grew up around the church of a 6th-century Celtic saint, Wddyn. Later it became part of the principality of Powys and in the 13th century was acquired by the Jerusalem Knights of St John.

Leave Llanwddyn on the B4393 Llanfyllin road, passing through rolling hill scenery. In 7¾ miles turn right on to the A490 to enter Llanfyllin.

LLANFYLLIN, Powys

This little market town on the River Cain centres on a pleasant square where the town hall used to stand. In olden days, Llanfyllin had a dubious reputation for strong ale — Old ale fills Llanfyllin with young widows — ran the saying. During the Napoleonic Wars French prisoners were quartered here and a room in the chemist's shop still displays frescoes painted by them during their captivity.

Follow the Welshpool road and in 2 miles turn left on to the B4393, SP 'Llansantffraid' and 'Oswestry'. Continue along the Cairn valley then in 3¾ miles turn left on to the A495 to enter Llansantffraid-ym-mechain.

LLANSANTFFRAID-YM-MECHAIN, Powys

The village strays along the main road in 3 stages. First comes the church, with vicarage, school hotel and timbered brick cottages gathered close around it. Next, a group of new houses spread out around the flour mill, and finally set around the 18th-century arched bridge stands a collection of tidy Victorian houses.

Follow the Vyrnwy valley before crossing the border into Shropshire. Later, at the T-junction turn right, then in 2¼ miles turn left on to the A483 for the return to Oswestry.

THE FEN COUNTRY

For centuries farmers have been draining the fens and creating new fields, but Oliver Cromwell, the farmer's son who became Lord Protector of England, would still recognise the broad horizons of the Cambridgeshire-Northamptonshire border, his old school in Huntingdon, and his family home — Hinchingbrooke House.

PETERBOROUGH, Cambs
Factories, office blocks and extensive housing estates have turned the ancient settlement of Peterborough into a 'New Town', unfortunately with little charm. Until the 19th century and the development of the railway, it was a peaceful river port on the Nene with an outstanding cathedral. The latter, built of local Barnack stone, is still magnificent and the triple-arched front is its chief glory. Catherine of Aragon and Mary, Queen of Scots were buried here, although Mary's body was subsequently reburied in Westminster Abbey by James I. Another fine building still standing is the old Guildhall in Market Place. It was built to commemorate the Restoration of Charles II and at one time was used as a Butter Market. A few old stone houses have also survived such as those in Preistgate and among them is the Museum and Art Gallery. Here there are bone carvings made by French prisoners during the Napoleonic Wars.

From Peterborough city centre follow SP 'Leicester (A47)' and cross the railway bridge. In 1¾ miles, at the roundabout, take the unclassified road for Longthorpe.

LONGTHORPE, Cambs
Longthorpe Tower (AM) was added to the village manor house in the 14th century as fortification. On one floor of the square tower there are some rare wall-paintings dating from about 1330, but they were not discovered until after World War II. The paintings represent religious and allegorical tales such as the Three Living and the Three Dead, and the Wheel of the Five Senses, figured as animals.

Beyond the village, at the T-junction, turn right. At the roundabout take the A47, SP 'Leicester', and continue to Castor.

CASTOR, Cambs
When the Romans occupied Britain they built *Durobrivae* by the Nene and took over the potteries at Castor, and Castor ware was subsequently sent to all corners of their Empire. The Normans built the village church, using Roman remains, and it is the only one in England dedicated to St Kyneburgha, the sister of King Peada who founded Peterborough Abbey.

After 3 miles cross the A1 then turn left on to the A6118 for Wansford.

WANSFORD, Cambs
Crossing the River Nene at Wansford is a medieval 10-arched bridge which links the village on either side of it. Wansford is sometimes known as Wansford in England, and this dates from the 17th century when a traveller called Drunken Barnabee arrived at the village inn (now called Haycock Inn) and, finding a plague sign on the door, slept on a haycock. During the night the Nene swept him downstream and when he awoke people said to him: 'Whereaway, from Greenland?' to which he replied: 'No; from Wansford Brigs in England.'

Continue on the B671, then in 3½ miles turn right on to the A605, SP 'Oundle', and enter Elton.

The 15th-century roof of the presbytery and chancel in Peterborough Cathedral

ELTON, Cambs
Along the village's 2 main streets — Over End and Middle Street — are ranked stone-built cottages and houses, many with mullioned windows. All Saints Church has 2 Saxon crosses in its churchyard which indicates there may have been a church on this site since the 10th century. Elton Hall (OACT) in Elton Park, dates from the 15th century but has had 18th- and 19th-century alterations

Continue on the A605 to Oundle.

OUNDLE, Northants
This lovely old county town has been unspoilt by time; alleyways thread their way past ancient inns, tall stone houses with steep roofs and tiny cottages with the smallest of windows. Oundle's famous public school was founded in 1556 by William Laxton, a grocer of the town who became Lord Mayor of London; the school is still owned by the Grocers' Company. The Nene flows round the town, making it a very popular sailing centre with beautiful views of the surrounding countryside.

Leave by the Kettering road. Cross the river and pass Barnwell Country Park. Join the A605 then in 1¾ miles (on right) is the turning for Lilford Park.

Wansford Bridge has been added to over the years which accounts for its irregular arches

LILFORD PARK, Northants
The 4th Baron Lilford, a keen ornithologist and naturalist, focused attention on Lilford Park at the end of the last century through the aviaries and gardens he built here. These have been restored or rebuilt, and the gardens are stocked with hundreds of birds, including the Lilford crane, named after the baron, and the Little owl, which Lilford introduced to Britain from Europe by releasing breeding pairs from aviaries in this park. The grounds, covering about 240 acres, offer a range of attractions for the whole family, including a children's farm, a craft and museum centre and an antique centre. The 17th-century house, Lilford Hall, is only open for special events such as motor shows and craft markets.

Continue on the A605 and in 1 mile pass the edge of Thorpe Waterville, then in another mile turn left on to an unclassified road for Titchmarsh.

TITCHMARSH, Northants
There is a splendid Perpendicular tower on the village church, which has a ha-ha (sunken ditch which cannot be seen from a distance) as a boundary. Two painted monuments inside the church are by Mrs Elizabeth Creed, cousin of John Dryden, the poet. The delightful thatched almshouses which stand to the south of the church and green, were provided by the Pickering family in 1756.

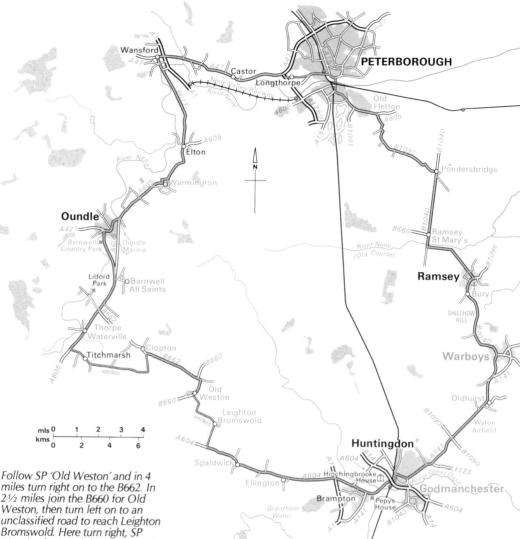

From the Ring Road (one way) follow the A141, SP 'March'. Pass RAF Wyton before reaching the edge of Oldhurst. In ½ mile turn left on to the B1040, SP 'Ramsey'. Pass through Warboys and Bury before entering Ramsey.

RAMSEY, Cambs

Ramsey Abbey, built in 969 on a tiny island in the marshland of the Fen country, prospered to become one of the 13th century's most important abbeys. As a result of this prosperity a town grew up around it. The Dissolution, however, brought an end to both: the abbey was destroyed and the lands sold off. Thereafter a series of misfortunes befell the town: the Parliamentarians destroyed many buildings during the Civil War; the Great Plague struck in 1666, and a series of devastating fires ravaged the town in the 17th and 18th centuries. All that remains of the abbey now is the gatehouse (NT) which looks across the smooth lawns of Abbey Green. A few 18th-century houses surround the green, but the rest of Ramsey is mostly 19th century. Great Whyte is the town's wide, main street, built in 1852 over Bury Brook which flowed through the town.

Turn left to continue on the B1040, SP 'Pondersbridge'. In 2¾ miles turn right and cross the river bridge then at Pondersbridge turn left on to the B1095, SP 'Peterborough'. In 4 miles turn left on to the A605 and pass through Old Fletton before the return to Peterborough.

Follow SP 'Old Weston' and in 4 miles turn right on to the B662. In 2½ miles join the B660 for Old Weston, then turn left on to an unclassified road to reach Leighton Bromswold. Here turn right, SP 'Huntingdon', and descend, then in 1 mile turn left on to the A604. Nearly 6 miles farther, at the roundabout, take the 2nd exit, then join the A141 before reaching the edge of Brampton.

BRAMPTON, Cambs

Among the reddish-yellow cottages in Brampton is the gabled house once owned and lived in by diarist Samuel Pepys's family (open by appointment). It is said that Pepys buried his money here when an invasion from Holland was feared.

At the roundabout go forward and in 1 mile pass (left) Hinchingbrooke House.

HINCHINBROOKE HOUSE, Cambs

A medieval nunnery was the foundation of Hinchinbrooke House (OACT), the remains of which were given to Oliver Cromwell's grandfather in 1538, but it was Oliver's father who began to adapt the ruins and build a country home. The house was damaged by fire in 1830 but afterwards restored by Edward Bore. One of the best features of the interior is the 17th-century carved staircase, which was installed during the 1950s from a house in Essex (now demolished). Hinchinbrooke has been used as a school since 1962.

Continue into Huntingdon.

HUNTINGDON, Cambs

Once a county town, Huntingdon has ancient origins, its history stretching back to Roman times — coins and pottery of that era have been found here. By the end of the 10th century a market and a mint were established, and the town grew in prosperity. However, the Black Death of 1348 drastically reduced the population, and the town sank into obscurity. Always a centre for local agriculture, Huntingdon survived the setback, and was again a substantial little market town by the 18th century, when the impressive town hall was built. In 1599 Oliver Cromwell was born here, and both he and Samuel Pepys attended the grammar school (OACT), now a museum of relics associated with Cromwell. The famous poet William Cowper lived in Cowper House in 1765. Most of the town is Georgian, but the George and Falcon inns are fine examples of 17th-century building and the finest medieval bridge in the county links the town with Godmanchester.

The George Inn in Huntingdon retains its courtyard, galley and external staircase of the 17th century.

ROSS-ON-WYE, Herefs & Worcs
High above the roofs of this attractive town rises the splendid 208ft spire of St Mary's Church, the topmost part of which was rebuilt in the 17th century with money donated by the philanthropic John Kyrle. Inside the main church, which dates mainly from the 13th century, are numerous interesting monuments. An important feature of the High Street is the red-sandstone Market Hall (AM) of 1670, which features a Charles II medallion set into the gable overlooking Man of Ross House – where Kyrle lived. The most conspicious reminder of Kyrle's many benefactions is the Prospect – a garden with excellent views over the river. Several ancient and attractive groups of buildings are preserved in the town, including a number of almshouses and the 16th-century Wilton Bridge.

Leave Ross-on-Wye by the B4260 SP 'Monmouth (A40)'. After ¾ mile cross the River Wye into Wilton.

WILTON, Herefs & Worcs
The splendid 16th-century bridge that spans the Wye here features a curiously inscribed sundial which was added in the 18th century. Near by are a group of old buildings and the picturesquely overgrown ruins of a 13th-century castle.

At the roundabout take 1st exit A40 and in 2 miles ascend to Pencraig. Continue for ½ mile, then turn left on to an unclassified road. Proceed to Goodrich.

GOODRICH, Herefs & Worcs
Imposing ruins of moated Goodrich Castle (AM), built in the 12th century as a defence against Welsh raiders, stand on a wooded hill overlooking the beautiful River Wye.

Branch right with SP 'Symond's Yat' then turn right on to the B4229. After ¾ mile turn left on to an unclassified road SP 'Symond's Yat East' and cross Huntsham Bridge. After 1 mile keep left and steeply ascend a narrow road to reach Symond's Yat Rock.

SYMOND'S YAT, Herefs & Worcs
This famous beauty spot lies in a narrow loop of the River Wye. An AA viewpoint at the summit of 473ft Yat Rock affords magnificent views over the Yat (gap or 'gate') itself, and of the river as it winds through the rich woodlands of its deep valley.

Join the B4432 SP 'Coleford' and continue to Christchurch, then turn right on to the B4228. After ½ mile meet crossroads and turn right on to the A4136 SP 'Monmouth'. Proceed to Staunton.

STAUNTON, Glos
Fine views of the Wye Valley can be enjoyed from many vantage points around this old village. The local

THE FOREST OF DEAN
Carpets of daffodils in spring and a leafy canopy in summer provide a backcloth for the one-man craft industries for which the forest is famous. West are the silvery coils of the majestic River Wye, which borders this outstanding region and divides England from Wales.

The Forest of Dean is a place of beauty and interest at all times of the year.

church has Norman origins and is often referred to as the 'Mother Church of the Forest of Dean'. An isolated rock known as the Buckstone makes a fine viewpoint. It used to move to the touch, but after having been dislodged in 1885 it was firmly fixed in its original position.

Descend into Wales through beautifully wooded scenery and after 4¼ miles turn left on to the A466 SP 'Chepstow'. A short detour to Monmouth can be made by remaining on the A4136.

MONMOUTH, Gwent
Strategically placed where the rivers Wye and Monnow meet, this ancient town played a vital role in subjugating South Wales from the Roman period till the Middle Ages. The outstanding reminder of these troubled times is a unique fortified bridge (AM) which has spanned the Monnow and guarded the town since 1260. The once-powerful castle (birthplace of Henry V) preserves an interesting 12th-century building among its remains. Near by is the Great Castle House (exterior AM), a 17th-century structure noted for its fine interior decorations. Other historic buildings include a ruined priory, several fine churches, an 18th-century shire hall, and venerable houses of the Tudor and Georgian periods. The Monmouth Museum in the Market Hall contains notable Nelson relics. East of the town is wooded Kymin Hill (NT), an excellent viewpoint which carries an 18th-century Naval Temple at its summit.

Shots from a cannon called Roaring Meg battered Goodrich Castle into submission during the Civil War.

Continue along the Wye Valley and pass through Redbrook, where the river forms part of the border between England and Wales. East of the road are traces of Offa's Dyke.

OFFA'S DYKE, Gwent etc
King Offa of Mercia constructed the banks and ditches of these extensive earthworks some time during the 8th century. The dyke, broken in places, stretches from Chepstow to Prestatyn and for many centuries was accepted as the boundary between England and Wales.

Cross Bigsweir Bridge and drive through Llandogo. Continue to Tintern Abbey.

TINTERN ABBEY, Gwent
Set amid the soft hills of Gwent and surrounded by the remains of ancient monastic buildings is the beautiful roofless church of Tintern Abbey. This once-important Cistercian foundation was created in 1131, and its size gradually increased along with its influence and importance – mainly in the 13th and 14th centuries. Close by is the little village of Tintern Parva.

Continue along the A466 and after 3 miles pass a path on the right leading to Wyndcliff Viewpoint. Drive through St Arvans and pass Chepstow Racecourse on the left. At the roundabout take the first exit into Chepstow.

CHEPSTOW, Gwent
Spectacularly perched above a bend of the Wye are the extensive remains of Chepstow Castle (AM), a massive fortification that was begun in stone only a year after the Norman invasion of England. The quaint old town, includes many old houses. A fine 18th-century house contains the town's museum, and the West Gate (AM) of the town wall still survives.

Leave Chepstow on the A48 SP 'Gloucester' and cross the River Wye into England. Ascend, and after ¼ mile at crossroads turn left on to the B4228, SP 'Coleford'. Continue to the edge of Hewelsfield.

HEWELSFIELD, Glos
Norman workmanship is evident in the fabric of Hewelsfield Church, which is said to be one of the oldest in the Forest of Dean.

Continue, with views of the River Severn to the right, and later turn left into St Briavels.

ST BRIAVELS, Glos
During the Middle Ages this quiet little village was the administrative centre for the Forest of Dean. Its church was built in 1089 and maintains a custom in which small cubes of bread and cheese are distributed among the parishioners after evening service on Whit Sunday. This practice is probably 700 years old. St Briavels Castle, now a youth hostel, has a magnificent 13th-century gatehouse and a 12th-century great hall.

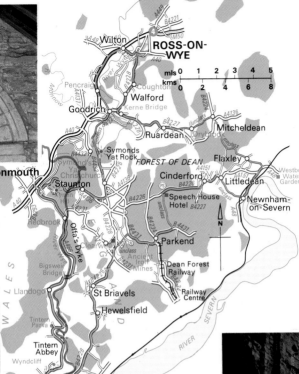

Ruardean's parish church has a fine tympanum made by a local school of sculptors.

The tower on Monnow Bridge was built as a fortified entrance to Monmouth.

Chepstow was one of the earliest stone castles to be built in Britain.

The writer C S Lewis was so moved by the majestic roofless ruin of Tintern Abbey that he wished all churches were open to the sky.

Keep forward through St Briavels and after ¼ mile reach crossroads and turn left rejoining the B4228. After 1¾ miles turn left on to the B4231 and after ¼ mile turn right to rejoin the B4228. After ¾ mile turn right on to an unclassified road SP 'Parkend', and after 1 mile meet a T-junction. Turn right on to the B4431 and continue to Parkend.

PARKEND, Glos
This rather undistinguished village has an interesting 'gothicky' church dating from 1822. Close by is the Dean Forest Railway.

DEAN FOREST RAILWAY, Glos
Plans are underway to open a working steam railway from Lydney to Parkend in the near future. A collection of locomotives and rolling stock is kept at the Norchard Railway Centre north of Lydney.

Continue on the B4431, and after 1¼ miles turn left on to an unclassified road SP 'Speech House'. Approach Speech House through the Forest of Dean.

FOREST OF DEAN, Glos
Within the boundaries of this historic area – the first National Forest Park to be created in England – is some of the finest woodland scenery to be found anywhere in Britain. Since 1016 the forest has been Crown property (although it is now cared for by the Forestry Commission) and it is

famous for a number of privately run industries, including coal mining and traditional charcoal burning. Specially laid-out forest trails and a forest drive help visitors appreciate the best that the area has to offer.

SPEECH HOUSE HOTEL, Glos
This handsome building succeeded St Briavels to become the administrative centre for the Forest of Dean, on its completion in 1676 it now serves as an hotel, but the old Verderers Court of Foresters is still held there.

Turn right on to the B4226 and pass a picnic site on the left. Continue to the edge of Cinderford.

CINDERFORD, Glos
Typical of early 19th-century development, this village was largely created to house the workforce required to operate the Forest Vale Ironworks.

Continue on the B4226 and ascend. After ¾ mile turn right on to the A4151 SP 'Gloucester' and proceed to Littledean.

LITTLEDEAN, Glos
Features of this small place include an attractive old church, an 18th-century gaol which now serves as a police station, and Littledean Hall (open), incorporating Roman, Saxon and Norman work, with a museum, watergardens and a large Roman temple.

At the T-junction turn right SP 'Newnham' on to an unclassified road. Descend to Newnham-on-Severn.

NEWNHAM-ON-SEVERN, Glos
Many old houses survive in this pleasant little town, which has a grassy bank down the centre of its high street. The local church affords enchanting views across the River Severn to the Cotswold Hills.

Turn left on to the A48 'Gloucester' road. After 2 miles turn left on to an unclassified road SP 'Mitcheldean'. Continue to Flaxley.

FLAXLEY, Glos
Unspoilt Flaxley is a cluster of houses with an unpretentious church and an historic abbey. The latter was originally created in the 12th century, but after a great fire in 1777 much of the monastic complex was rebuilt in the Georgian style. It is now used as a private dwelling.

Continue and in 1 mile turn right. Two miles farther cross a main road to enter Mitcheldean.

MITCHELDEAN, Glos
The beautiful 18th-century spire of Mitcheldean Church rises grandly over the roofs of much older half-timbered cottages in the village.

At Mitcheldean Church turn left for Drybrook. At Drybrook crossroads go straight across, then keep left. In ¾ mile meet a T-junction and turn right on to the B4227. Continue to Ruardean.

RUARDEAN, Glos
Above the inner doorway of Ruardean's notable church is a beautifully-preserved Norman tympanum depicting St George's battle against the dragon.

Bear right and descend, and after 1½ miles turn right on to the B4228 SP 'Ross'. Follow the River Wye and drive through Kerne Bridge to reach Walford.

WALFORD, Herefs & Worcs
This Wye-side village has a 13th-century church and stands on the site of a Roman camp.

Continue on the B4228 to return to Ross-on-Wye.

POETRY AND SHROPSHIRE IRON

Inspiration lives in the Shropshire hills and along Wenlock Edge. Housman captured its essence in the lovely poems of 'A Shropshire Lad', and the early ironmasters distilled it in a graceful bridge that was to herald the industrial revolution.

SHREWSBURY, Salop

Superbly set in a huge loop of the Severn, this beautiful and unspoilt town is famous for its half-timbered buildings and picturesque streets. Also here are many excellent examples of 18th- and 19th-century architecture. Traditionally founded during the 5th century by the Romans, Shrewsbury has been occupied by various peoples interested in its strategic position. Two notable 18th-century bridges span the Severn into the town centre, and the remains of a castle that defended the vulnerable north-eastern entrance dominate the imposing railway station. Fortification of the castle site was begun in the 11th century, but the remains date mainly from the 13th and were incorporated in a private house about 200 years ago. Near by are the 17th-century buildings of old Shrewsbury School, which now houses the civic library. Outstanding churches in Shrewsbury include the Norman and later Abbey Church, 12th- to 17th-century St Mary's, and mainly 18th-century St Julian's, with its ancient towers. Amongst the outstanding buildings are Rowley's Mansion, which houses a museum of local history and art; Whitehall of 1582; the gateway of the Council House; the Lion Coaching Inn; and the small complex of 14th-century cottages, shops and fine old hall called Bear Steps.

Leave Shrewsbury on the A49 'Leominster' road, and ¼ mile beyond Baystonhill turn left on to an unclassified road to reach Condover.

CONDOVER, Salop

Pink sandstone was the predominant material used to build both the 17th-century local church and Condover Hall (open on application), a splendid example of Elizabethan architecture.

At Condover turn left SP 'Pitchford' and after ¼ mile bear left. After 1¼ miles meet crossroads and turn right to enter Pitchford.

PITCHFORD, Salop

Half-timbered Pitchford Hall (not open) is a perfect example of a 16th-century black-and-white building, and the adjacent church retains good Norman details.

Continue to Acton Burnell.

ACTON BURNELL, Salop

Edward I held what is said to have been the first English parliament here in 1283. Ruined Acton Burnell Castle (AM) dates from the 13th century and was built by Robert Burnell, Bishop of Bath and Wells, partly as a castle and partly as a palace.

Meet crossroads, turn right SP 'Church Stretton', and after 2 miles bear right. Enter Longnor.

LONGNOR, Salop

In a grove of trees here is a perfect 13th-century church with 18th-century furnishings. Longnor Hall (not open) stands in a large deerpark and dates from 1670. Near by is black-and-white Moat House.

Continue, and after a short way turn left on to the A49. Enter Leebotwood.

Winter sunshine on Wenlock Edge.

LEEBOTWOOD, Salop

The finest of several half-timbered buildings in this village is the thatched Pound Inn. A 1,236ft hill known as The Lawley rises high above the village nearby.

Continue, with Caer Caradoc Hill to the left and the Long Mynd moorland to the right.

CAER CARADOC HILL, Salop

Earthworks of an iron-age hillfort said to have been defended by King Caractacus crown this miniature mountain, which is only 1,500ft high.

Amongst Shrewsbury's many beautiful half-timbered buildings is the Old Council House gateway.

THE LONG MYND, Salop

Rising like the armoured back of some prehistoric monster from the ordered fields of lowland Shropshire, the Long Mynd is a heather-covered mass of ancient grits and shales, largely owned and protected by the National Trust. Where the moorland hills fall towards Church Stretton they are scored by numerous ravines; the lovely Cardingmill Valley is possibly the most beautiful.

Continue and meet crossroads. Turn right on to the B4371 SP 'Town Centre' and enter Church Stretton.

CHURCH STRETTON, Salop

During the late 19th century the district around Church Stretton became known as 'Little Switzerland', and the town itself developed into a popular inland resort. Red-brick and half-timbered Victorian villas mingle with older black-and-white buildings to create a pleasant character complemented by the Church of St Lawrence, which has been adapted through many periods. Above the Norman north doorway is a Celtic fertility symbol. There are three Strettons in the valley – Church Stretton at the centre, All Stretton to the north, and Little Stretton to the south. The latter has many half-timbered buildings.

Return to crossroads and turn left on to the B4370. Pass through the pretty village of Little Stretton. Turn right on to the A49, and continue to Craven Arms.

CRAVEN ARMS, Salop
Originally the hamlet of Newton, this 19th-century town development was renamed after a coaching inn that just preceded its expansion. Today it is an important centre for livestock auctions.

A detour of ¾ mile from the main tour route can be made by continuing on the A49 to Stokesay Castle.

STOKESAY CASTLE, Salop
Wooden beams, overhanging walls, steep roofs, and decorated woodwork, make Stokesay a picture-book castle. It is of the oldest surviving examples of a fortified manor house set in a romantic setting with a quaint Elizabethan gatehouse and dating from c 1280. The castle (AM) owes its superb condition to a singularly uneventful history. Beyond the moat is a church that was damaged during the Civil War and subsequently refurbished during the Commonwealth. Interior furnishings and fittings of that time remain intact.

Leave Craven Arms on the B4368 SP 'Bridgnorth' and enter Corve Dale. Shortly reach Diddlebury.

DIDDLEBURY, Salop
Diddlebury enjoys a picturesque setting beside the river in Corve Dale, beneath the high ridge of beautiful Wenlock Edge. Saxon masonry in the local church includes attractive herringbone work on the north wall.

Continue to the White House at Aston Munslow.

THE WHITE HOUSE, Salop
Many periods are represented in the complex of buildings associated with this mansion, and the house itself has a 14th-century hall and 16th-century cross-wing. A fascinating museum of country life accommodated here displays a variety of farm relics.

Continue through Munslow, with Wenlock Edge to the left and the River Corve to the right. Reach Shipton.

SHIPTON, Salop
Famous and beautiful Shipton Hall (open) is the focal point of this Corve Dale village. Built in c 1587 and enlarged at the back during the mid-18th century, it comprises a large range of buildings, including a fine stable block which dates from the 18th century.

At Shipton bear left on to the B4378 SP 'Much Wenlock' and continue to Much Wenlock.

MUCH WENLOCK, Salop
Poet A E Housman celebrated the beauty of this region in his collection *A Shropshire Lad.* The town is a charming little market centre with

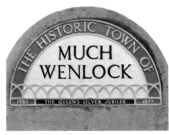

The traceried stonework of Wenlock Priory is echoed in the symbolic design of Much Wenlock's attractive town nameplate.

many excellent half-timbered and other buildings, including such notable examples as Raynald's Mansion, the Manor House, and the Guildhall. Remains of Wenlock Priory (AM), which was founded in the 7th century and became a Cluniac house in 1080, include beautiful interlocking Norman tracery. Near by is splendid Priors Lodge of 1500.
Leave Much Wenlock on the A458 'Bridgnorth' road and continue to Morville.

MORVILLE, Salop
Morville Hall (NT) was rebuilt in the 18th century, and the local church contains a wealth of details from many periods.
Continue and later at roundabout take the 1st exit to join the B4364 and enter Bridgnorth.

BRIDGNORTH, Salop
Bridgnorth is an ancient town, with many interesting buildings.
Leave Bridgnorth on the B4373 and after 5¼ miles bear right SP 'Wellington'. Descend into the Severn Gorge and cross the river to reach a T-junction. Turn left and in ¼ mile at roundabout join the A4169 to enter Ironbridge.

IRONBRIDGE, Salop
Across the River Severn here is a splendid iron bridge that was built in

Right: Abraham Darby designed the revolutionary bridge at Ironbridge in the 18th century, unconsciously creating a memorial to the British industrial revolution. Below: a detail of the bridge's ironwork.

1779, the first of its kind in the world. This must surely be the most beautiful monument there is to the industrial revolution, which had its birth in this area. The Ironbridge Gorge Museum, covering six square miles, includes a reconstructed Victorian village and museums of iron and steel making and of the Coalport China Company and a visitor centre. The streets and buildings of Ironbridge itself cling to the sides of the Severn Gorge.
Beyond Ironbridge keep forward on to the B4380 SP 'Shrewsbury'. Continue to Buildwas.

BUILDWAS, Salop
Concrete cooling towers looming from a local power station otherwise hidden by trees make a controversial counterpoint to the 12th-century remains of Buildwas Abbey (AM), near the River Severn. Stone from the ruin was incorporated in the local church. North of the hamlet is the 1,334ft bulk of The Wrekin.
Continue through Leighton, along the Severn Valley, to the edge of Wroxeter.

WROXETER, Salop
During Roman times the important town of *Uriconium* stood here. Excavated remains (AM) include the baths and fragments of other buildings. Near by is a church which incorporates Roman bricks and masonry in its fabric, and displays architectural features from many ages. Inside are several very fine monuments and memorials.
Continue on the B4380 and after ¾ mile turn left on to the A5. Enter Atcham.

ATCHAM, Salop
Spacious wooded parklands and two 18th-century bridges are the main features of this pretty, village which also has a church uniquely dedicated to St Eata. The Myton and Mermaid Inn is of Georgian origin, and Longer Hall was built in 1803 to designs by John Nash. Humphrey Repton laid out the grounds of both Longner and nearby Attingham Hall (NT) (open), a magnificent house of 1785.
Cross the Severn and return to Shrewsbury.

SKEGNESS, Lincs

In 1863 a rail service was begun at Skegness, with trains running to and from the teeming towns of the industrial Midlands. The result was a boom in seaside tourism, and the holiday crowds of today continue to enjoy the excellent sands and bathing facilities that prompted the transformation of this one-time fishing village into one of the east coast's most popular resorts. Magnificent seafront gardens border a long promenade where, in simpler days, Lord Tennyson and his brothers strolled to take the bracing sea air. A vast swimming pool, the Natureland Zoo, and various first-class entertainments vie for attention with 6 miles of sandy beach. The Church Farm Museum has the Farmhouse and cottage furnished as it would have been in the 19th century. At the southern end of the beach is Gibraltar Point, where there is a nature reserve and bird observatory.

Leave Skegness on the A158 'Lincoln' road and drive to Burgh-le-Marsh.

BURGH-LE-MARSH, Lincs

One of the main features of this area is a fine 5-sailed tower windmill that is still in working order. The impressive local church has two porches and a tower with 16 iron crosses. Inside is a restored screen.

Drive for 2¾ miles beyond the village and approach a roundabout with Gunby Hall to the left.

GUNBY HALL, Lincs

Lord Tennyson described this imposing red-brick building (NT) as 'a house of ancient peace'. It was built c1700 by Sir William Massingberd and shows the influence of Sir Christopher Wren. Features of the interior include an oak staircase, wainscoted rooms containing portraits by Reynolds, and various pieces of fine furniture. The house and its formal gardens are open by prior written appointment.

Continue along the A158 and drive through Candlesby, with Welton High Wood to the right. Proceed to Scremby.

SCREMBY, Lincs

Notable features of the good 18th-century church in Scremby include a panelled chancel and a monument to Charles Brackenbury.

Beyond Scremby meet crossroads and turn right on to an unclassified road to Skendleby.

SKENDLEBY, Lincs

Attractively set in the Lincolnshire Wolds, this pleasant village features a partly greenstone church and a mid 18th-century hall. Near by is a prehistoric site known as the Giant's Hill, where there are two long barrows. The most prominent measures 200ft long and stands 5ft high; the other has been severely reduced by ploughing.

Drive to the end of Skendleby and bear right SP 'Willoughby', then

BETWEEN THE WOLDS AND THE SEA

Attractive resorts and beaches of fine sand are interspersed with charming little fishing villages on Lincolnshire's holiday coast. Inland are picturesque hamlets clustered round greenstone churches, hills crowned by solitary windmills, and the enchanting lanes of the Wolds country.

Skegness prepares for the holiday season.

ascend to cross a main road. Descend, and in 1¾ miles turn left on to the B1196 SP 'Alford'. Approach Alford, with Well Vale to the left, and turn sharp left on to an unclassified road to enter the village of Well.

WELL, Lincs

Set on the eastern slopes of the Wolds, in the pastoral beauty of Well Vale, this tiny village takes its name from a spring that bubbles from the chalk to fill two lakes in a closely-wooded valley. Close to the village the beautiful Georgian red-brick building of Well Vale Hall stands in 170 acres of fine parkland.

Return to the B1196 and turn left to enter Alford.

ALFORD, Lincs

One of Lincolnshire's finest windmills can be seen here. Its 6-storey brick tower carries five sails and is topped by an ogee cap. It dates from 1813 and, although intact, is no longer in use. Merton Lodge is a good example of the many Georgian and later houses to be seen in the town.

Leave Alford on the A1104 'Louth, Lincoln' road and ascend. Reach Ulceby; cross a roundabout and take the 2nd exit on to the A16, then in ½ mile turn right on to the unclassified 'Harrington' road. Continue, with panoramic views, into Harrington.

HARRINGTON, Lincs

Harrington Hall (open) was rebuilt in 1673 and features a good Elizabethan facade and contains fine 17th- and 18th-century paintings, china and furniture and beautiful gardens.

Continue through pleasantly wooded countryside to Somersby.

Burgh-le-Marsh church clock urges a greater regard for time.

SOMERSBY, Lincs

The poet Alfred Lord Tennyson was born in this tiny Wolds village. His house, which still stands but is not open to the public, was adapted by his father to include a dining room with high gothic windows that entirely suited that era of romanticism. Various memorials to the Tennyson family can be seen in the local church, and a fine carved cross stands in the churchyard.

Keep forward into a narrow road for Salmonby and turn left SP 'Horncastle'. Continue for 2 miles, then meet crossroads and turn right SP 'Belchford'. Climb to a road summit of 455ft, with good all-round views, then descend into Belchford and turn right SP 'Alford'. After a short distance ascend Belchford Hill and meet a T-junction. Turn left SP 'Louth' and continue, with magnificent views, to a road summit of 487ft. In 3¼ miles meet crossroads and turn right on to the A153, passing the entrance to Caldwell Park Motor Cycle Racing Circuit on the right. In ¾ mile branch right (no SP) on to an unclassified road and continue to Tathwell.

TATHWELL, Lincs

Attractively situated in a sheltered position above a lake, this village has a good church that features a Norman tower and contains various interesting monuments.

Beyond Tathwell meet crossroads and drive forward SP 'Legbourne'. A short detour from the main route can be taken by turning right at the crossroads and driving to Bully Hill.

BULLY HILL, Lincs

Some of the finest prehistoric barrow groups to have survived in the whole county of Lincolnshire can be seen here. The largest of seven measures 60ft in diameter by 10ft high, and they are thought to date from the late stone or early bronze age.

On the main route, drive 1¼ miles beyond the crossroads and turn right on to the A16. After another 1¼ miles turn left on to the unclassified 'Little Cawthorpe' road, descend through Maltby and Haugham Woods, and turn right at Little Cawthorpe. Reach the village church and turn left (no SP), then pass through a ford and meet a T-junction. Turn right, and in ½ mile turn right again on to the A157. Continue to the end of Legbourne and bear right, then turn left on to the unclassified 'Manby' road. Continue to Little Carlton, turn left to reach Manby village.

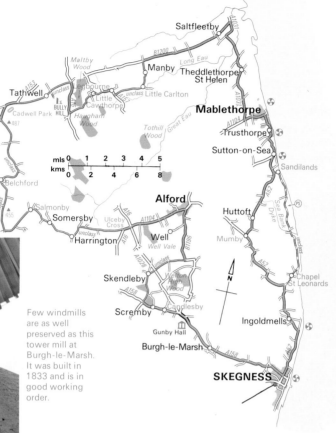

Few windmills are as well preserved as this tower mill at Burgh-le-Marsh. It was built in 1833 and is in good working order.

The solid Norman tower of St Vedast's Church, Tathwell, is well sheltered from the elements.

Gunby Hall's austere face conceals a wealth of fine decoration.

MANBY, Lincs
The greenstone church of this pleasant little village has a tall tower and contains a remarkably well-preserved Saxon slab decorated with a distinctive rope design.

Meet crossroads beyond Manby and turn right on to the B1200. Continue to Saltfleetby.

SALTFLEETBY, Lincs
Close to St Peter's Church in Saltfleetby is the isolated tower of a church that the present greenstone building replaced. The recent building incorporates a few early-English fragments from its predecessor.

Meet a junction with the A1031, turn right, and continue to Theddlethorpe St Helen.

THEDDLETHORPE ST HELEN, Lincs
This tiny coastal village is near a scrub-covered foreshore that forms part of a national nature reserve and is one of the few remaining habitats of the Natterjack toad. This curious amphibian runs instead of hops, and is easily identifiable by the pale stripe down its back. Signposts and warning flags mark the site of an RAF bombing range on the sands.

Proceed along the A1031 for 3 miles, then turn left on to the A1104 into Mablethorpe.

MABLETHORPE, Lincs
Thanks to a highly expensive system of groynes this popular resort boasts a beautiful beach of firm golden sand. In normal weather swimmers can enjoy safe bathing here, but rough conditions make the water treacherous and red flags are flown to warn people away. Low tide reveals old stumps that are the sole remains of a woodland village swamped by the sea in 1289. All that survived was the fine old Church of St Mary, which contains various medieval relics. Today the town is guarded by a concrete promenade.

Leave Mablethorpe on the A52 'Skegness' road and continue to Trusthorpe.

TRUSTHORPE, Lincs
Fine sands and good bathing facilities make this a popular resort, but it is also the base for Humber Radio – an important Post Office link with ships and oil rigs in the North Sea. The tall radio mast dominates the village.

Continue on the A52 and drive into Sutton-on-Sea.

SUTTON-ON-SEA, Lincs
Safe bathing and a level sandy beach are the main features of this little coastal resort. The 4,500-year-old stumps and roots of a forest that was flooded by the sea can be seen at low tide.

From Sutton-on-Sea it is possible to take a pleasant detour from the main route, along the shore below the Sea Bank Dyke. In 1 mile meet a roundabout and turn left on to the unclassified road to Sandilands and drive straight on beside the sea wall. Reach Chapel St Leonards and turn left across a river bridge, then turn right with SP 'Skegness' to rejoin the A52 before Ingoldmells. On the main route, continue along the A52 to Huttoft.

HUTTOFT, Lincs
A tall windmill of the tower type can be seen here, with an interesting early-Victorian grain store.

Continue along the A52 and drive through Mumby to Ingoldmells.

INGOLDMELLS, Lincs
This little resort offers 3 miles of firm golden sand and a host of holiday diversions, including a funfair. Remains of an early iron-age salt-panning site between Ingoldmells and Chapel St Leonards include various structures that can only be seen at low tide.

Continue along the A52 for the return to Skegness.

SPALDING, Lincs

This historic fenland town stands on the banks of the Welland in an area of drained marshland where market gardeners and bulb growers raise crops in soil of almost legendary richness. In springtime the district is glorious with tulips, daffodils, narcissi, and hyacinths that form a carpet of blazing colour comparable only with the bulb fields of Holland. Every May the town holds a spectacular Flower Festival that attracts visitors from all

BULB FIELDS IN THE FENS

Spring in the Fens is an explosion of colour. Daffodils, tulips, and hyacinths cover acre after flat acre of reclaimed land, stretching away from the bulb towns in gloriously-variegated carpets reminiscent of the Dutch countryside rather than rural England.

mutiny. He became a pioneer of Australian exploration and wrote a book about his voyages. He died in 1814, on the day that his book was published.

Continue through fenland along the A52.

THE LINCOLNSHIRE FENS, Lincs

The Fens of Lincolnshire covered an area that is barely above sea level and have been reduced by centuries of land reclamation. The Romans built the first sea wall here and drained the land behind it; in subsequent centuries their work was continued, and much later the expertise of Dutch engineer Vermuyden was used to make many acres of ground into rich arable land. A giant reclamation scheme begun in the 17th century used the talents of such famous men as Rennie and Telford, and was largely responsible for the shape of the landscape as it exists today. Everywhere the flat fields and pastures are criss-crossed by drains and dykes that stretch away to an almost treeless horizon.

Continue along the A52, with Swaton Fen on the right and Horbling Fen to the left. In 4 miles turn left on to the B1177 'Bourne' road and proceed to Horbling.

HORBLING, Lincs

Spring Well, situated a little way north of Horbling's Norman and later church, was once a communal washing trough. The village itself is a charming collection of mainly Georgian houses.

Proceed along the B1177 to Billingborough.

BILLINGBOROUGH, Lincs

The local church carries a 150ft spire that can be seen for a long way over the surrounding flat countryside. An unusual façade is displayed by the George and Dragon Inn, which dates from the 17th century.

Continue for ¾ mile by Billingborough Fen and pass a track leading right to the site of Sempringham Abbey.

SEMPRINGHAM ABBEY, Lincs

Sir Gilbert of Sempringham founded the Gilbertine order here c1130. He was the son of the local lord, and the Gilbertines were the only monastic order to have been founded in Britain. Close to the site an uneven area of grassland covers the remains of the village, but the superb Norman church survives as an outstanding example of its period.

Continue along the B1177 and drive through Pointon to Dowsby.

DOWSBY, Lincs

Dowsby Hall was built c1603, and the local church contains many fine moulded arches.

Stay on the B1177 through Dunsby, passing Dowsby Fen and Dunsby Fen on the left. Join the A15, with Bourne North Fen to the left, and continue to Bourne.

over the country. On the eastern outskirts are the beautiful Springfield Gardens, 25 acres of lawns and water features designed to show over a million bulbs to their best advantage. In summer the early freshness of the bulbs is replaced by the mature beauty of more than 80 species of rose in the magnificent Summer Rose Garden. The town itself has many old buildings in charming streets on both banks of the river, including several good examples of 18th-century design. One of the oldest is the greatly restored Ayscoughfee Hall, which dates from the 15th century and now houses a museum of local history. Its mellow stone and graceful lines are complemented by well-kept lawns enclosed by yew hedges. A small museum in Broad St (open by appointment) was founded by the Gentleman's Society in 1710. Spalding has many good churches, but the best is the late 13th-century Church of SS Mary and Nicholas. This has an angel-carved hammerbeam roof in the nave and was extensively restored by the Victorian architect Sir G G Scott.

Leave Spalding on the A16 'Boston' road and drive to Pinchbeck.

PINCHBECK, Lincs

Situated on the River Glen in a bulb-growing district, this village has preserved its old wooden stocks and has a restored church with a leaning tower. A fine 18th-century group of buildings includes the rectory and a stable block.

Continue on the A16 to Surfleet.

The area around Spalding is ablaze with tulips in the spring.

SURFLEET, Lincs

The spire on the church in this fenland village leans 6ft out of true – considerably more than the tower at Pinchbeck. Naturalist Gilbert White described a local heronry in his early work *Natural History*, but this has since been abandoned.

Cross the River Glen and proceed along the A16 to Gosberton.

GOSBERTON, Lincs

An outstanding feature of this pleasant little village is its cruciform church, which displays a curious tower gargoyle fashioned in the shape of an elephant.

Fleet Fen is part of Lincolnshire's extensive 17th-century drainage works.

Leave Gosberton, keep forward on the A152, and continue to Donington.

DONINGTON, Lincs

In Roman times the area around Donington was drained in the first of many attempts to reclaim agricultural land from the Fens. Much later the town was a centre of the flax and hemp industry, and nowadays it is a popular touring base. Its cobbled market square is surrounded by pleasant Georgian buildings, and its church carries a fine tower surmounted by an elegant spire. Inside is a tablet commemorating Captain Matthew Flinders, a great sailor who was born in Donington and travelled with Captain Bligh after the *Bounty*

The beautiful water gardens near Peakirk are the home of various water birds, including trumpeter swans.

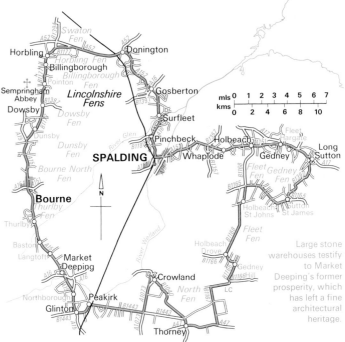

Large stone warehouses testify to Market Deeping's former prosperity, which has left a fine architectural heritage.

BOURNE, Lincs
Bourne is an ancient market town and reputedly the birthplace of Hereward the Wake, the last Saxon to resist the invading Norman army. The town was the former manufacturing base of the BRM racing car and is renowned for the purity of its water. The many watercress beds in the area are ample proof of the latter. Good domestic architecture in the town includes attractive Tudor cottages in South Street and a generous scattering of Georgian houses and shops. The Burghley Arms Hotel was the birthplace of Sir William Cecil, Lord High Treasurer to Elizabeth I, in 1520. Other famous natives of the town include Frederick Worth, founder of the House of Worth in Paris, and Robert Mannying, who founded an Augustinian abbey here in the 13th century. Remains of the monastic buildings are incorporated in the nave of the parish church. A Roman canal known as the Car Dyke runs close to the town, and castle earthworks can be seen a little way south.

Continue along the A15 'Peterborough' road and drive through Thurlby. Cross the River Glen and continue through Baston and Langtoft to Market Deeping.

MARKET DEEPING, Lincs
Several fine old houses testify to the one-time prosperity and importance of this ancient market town, situated on the River Welland at the edge of the Fens. Its restored church has an unusual rood loft doorway, and the 13th-century parish rectory is thought to be the oldest inhabited parsonage in England.

Leave Market Deeping on the A15, cross the River Welland, and pass the village of Northborough. Proceed to Glinton.

GLINTON, Cambs
Among the pleasant stone cottages of this attractive village is a fine 17th-century manor house; the entire group is centred on the slender spire of the local church.

Leave Glinton and turn left on to the B1443 'Thorney' road. Continue to Peakirk.

PEAKIRK, Cambs
A rare 14th-century lectern and numerous paintings can be seen in Peakirk's church, the only one in Britain dedicated to St Pega. Close to the village is the Wildfowl Trust gardens.

Leave Peakirk and continue east for 4 miles, then turn left on to the A1073. After another 2 miles turn left again on to an unclassified road and drive into Crowland.

CROWLAND, Lincs
One of the most interesting features of this pleasant little town is its unique Triangular Bridge (AM), which was built in the 14th century to span several streams of the River Welland. Its three arches, which meet at an angle of 120 degrees, now stand on dry land. In 1720 a carved figure of the Virgin Mary was taken from the partly ruined abbey that now serves as the parish church and placed on the bridge. The original abbey was founded in 716 by King Ethelbald in memory of St Guthlac.

From Crowland follow the B1040 to Thorney.

THORNEY, Cambs
It was here that the Saxon hero Hereward the Wake made his last stand against the invading Norman armies under William the Conqueror. Remains of a 12th-century abbey built by William after his victory can be seen near by, and the restored abbey church shows Norman and later workmanship. Abbey House is a largely 16th-century building with 17th-century additions. A good 18th-century windmill stands in the grounds.

From Thorney turn left on the A47 'Wisbech' road and in 1½ miles turn left again on to the B1167 SP 'Gedney Hill'. Continue for 4½ miles, then turn left on to the B1166 to Gedney Hill. At Gedney Hill turn left and continue to Holbeach Drove, then turn right on to the B1168 with Fleet Fen to the right. Meet crossroads 1 mile beyond Holbeach St Johns and turn right on to the B1165 for Sutton St James. Drive to the end of this village, turn left on to the B1390 to Long Sutton.

LONG SUTTON, Lincs
Many different architectural periods are represented in the fabric of this pretty market town's church, but the main feature is its detached, 162ft tower. This has a lead and timber spire that is considered one of the finest in Britain.

Leave Long Sutton on the A17 SP 'Sleaford', passing Gedney to the left.

Whaplode Church never came to the attention of 19th-century restorers, whose enthusiasm often outstripped their ability.

GEDNEY, Lincs
The fine marshland church in Gedney features a notable west tower and contains a 14th-century brass. Also inside are a number of alabaster effigies.

Leave the village and in a short distance turn left on to the A151 'Spalding' road, passing through Fleet Hargate into Holbeach.

HOLBEACH, Lincs
One of the county's major bulb-growing centres, this ancient market town boasts many good Georgian houses and a 14th-century church with a lofty spire and fine traceried windows. William Stukely, a founder of the Society of Antiquaries, was born here in 1718.

Proceed along the A151 to Whaplode.

WHAPLODE, Lincs
The splendid Norman and later church in this little marshland village has a presence that is out of all proportion to the size of the community that it serves. Inside is a notable 17th-century monument to Sir Anthony Irby.

Continue along the A151 for the return to Spalding.

STAFFORD, Staffs

New buildings encircle the county town, but despite this the old centre retains its dignified character. In Greengate Street stands the aptly named High House, 4 storeys high, and a beautiful example of timberframe construction. St Chad's is a fine Norman church with carvings said to have been the work of Saracens brought back to England after the Crusades by Lord Biddulph. The parish church, St Mary's, contains a monument to Izaak Walton, the noted angler, who was born at Stafford in 1593. Noel's Almshouses in Mill Street, a group of stone houses round a spacious courtyard, date from 1660. The William Salt Library in Eastgate Street is a remarkable collection of old deeds, drawings and books on Staffordshire history amassed by William Salt.

Leave on the A518, SP 'Telford' and 'Newport', and pass through Haughton for Gnosall.

GNOSALL, Staffs

Gnosall's church has a superb Norman interior, featuring massive pillars and decorated arches. An interesting item near the altar, in the pavement of the south aisle, is the rough carving of a pair of sheep-shearer's shears, no doubt a tribute to the importance of the wool trade. High on the tower outside can be seen a mason's mark of shield and hammer.

WHERE A HUNTED KING FOUND REFUGE

The capital of the Black Country is, unexpectedly, the gateway to the leafy woodlands and deer-haunted glades of Cannock Chase — noble remnant of a royal forest — and to the quiet pleasures of Staffordshire's unassuming countryside, where a succession of stately homes once gave shelter to the exiled Charles II.

Continue to Newport.

NEWPORT, Shrops

A town of great charm, Newport's broad main street passes on either side of its imposing church, whose 14th-century tower looks out on a vista of handsome 18th-century houses. There is a famous grammar school near the church, founded by William Adam in the Commonwealth period, that still has its original 17th-century clock. One of its most famous pupils was Sir Oliver Lodge, who was one of the pioneer experimenters in wireless telegrams.

Turn left then right, still SP 'Telford', to remain on the A518. In 2 miles turn left on to an unclassified road and enter Lilleshall. In 1¼ miles turn left, SP 'Lilleshall Abbey', and pass the remains in 1 mile (left).

LILLESHALL ABBEY, Shrops

Lilleshall Abbey (AM) now consists of graceful ruined arches and walls but some idea of its former magnificence can be gained by looking through the west front down the length of the ruins to the east window. It was founded in 1148 and after the Dissolution Henry VIII gave the abbey to the Leveson family, who were local landowners at that time. It stands in the grounds of the Hall that has now been turned into the National Sports Centre, which is where the English team trained before winning the World Cup in 1966.

In 2 miles turn left on to the B4379, then turn right, SP 'London'. Later cross the A41 to join the B5314. In another 2 miles turn left on to the A5, then take the next turning right on to an unclassified road and pass the entrance to Weston Park.

WESTON PARK, Staffs

This Classical 17th-century house (OACT) has been the family home of the Earls of Bradford for 300 years. The rooms are mainly of 18th and 19th-century inspiration, and the tapestry room, lined with rose-pink Gobelin tapestries, is particularly notable. However, the real treasure of Weston is the magnificent collection of paintings, which includes portraits of the Bradfords and works by leading Dutch, Italian and French masters.

Continue along the unclassified road to Tong.

TONG, Shrops

Thatched cottages, a distant mock-castle, wooded slopes and an ancient church give Tong its charm and character. When Charles Dickens wrote *The Old Curiosity Shop* he had this village in mind as the final haven of Little Nell and her grandfather. The red sandstone church, with unusual battlements, has one of the most splendid arrays of monuments in the Midlands. Many are of Lady Elizabeth Pembruge — who founded the church in the early 15th century — and her husband. Others include effigies of the Vernon family, including Sir Richard, Speaker of the House of Commons in 1428.

The Shropshire Union Canal at Gnosall, which links the Mersey to the Severn

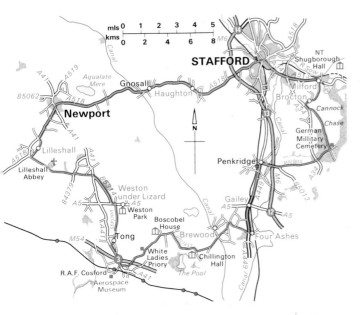

At the church turn left, then shortly turn left again on to the A41. In almost 1 mile, at the start of the dual-carriageway, turn left on to an unclassified road (no SP). Alternatively, turn right to visit the Aerospace Museum.

AEROSPACE MUSEUM, Shrops
Two hangars within the grounds of Cosford RAF station house the museum. One hangar concentrates on rockets, ranging from the earliest German model to more modern ones. The other hangar has over 50 aircraft, including a World War II Lincoln Bomber which is being meticulously restored by teams of volunteers. Here too is a prototype of the TSR2 — a new fighter-plane which Harold Wilson cancelled because it was costing too much money. Each exhibit has a placard describing its history, and outside there are picnic sites and a souvenir shop.

The main tour later joins a narrow byroad, SP 'Shackley', and continues to Boscobel House.

BOSCOBEL HOUSE, Shrops
Built in 1600 for the Roman Catholic Gifford family, Boscobel House (AM) was amply provided with secret hiding places to shelter priests, and it was here that Charles II, defeated and weary, found refuge in 1651 after the Battle of Worcester. Hunted high and low by soldiers, he spent the day in an oak tree near the house hidden by the loyal Penderel family, who were Boscobel's tenants. The present oak tree, although ancient, is not the original, but grew from one of its acorns. Whiteladies nearby, is a ruined 12th-century nunnery where the king also sheltered from pursuit.

At the T-junction turn right, then branch left on to another byroad (no SP). In ¾ mile turn right and 1¼ miles farther pass (right) Chillington Hall.

CHILLINGTON HALL, Staffs
For 800 years, Chillington Hall (OACT) has belonged to the Gifford family through direct male descent, but it was not until 1724 that Peter Gifford began to build the existing redbrick mansion. He demolished part of the Tudor house and bought in Francis Smith of Warwick as the architect. Later, in about 1750, Sir John Soane built the east front and one of the most interesting rooms is Soane's saloon, which replaced the Tudor great hall. It has an oval ceiling which leads up to an oval lantern and over the chimneypiece is the Gifford family arms. Capability Brown landscaped the grounds in the 18th century and formed the beautiful ornamental lake that occupies 75 acres.

After passing the main gateway turn left then in 1 mile turn left again. In ¾ mile go over the crossroads, SP 'Four Ashes', then in another ¾ mile, at the T-junction, turn left. At the next T-junction turn right and cross the river bridge then turn right again, still SP 'Four Ashes'. In 1¼ miles turn left on to the A449, SP 'Stafford', then at the Gailey roundabout take the 2nd exit and continue to Penkridge.

PENKRIDGE, Staffs
Of the several pleasing old buildings in this quiet little town near the River Penk, the old stone and timber deanery, dating from the 16th century is the most outstanding. The large parish church is packed with interesting monuments and was once the collegiate church of the area which maintained a dean and 4 canons. North of the church is the timber-framed Old Deanery.

At Penkridge turn right on to the unclassified road, SP 'Cannock', then turn right again. Cross the M6 then in ½ mile turn left, SP Rugeley'. In 2 miles cross the A34 and enter Cannock Chase.

CANNOCK CHASE, Staffs
Conifers, silver birches, heathland and little valleys cover a wide area of countryside that was for centuries the royal hunting forest of Cannock Chase. Fallow deer, descendants of the vast herds that roamed the Chase in medieval and Tudor times, graze among the surviving areas of oakwood, and in marshy areas the rare sundew flourishes. Soaring up above the treeline, the Post Office tower looks down on the German Military cemetary where the dead of 2 wars lie buried, including the crew of the first Zeppelin shot down in World War I.

At the next crossroads turn left, SP 'Brocton' and 'Stafford', and pass the German Military cemetary. Descend to the A34 and turn right. In ¼ mile, at the crossroads, turn right into Brocton, then continue to Milford. From here a short diversion to the right along the A513 leads to Shugborough Hall.

SHUGBOROUGH HALL, Staffs
The white, colonnaded mansion (NT) set in beautiful grounds has been the home of the Anson family, Earls of Lichfield, since the 17th century. The fortune of

The dining room fireplace and a portrait of Admiral Lord Anson at Shugborough

George Anson, the celebrated admiral and circumnavigator of the world, paid for much of the splendour of house and park. Mementoes of the admiral's voyages and victories are an outstanding feature of the house, which also contains fine paintings and 18th-century furniture. In the park, the flamboyant Triumphal Arch, modelled on that of the Emperor Hadrian at Athens, commemorates Admiral Anson's victory over the French in 1747. Other particularly charming features are the elegant little Tower of the Winds and, on an island in the lake, the Cat's Monument in memory of a favourite pet of the Admiral that sailed round the world with him. The Staffordshire County Museum and Farm Park are also contained in the grounds of Shugborough Hall. Museum exhibits include social history, crafts and agricultural subjects, and the park has rare farm livestock.

The main tour leaves Milford on the A513 and later joins the A34 for the return to Stafford.

STAFFORDSHIRE'S VALLEYS

Three valleys, Dovedale, the Manifold and the Churnet, offer some of the loveliest scenery to be found anywhere England. Often, and unfairly, dismissed for the industrial sprawl of the Potteries, the countryside of north Staffordshire changes from a patchwork of small, hedged fields to the bleak grandeur of the open moors.

STOKE-ON-TRENT, Staffs

In 1910, the towns known as the Potteries — Hanley, Burslem, Tunstall, Fenton, and Longton — were amalgamated and named Stoke-on-Trent. Pots dating from before the Roman era have been discovered in the area, but the great English porcelain companies, Wedgwood, Minton, Spode and Doulton, were all established in the late-18th and early-19th centuries. Most of the factories organise conducted tours and the Gladstone Pottery Museum in Longton, with its carefully restored and preserved traditional bottle-shaped kilns has practical demonstrations of the craft as well as exhibitions. Hanley's City Museum contains one of the finest collections of pottery and porcelain in the world. Novelist Arnold Bennet, who wrote books about the Potteries, or 5 Towns was born in Hanley in 1867. Drawings, manuscripts, letters and other relics of the writer can be seen in the City Museum. Another native of the Potteries represented in the museum is the aeronautical engineer R J Mitchell who designed the first 'Spitfire' aeroplane in 1936 which became famous as a World War II fighter. Also near Cobridge is Ford Green Hall (OACT), a 16th-century timber-framed mansion built for the Fords, a family of yeoman farmers, which contains English furniture and domestic items of the 16th to 18th centuries. Some idea of the development of mining technology can be gained from

A piece of 'jasperware' pottery made by Wedgwood in Stoke-on-Trent

the Chatterley Whitfield Mining Museum near Tunstall. Guided tours take you 700ft below the ground around the workings and there is a colliery lamphouse exhibition and museum

From the city centre at Hanley follow SP 'Burslem A50', and in ¾ mile turn right on to the A53. Pass through Baddeley Green and Endon then in 1¼ miles turn left, SP 'Rudyard', into Dunwood Lane, and continue for 2½ miles to Rudyard.

RUDYARD, Staffs

This charming little village was made famous by the parents of the novelist and poet Rudyard Kipling, whom they named after the place where they had spent many holidays, and where it is said Lockwood Kipling proposed to Alice Macdonald. The lake lies in a deep wooded valley surrounded by high moors, and along the shores of the nearby reservoir are pleasant walks, with picnic sites.

Turn right on to the B5331. In 1 mile, at the T-junction, turn right on to the A523 then take the next turning left, SP 'Meerbrook'. In ½ mile turn left again and later skirt Tittesworth Reservoir before reaching Meerbrook.

MEERBROOK, Staffs

A lonely village surrounded by bleak moorland, Meerbrook lies in the shadow of Hen Cloud (1,250ft). Nearby are the Staffordshire Roaches, a forbidding outcrop of dark millstone grit rocks rising to 1,658ft which have been weathered over the ages into fantastic shapes.

Turn right at the church, SP 'Blackshaw Moor' and 'Leek' and in 1¼ miles turn left on to the A531. In 2 miles go forward over a crossroads then turn right, SP 'Longnor'. A long descent leads to the Manifold valley and Longnor.

LONGNOR, Staffs

Longnor is the market centre of the far north of Staffordshire, a charming stone-built place surrounded by superb hill scenery, whose narrow streets and alleys end abruptly in magnificent views of the Peak District.

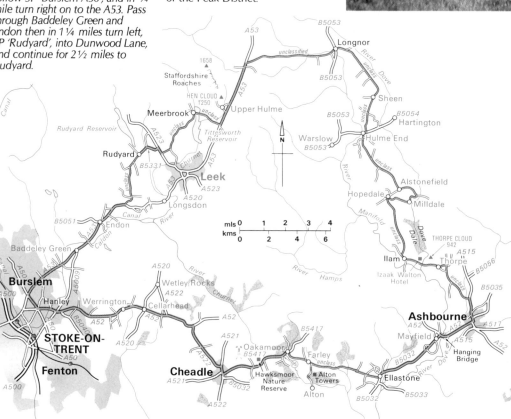

Dovedale's alpine scenery has earned it the title Little Switzerland

Follow SP 'Bakewell' and in ½ mile branch right, SP 'Hulme End'. Continue, through Sheen, then in 1½ miles turn right on to the B5054 into Hulme End, and at the Light Railway Hotel turn left on to the unclassified road for Alstonefield. Here keep left, SP 'Ashbourne', and in 1¼ miles turn sharp right (care needed) SP 'Milldale'. At Milldale, turn right and ascend a narrow gorge to Hopedale. At the Watts Russell Arms turn left, SP 'Ilam', and in 100 yds turn left again. After 2 miles descend into Ilam.

ILAM, Staffs
Ilam owes its delightful and unique appearance to the 19th-century manufacturer Jesse Watts Russell, who bought the village and estate. The cottages he built are completely different in design from the traditional Staffordshire style, with steep-pitched, gabled roofs covered with dark red, shaped tiles. Ilam Hall is now a youth hostel, but the spacious park in the lower reaches of the Manifold valley belongs to the National Trust.

At the war memorial turn left, SP 'Dovedale, Thorpe'. In ¾ mile, by the entrance to the Izaak Walton Hotel, a short detour can be made by turning left to reach a car park at the entrance to Dovedale (reached on foot).

DOVEDALE, Staffs
Dovedale, at the southern edge of the Peak District National Park, is one of the most beautiful valleys in England. The River Dove, the boundary between Staffordshire and Derbyshire, runs through a deep, wooded limestone gorge, where high white cliffs,

Below: 150 years ago Alton Towers was no more than a bare and rocky wasteland

honeycombed with caves, have been weathered into distinctive shapes — the 12 Apostles, Dovedale Castle, Lion's Head, and so on. At the southern end of the valley, annual sheepdog trials draw crowds at the end of August from all over the region.

Cross the River Dove into Derbyshire then skirt the village of Thorpe and in ½ mile, at the Dog and Partridge Hotel, turn right, SP 'Ashbourne'. In 2 miles turn right on to the A515 to enter Ashbourne.

ASHBOURNE, Derbys
Ashbourne has some fine architecture, particularly in Church Street, where 2 sets of almshouses, an Elizabethan grammar school, a mansion house and an old inn make a pleasing group. The parish church, St Oswald's, is considered one of the best examples of Early English style in the North Midlands. Ashbourne holds a traditional football game on Shrove Tuesday, when the inhabitants of the 2 banks of Henmore Brook compete in a riotous game with few rules and unlimited numbers. The locally famous Ashbourne gingerbread is still made to a secret recipe, taught to the town's bakers by French soldiers held prisoner during the Napoleonic Wars.

Leave on the A52, SP 'Uttoxeter (B5032)', and in 1½ miles cross the Hanging Bridge.

HANGING BRIDGE, Staffs
The Hanging Bridge leads the way from Derbyshire across the River Dove to the small stone-built village of Mayfield, clinging to the Staffordshire bank. The name is said to commemorate the hanging of Jacobite supporters of Bonnie Prince Charlie in 1745 — his army had reached Derby on the march south, but then retreated back to Scotland. Records show, however, that the name is much older than the 18th century.

Beyond the bridge turn immediately left on to the B5032. Continue through Mayfield following the Dove valley, to reach Ellastone.

ELLASTONE, Staffs
Robert Evans, father of the novelist George Eliot (Mary Ann Evans), worked as a carpenter here for a time, and the village features in her novel *Adam Bede* under the name Hayslope. Not far from the village, Wootton Lodge (not open) looks out over the Churnet valley. A tall, graceful building, it is one of the finest examples of Jacobean architecture in the county.

Turn left in the village then in ¼ mile turn right on to an unclassified road. In ½ mile go forward over crossroads and in another ½ mile turn left. In 1½ miles, at the edge of Farley, a detour can be made by turning left, 'SP 'Alton', for Alton Towers.

ALTON TOWERS, Staffs
The 15th Earl of Shrewsbury, whose family had acquired vast estates in Staffordshire, came to Alton in the early 19th century and fell in love with the rugged scenery of the Churnet valley. The 600-acre gardens of Alton Towers (OACT) are the result of his work. Thousands of trees and flowering shrubs — rhododendrons, azaleas, Japanese maple, cedars, dwarf and giant conifers, tulip trees — cover the hillsides and set off a series of gardens, ornamental ponds and fountains, connected by winding paths designed to offer an ever-changing succession of views. Soaring above the gardens, the towers and pinnacles of Alton Towers seem like something from a fairy tale. Most of the house, built by the 16th Earl, is just a shell, but the chapel, with its splendid roof designed by the Victorian architect, Pugin, is intact and now houses a superb model railway. Other modern innovations include a miniature scenic railway, an aerial cable car and numerous amusements for children.

The main tour continues into Farley. At the end of the village turn left, SP 'Oakmoor', and in 1 mile turn left again on to the B5417. Cross the River Churnet into Oakmoor and later pass (right) the Hawksmoor Nature Reserve.

HAWKSMOOR NATURE RESERVE, Staffs
This part of the Churnet valley, between Oakmoor and Cheadle, was presented to the National Trust in 1926 by J. R. B. Masefield, a well-known Staffordshire naturalist and cousin of the poet John Masefield. Several rare varieties of tree, such as the lodge pole pine and the red oak flourish alongside the native plants, and many birds — curlews, pheasants, redstarts, nightjars and warblers — have found refuge in the woodland. Nature trails are well marked.

Continue on the B5417 to Cheadle.

CHEADLE, Staffs
High moorland surrounds this small market with a high street of pleasant 18th-century and Victorian buildings, but dominating it all is the massive Roman Catholic church whose lofty spire (200ft) is a landmark for miles around. The church was built in 1846 by Pugin and is regarded as one of his masterpieces. The interior is a magnificent tableau of rich colour, creating an atmosphere of 19th-century opulence.

At the town centre turn right on to the A522, SP 'Leek', and in 2¼ miles turn left on to the A52 for Cellarhead, Werrington and Bucknall. At the traffic signals beyond Bucknall turn right, then at the next traffic signals go forward on the A5008 for the return to Hanley (Stoke-on-Trent).

STRATFORD-UPON-AVON, Warwicks

Sir Hugh Clopton's 14-arched medieval stone bridge is still, as it has been since Shakespeare's day, the main gateway to Stratford. The house in Henley Street, where the poet was born on 23 April 1564, is a substantial timber-framed building preserved by the Shakespeare Birthplace Trust (OACT) as a museum, but the house he bought after becoming successful, New Place, was wantonly destroyed by an 18th-century owner. The foundations remain, however, and a delightful Elizabethan knot garden has been planted on the site. Hall's Croft, where the poet's daughter Susanna lived with her husband, Dr John Hall, contains a fascinating collection of Elizabethan medical implements. The most elaborate timbered house in Stratford is Harvard House, built in 1596 by the grandparents of John Harvard, who sailed to America, and on his death left £799 17s 2d with which to found Harvard University. The Royal Shakespeare Theatre, built in 1932, dominates the riverside, striking a startlingly modern note amid the old buildings of the town. It incorporates a museum and art gallery. Holy Trinity Church is Shakespeare's burial place: he died in 1616 and lies under the chancel with Susanna and John Hall. As a change from the Shakespearean connections of Stratford, the Motor Museum is a superb evocation of 1920s motoring history, specialising in sports and touring cars. There are several gardens laid out on the banks of the Avon which provide a welcome respite from the bustle of the town.

Leave Stratford on the A439, SP 'Evesham'. After ½ mile a short detour to the right may be taken along Shottery Road to the hamlet of Shottery.

The Tudor gatehouse of Coughton Court dominates the 18th-century west front that was built around it

SHOTTERY, Warwicks

Tourists flock to this pretty little hamlet across the fields from Stratford to see the idyllic thatched and timbered cottage (OACT) where Anne Hathaway lived and where Shakespeare came to woo her. Original Tudor furniture and fascinating domestic items are displayed in the old rooms. The Hathaway family lived in the house from 1470 until 1911, when it was acquired by the Shakespeare Birthplace Trust.

The main tour continues on the A439 along the shallow valley of the River Avon and later skirts Bidford-on-Avon.

A fascinating array of rural bygones can be seen in the barns belonging to Mary Arden's cottage in Wilmcote

SHAKESPEARE AND THE HEART OF ENGLAND

Among the winding lanes of Warwickshire and Worcestershire a wealth of timber, thatch and stone, seen in country cottage, village church and stately home, revives the atmosphere of Tudor England. From the interplay of forest and farmland, garden and park, Shakespeare drew the stirring imagery of his writing.

BIDFORD-ON-AVON, Warwicks

Shakespeare's connection with Bidford was the Falcon Inn, a handsome gabled building which still stands, though it is now a private house. The poet is known to have enjoyed many a drinking bout at the Falcon, and is popularly supposed to have composed the 4 lines of doggerel that end: 'Dodging Exhall, Papist Wixford, Beggarly Broom and drunken Bidford'.

Remain on the Evesham road and in 3 miles turn right on to an unclassified road to enter Harvington. Here turn right, SP 'The Lenches', then at the end of the village cross the main road and continue to Church Lench.

THE LENCHES, Herefs & Worcs

Five villages with the name Lench are dotted about the countryside north of Evesham, and 2 of them, Church and Rous Lench, lie on the route. Lench comes from an old English word meaning 'hill', and this part of the country, near the old Warwickshire border is an area of little hills. Each has a distinctive charm, but Rous Lench is perhaps the most interesting (see tour 30).

At Church Lench turn right to reach Rous Lench. Continue on the Inkberrow road and in 1 mile, at the T-junction, turn right, SP 'Alcester'. In another 1½ miles turn left for Abbots Morton.

ABBOTS MORTON, Herefs & Worcs

Often described as the most perfect village in the country, Abbots Morton is rich in black and white timbered cottages of all shapes and sizes. Its lovely 14th-century stone church stands surrounded by trees on a small mound overlooking the village, while on the green stands a thatched letterbox.

Bear right into the village and ¾ mile further, at the T-junction, turn left. In 1½ miles turn right on to the A441, then in another ½ mile, turn left on to the A435, SP 'Birmingham'. Later pass the entrance to Ragley Hall.

RAGLEY HALL, Warwicks

A stately Jacobean mansion of 15 bays, built between 1680 and 1690 by Robert Hooks for the 1st Earl of Conway, Ragley Hall (OACT) is one of the finest houses in England. Much of the sumptuous interior, however, was designed in the 18th century by James Gibbs for the 2nd Baron Conway, later created Earl, the Marquess of Hertford. Showpiece of the house is the great hall, 70ft long, 40ft wide and 40ft high, decorated with exquisite rococo plasterwork. Paintings by great European masters such as Reynolds and Hoppner, and collections of fine porcelain are on display.

Continue to Alcester.

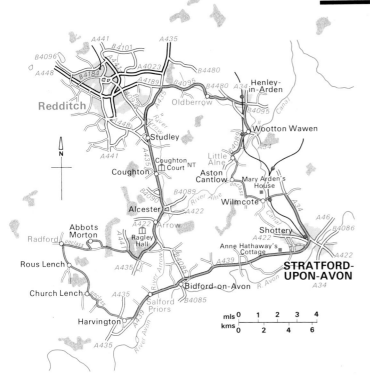

Malt Mill Lane in Alcester is lined by a remarkable collection of ancient houses which were renovated in 1975

ALCESTER, Warwicks
This attractive little market town (pronounced Olster) lies at the confluence of the Rivers Arrow and Alne. Its oldest building is the Old Malt House, a gabled, half timbered structure dating from 1500, but the narrow streets contain many charming Jacobean and Georgian houses; Butter Street in particular is a delight, with its rows of picturesque old cottages. Tudor cottages cluster about the parish church with its 14th-century west tower, the nave and aisles having been rebuilt in the 18th-century. It contains the fine alabaster tomb of Fulke Greville, the grandfather of the Elizabethan poet who was his namesake. Alcester Mop is a pleasure fair held in the town each October.

Leave on the A435 Birmingham road and continue to Coughton.

COUGHTON, Warwicks
The influence of the Throckmortons predominates in the 16th-century church, where monuments and brasses commemorate generations of this staunchly Roman Catholic family. Coughton Court (NT) was the family home, its Tudor stone gatehouse flanked by warm-toned stucco giving entrance to a courtyard with 2 timbered wings. As befits a Roman Catholic house, there is a hidden chapel, reached by a rope ladder, in one of the turrets, and many Jacobite relics. The Throckmortons were implicated in the 1605 Gunpowder Plot, and it was at Coughton that the family and friends of the conspirators waited anxiously for news. In the saloon is the famous Throckmorton coat, made for a bet in 1811 from wool sheared at sunrise and woven into a coat by sunset of the same day.

Continue through Studley.

STUDLEY, Warwicks
Pleasant countryside surrounds this small town which is possibly the largest centre of needle-making in Europe. Since 1800, when steam power was introduced, the industry has been mechanised, but the tradition goes back for more than 300 years, and there are many old houses dating from the 17th century.

At the end of the town go forward at the roundabout, SP 'Birmingham'. Nearly 2 miles farther turn right on to the B4095 and continue to Henley-in-Arden.

HENLEY-IN-ARDEN, Warwicks
Once, as the last part of the name suggests, Henley lay in the great Forest of Arden. Its ¾ mile-long broad main street is bordered by timbered houses and inns of all periods and makes a charming picture. Many of the inns date from the great coaching age of the 18th-century when Henley was served daily by a mail coach and 4 post coaches.

Leave on the A34 Stratford Road to reach Wootton Wawen.

WOOTTON WAWEN, Warwicks
The fine village church exhibits features of almost every style of English architecture, from Anglo-Danish to the late Middle Ages. Parts of the crossing tower are the most ancient, but there are examples of Norman, early English, Decorated and Perpendicular styles as well as features of the 17th, 18th and 19th centuries. The village is attractive, with a graceful 17th-century hall (not open) which was the childhood home of Mrs Fitzherbert whom the Prince Regent, later George IV, loved and with whom he illegally contracted a secret marriage in 1785.

Leave on the B4089 Alcester Road. In 2 miles branch left, SP 'Aston Cantlow'. Cross the river bridge and turn right for Aston Cantlow.

Ragley Hall commands sweeping views over its parkland to the distant Cotswolds

ASTON CANTLOW, Warwicks
This church is very probably the one in which John Shakespeare and Mary Arden, Shakespeare's parents, were married in 1557, though the church records begin only in 1560. The Victorian architect William Butterfield designed the pretty cottages, vicarage, school and master's house near the church, and the rest of the village is a pleasing mixture of black and white timbered houses offset by terraces of red brick. The name Cantlow comes from the Cantelupe family, and Thomas Cantelupe, rector of the village church later became Chancellor of England and Bishop of Hereford. In 1282 he died while on pilgrimage to Rome and was subsequently (1320) canonized, the only Warwickshire rector to be so honoured and the last Englishman to be canonized until after the Reformation.

Go forward through the village, then turn left, SP 'Wilmcote'. In 1 mile turn left again for Wilmcote.

WILMCOTE, Warwicks
The highlight of Wilmcote is the lovely timbered farmhouse that was the home of Mary Arden, Shakespeare's mother. Simply furnished, in period, the old timbered house, surrounded by a charming old-fashioned cottage garden, retains a strong sense of atmosphere, enhanced by the collection of old Warwickshire agricultural implements housed in the stone barns belonging to the house (OACT).

Turn left, SP 'Stratford', then in 1 mile turn right on to the A34 for the return to Stratford-upon-Avon.

WARWICK, Warwicks
Imposing Warwick Castle is one of the finest medieval strongholds in Europe. It stands on a Saxon site above this compact River Avon town, and its exceptional Norman and later structure hides an interior completely rebuilt during the 17th century. The castle is still occupied, but visitors have access to the state rooms, torture chamber, silver vault, ghost tower, and Avon-side grounds that were landscaped by Capability Brown. Also in the town are the remains of town walls, two gates, and a great number of building styles ranging from half-timbered to the conscious starkness of the 20th century. Lord Leycester's Hospital was founded as a guildhall in 1383 and converted to almshouses in 1571 (open), and the 18th-century Shire Hall is considered an excellent example of its type. Elizabeth Oken's House contains a Doll Museum, and 17th-century St John's House features both a museum of crafts, costume, and furniture, and the Museum of the Royal Warwickshire Regiment. The 18th-century Court House is an Italianate building.

Leave Warwick on the A425 'Banbury' road and continue for 2¼ miles to join the A41. Proceed for 1¼ miles and turn right on to the B4087 SP 'Wellesbourne'. Continue to Wellesbourne.

A magnificent collection of armour is housed in Warwick Castle.

WELLESBOURNE, Warwicks
Georgian houses and a Hall dating from c1700 are the main features of this pleasant village.

Follow SP 'Stratford B4086' for 1 mile and turn right on to the B4088 SP 'Charlecote' to reach the village of Charlecote.

CHARLECOTE, Warwicks
Charlecote Park (NT) is a fine Elizabethan house with a great hall and museum. The Avon flows through grounds where Shakespeare is said to have been caught poaching deer. Attractive old cottages survive in the village.

In Charlecote turn left on to the unclassified 'Hampton Lucy' road and cross the River Avon. Continue to Hampton Lucy.

SHAKESPEARE COUNTRY

England's heartlands are watered by the Avon and Stour, great rivers that wind through charming Elizabethan villages, country estates graced by stately houses, and historic towns where Shakespeare drew inspiration from the comedy and tragedy in the lives of his contemporaries.

HAMPTON LUCY, Warwicks
Of particular interest here is a cast-iron bridge that was built in 1829.

On entering Hampton Lucy bear left SP 'Stratford'. Proceed for 1¼ miles, bear left again, and in ¾ mile turn left on to the A46 for Stratford.

STRATFORD-UPON-AVON, Warwicks
William Shakespeare was born here in 1564. His childhood home contains a museum relating to his life, and the old Guildhall that housed his school still stands. A picturesque Elizabethan knot garden can be seen near the foundations of New Place, where he died, and his remains lie in Holy Trinity Church. A lovely thatched and timbered cottage (open) in the nearby village of Shottery is where his wife Anne Hathaway was born, and gabled Hall's Croft (open) was the home of their daughter Susanna. Many of the great man's works are staged in the Royal Shakespeare Theatre, which was built on an Avon-side site in 1932; it incorporates a museum and

The River Avon formed an essential aspect of Warwick Castle's defences.

picture gallery (open). Among many 15th- and 16th-century buildings preserved in the town are several lovely half-timbered houses and the 14-arch Clopton Bridge over the Avon. Harvard House was the home of the grandparents of John Harvard, founder of the US university of the same name. The World of Shakespeare specializes in scenes from Elizabethan England, the Motor Museum preserves a number of veteran and vintage cars, and an Arms and Armour museum exhibits some 800 pieces.

Leave the town by the A34 'Oxford' road and later pass Alscot Park to the right. Proceed to Alderminster.

ALDERMINSTER, Warwicks
Views across the Stour valley to Meon Hill and the Cotswolds can be enjoyed from the 13th-century church here.

The Guildhall schoolroom, where the poet and dramatist William Shakespeare took his first steps in learning.

Remain on the A34 to reach Newbold-upon-Stour. At the end of that village turn right on to an unclassified road and drive to Armscote. Turn right and continue to Ilmington.

ILMINGTON, Warwicks
Situated at the east foot of the Cotswolds, this village has several picturesque cottages and an old tithe barn. The rectory and manor house both date from the 16th century. Above the village is 854ft Ilmington Down, one of the highest points in Warwickshire.

Turn left and follow SP 'Campden' to climb Ilmington Down. Descend, meet crossroads, and turn left to reach Ebrington.

EBRINGTON, Glos
Delightful stone and thatched cottages complement a church with a fine Norman doorway in this lovely Cotswold village.

Join the B4035 and drive to Shipston-on-Stour.

SHIPSTON-ON-STOUR, Warwicks
Once one of the most important sheep markets in the country, this mainly Georgian town lies at the edge of the Vale of Red Horse.

Follow SP 'Banbury', cross the River Stour, and proceed for ¾ mile to crossroads. Turn left on to the unclassified 'Honington' road, then in ¾ mile turn right SP 'Tysoe' and proceed for 2¾ miles. Meet crossroads and drive forward. In ¾ mile a detour from the main route can be made by turning right to reach Compton Wynyates.

COMPTON WYNYATES, Warwicks
The estate in which this exceptional Tudor house stands has been in the same family since the 13th century. Sir William Compton built the magnificent red-brick extravagance that stands here today, and the interior has remained largely unaltered since Tudor times (not open). Close to the house the wild hillside parkland has been cultivated as a modern topiary garden.

Continue to Upper Tysoe.

UPPER TYSOE, Warwicks
One of a trio of villages named from the Norse God Tiw, this little place has a 16th-century manor house and stands in the Vale of Red Horse. The Vale itself derives its name from a turf-cut figure on Rising Hill, due east of Lower Tysoe. Until 1800 this was scoured annually, but it is now scarcely visible.

In Upper Tysoe turn left SP 'Kineton', then right SP 'Shenington' and 'Banbury'. Ascend Tysoe Hill, meet crossroads, and turn left to follow the ridge of Edgehill. Continue for 2 miles and drive forward on to the A422. A short detour from the main route can be made by continuing on the A422 for ½ mile to Upton House.

The superb Tudor architecture of Compton Wynyates.

UPTON HOUSE, Warwicks
Good views can be enjoyed from the lovely terraced gardens of this impressive 17th-century house (NT). Inside are collections of porcelain, pictures, and various pieces of 18th-century furniture.

On the main route, continue for ¼ mile after joining the A422 and bear left on to an unclassified road for Edgehill village.

EDGEHILL, Warwicks
An 18th-century folly which now forms part of a pub in the village affords extensive views over the countryside. North, on private ground by the B4086, is the field where the first major battle of the Civil War was fought in 1642. Here the horizon is dominated by the attractively wooded 700ft ridge of Edgehill, which extends for 3 miles.

Leave Edgehill village and in 1 mile bear left on to the B4086 SP 'Kineton'. Descend to Kineton with the Edgehill battlefield to the left.

KINETON, Warwicks
Near Kineton station are the remains of a motte and bailey castle, and ¾ mile north west is a sail-less tower windmill. The church has a splendid 13th-century doorway.

Turn right on to the B4451 SP 'Southam' and proceed to Gaydon. Turn right on to the A41 SP 'Banbury'. Proceed for 2 miles and turn left on to the unclassified 'Fenny Compton' road, then keep forward SP 'Burton Hills'. Ascend the Burton Hills (a country park) and pass the isolated village of Burton Dassett to the right.

BURTON DASSETT, Warwicks
Church Hill rises to 689ft above this pretty village and is surmounted by a lookout tower that may once have been part of a medieval windmill. The hill's summit, used as a beacon site during the Battle of Edgehill in 1642, is now a country park.

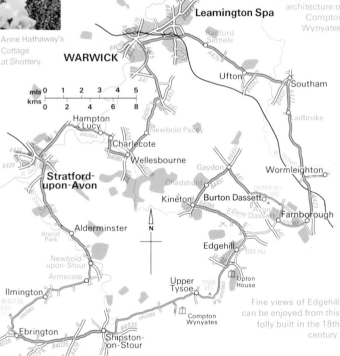

Continue for 1 mile to reach crossroads and turn right to descend to Avon Dassett. Drive to the end of the village and keep forward. Enter Farnborough.

FARNBOROUGH, Warwicks
Notable Farnborough Hall (NT) dates from the 17th and 18th centuries and features excellent rococo stucco-work with panels of scrolls, rays, shells, fruit and flowers. Delightful grounds include landscaped terraced lawns which afford superb views to the ridge of Edgehill. A classical air is given the gardens by a small Ionic temple and an oval pavilion.

Keep left through Farnborough and at the end of the village turn left on to the A423 SP 'Coventry'. In 2 miles it is possible to make a detour from the main route to Wormleighton by turning right on to an unclassified road.

WORMLEIGHTON, Warwicks
Prince Rupert slept at Wormleighton Manor the night before he gave battle to parliamentarian cavalry at Edgehill. The reputedly lovely house was destroyed later in the Civil War, but the imposing gateway survives, complete with its carved crests.

On the main route, proceed on the A423 to the edge of Southam.

SOUTHAM, Warwicks
At one time this ancient town was famed for a mineral spring and healing well which were both claimed to have wide-ranging medicinal powers. The Reverend Holyoake, a rector of the local 15th- and 16th-century church, compiled the first dictionary of the English language.

At the edge of Southam turn left on to the A425 SP 'Leamington' to reach Ufton.

UFTON, Warwicks
Views from this 380ft-high village extend beyond the ancient Fosse Way and River Avon to the distant Malvern Hills, known for their mineral springs. Inside the village church, which dates from the 13th century but has been extensively restored since, is a good 16th-century memorial brass.

Continue and pass through Radford Semele to reach Leamington Spa.

Fine views of Edgehill can be enjoyed from this folly built in the 18th century.

LEAMINGTON SPA, Warwicks
In the 18th century it was claimed that mineral springs in this lovely old town were beneficial in the treatment of various complaints. As the high-society fashion for taking the waters blossomed so also did Leamington, and today it boasts many grand old buildings that recall the prosperity of those times. The Pump Room of 1814, rebuilt in 1925, is an excellent focus for the terraces of Regency, Georgian, and Victorian houses that grace the streets around it. Between the buildings are wide parks and open spaces, the carefully tended Jephson Gardens, and the vagrant windings of the River Lea. The Warwick Art Gallery and Museum exhibits a good selection of paintings and examples of 18th-century glass.

Continue along the A425 and return to Warwick.

Key to Town Plans

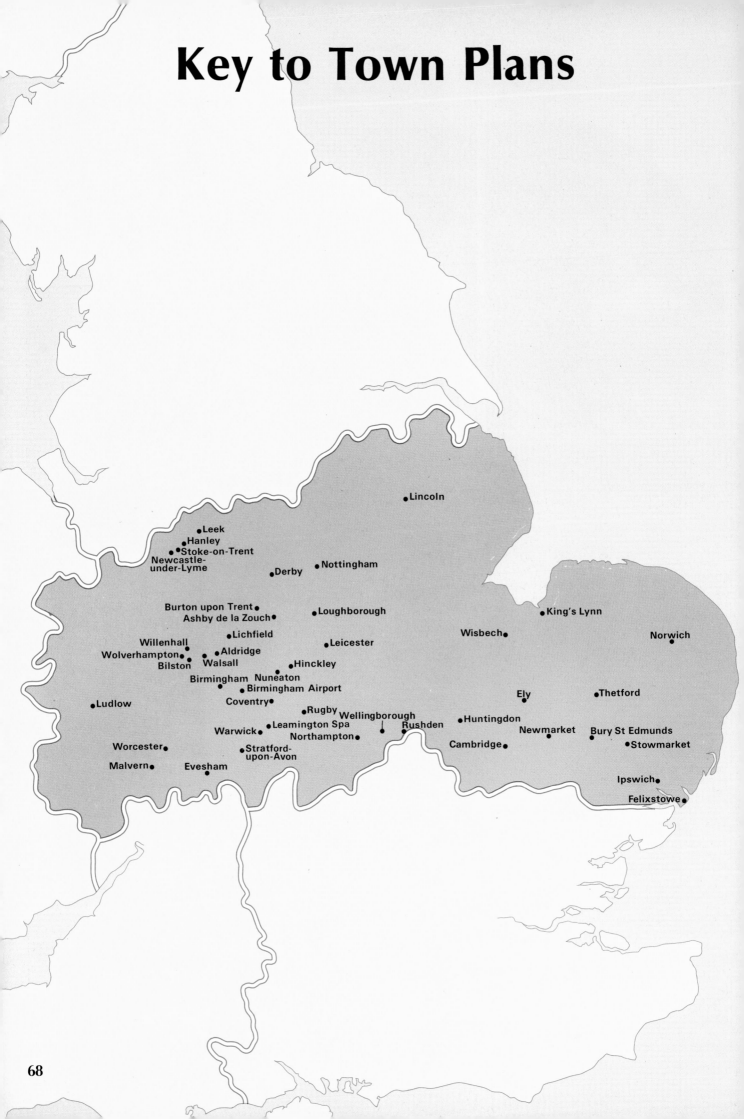

Lincoln

Leek
Hanley
Stoke-on-Trent
Newcastle-
under-Lyme
Derby
Nottingham

Burton upon Trent
Ashby de la Zouch
Loughborough
King's Lynn

Wisbech
Norwich

Lichfield
Leicester

Willenhall
Wolverhampton
Aldridge
Bilston
Walsall
Hinckley

Ely
Thetford

Birmingham
Nuneaton
Birmingham Airport
Coventry
Huntingdon

Ludlow

Rugby
Wellingborough
Warwick
Leamington Spa
Rushden
Newmarket
Bury St Edmunds

Northampton
Cambridge
Stowmarket

Worcester
Stratford-
upon-Avon

Malvern
Evesham
Ipswich

Felixstowe

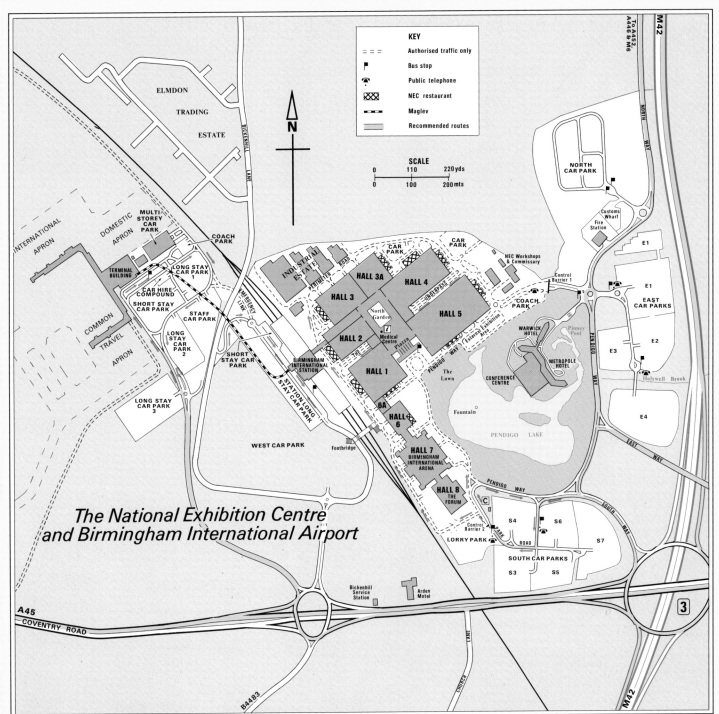

KEY

= = =   Authorised traffic only

⬛   Bus stop

☎   Public telephone

▨   NEC restaurant

▪-▪-▪   Maglev

▬   Recommended routes

SCALE

0   110   220 yds

0   100   200 mts

N

*The National Exhibition Centre
and Birmingham International Airport*

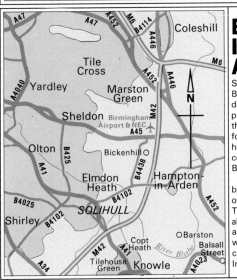

Birmingham International Airport and NEC

Situated just nine miles east of the city, Birmingham International Airport is a short distance from the M6 and M42 motorways, and provides quick and easy access from most parts of the country. This is a popular embarkation point for charter flights to a wide range of European holiday destinations, and it also provides a comprehensive network of scheduled flights to many British and European destinations.

A special viewing area with its own shop and buffet is situated on the third level, with its own access at the front of the terminal building. The airport's choice of buffets and licensed bars also includes the 150-seater Landside Restaurant, and all of them are open to the general public as well as to passengers. Multi-storey and surface car parking is available, while Birmingham International Station offers an 80-minute rail link with London (Euston), and connections to other British cities. The airport is also the site of the Maglev transit system, which sweeps travellers in 90 seconds from the three-storey airport terminal to the Birmingham International Railway Station, and to the National Exhibition Centre. The Maglev has three unmanned cars (each taking up to 32 passengers with their luggage), suspended by magnetic levitation 15mm above guidance tracks and driven without friction by linear induction motors, along a 600 metre elevated track.

National Exhibition Centre The new centre was opened by HM the Queen in February 1976 and lies about eight miles east of Birmingham city centre. The 10 exhibition halls have an interior area of 105,085 square metres and the landscaped setting covers 310 acres. The central feature of the complex — the Piazza — has shops, banks, medical and visitor services, including the Birmingham Convention and Visitor Bureau. The International Area is a multi-purpose hall for conventions, concerts and sporting events, with seating for up to 12,000, and the Forum is designed specifically for presentations and product launches.

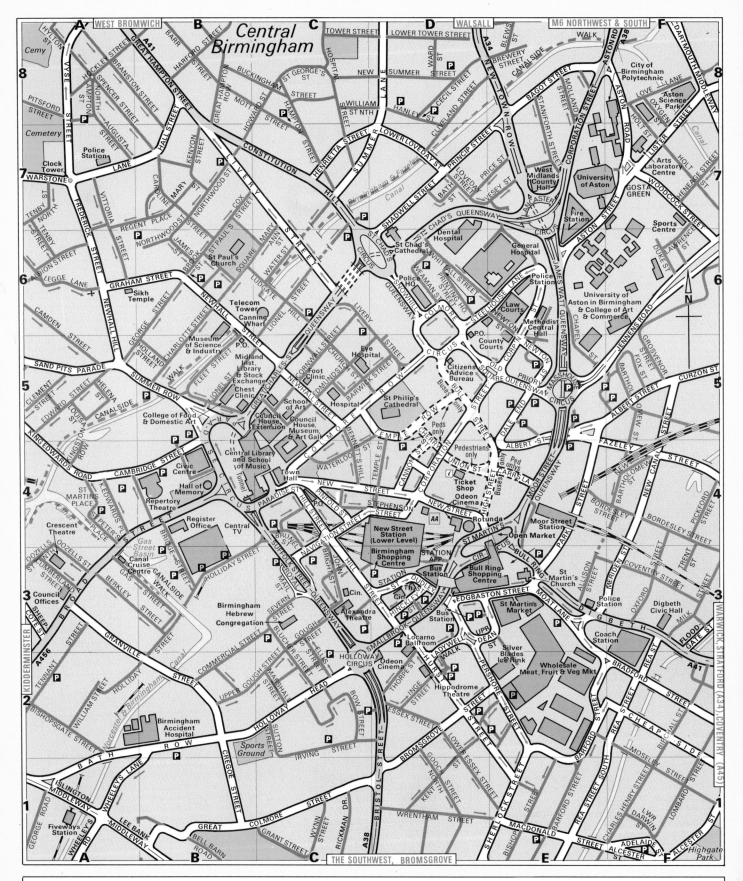

Birmingham

It is very difficult to visualise Birmingham as it was before it began the growth which eventually made it the second-largest city in England. When the Romans were in Britain it was little more than a staging post on Icknield Street. Throughout medieval times it was a sleepy agricultural centre in the middle of a heavily-forested region. Timbered houses clustered together round a green that was

eventually to be called the Bull Ring. But by the 16th century, although still a tiny and unimportant village by today's standards, it had begun to gain a reputation as a manufacturing centre. Tens of thousands of sword blades were made here during the Civil War. Throughout the 18th century more and more land was built on. In 1770 the Birmingham Canal was completed, making trade very much easier and increasing the town's development dramatically. All of that pales into near

insignificance compared with what happened in the 19th century. Birmingham was not represented in Parliament until 1832 and had no town council until 1838. Yet by 1889 it had already been made a city, and after only another 20 years it had become the second largest city in England. Many of Birmingham's most imposing public buildings date from the 19th century, when the city was growing so rapidly. Surprisingly, the city has more miles of waterway than Venice.

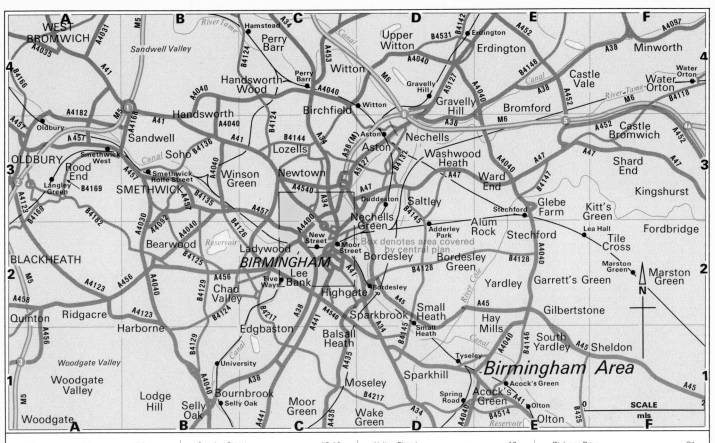

Key to Town Plan and Area Plan

Town Plan

AA Recommended roads

Restricted roads

Other roads

Buildings of interest   Station ▢

AA Centre   AA

Car Parks   P

Parks and open spaces

Churches   ✝

Area Plan

A roads

B roads

Locations   Meer End ○

Urban area

Street Index with Grid Reference

Birmingham

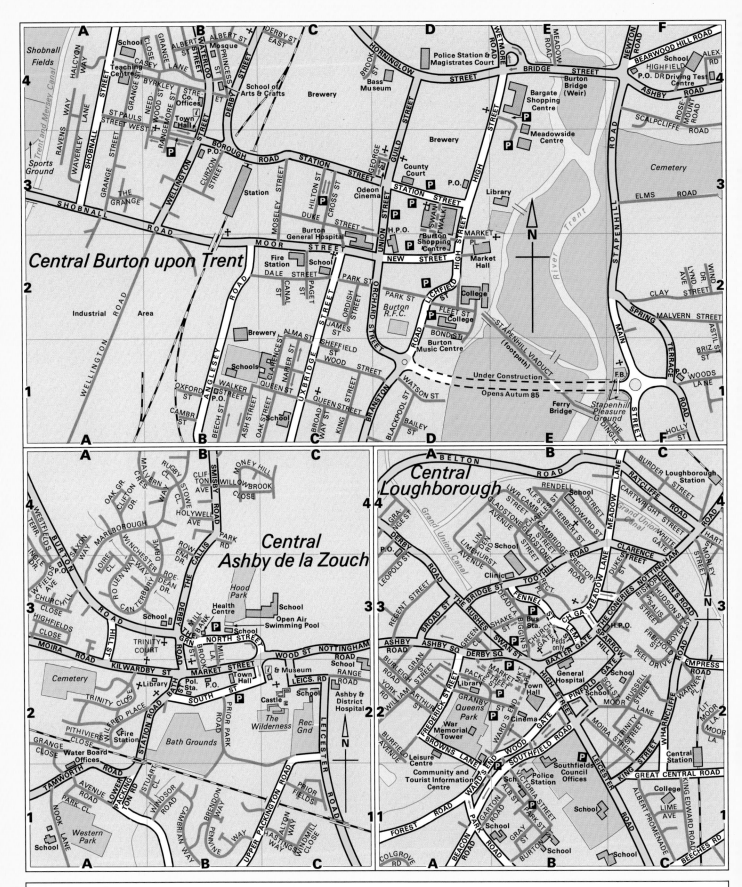

Burton upon Trent

Beer has been brewed here since medieval times and is still prevalent in the town, even though the number of breweries has diminished. The Bass Museum traces the history of the local brewing industry, and other places of interest include the Meadowside Centre, with its fine facilities for sports and the arts. Interesting old buildings can be seen, especially around Horninglow Street, and the Market Hall (now the new shopping centre) dates from the 19th century.

Loughborough Forty-seven locally-made bells ring out from the Queens Park Carillon Tower every Sunday during the summer, and many of Britain's churches have bells from Loughborough's John Taylor Foundry. A busy market and university town situated on the River Stour, Loughborough is also known for its colleges of technology and physical education. Its facilities include a modern Leisure Centre, and amongst local places of interest are the Parish Church of All Saints, dating from the 14th century, the much-restored Old Rectory, and Loughborough Central Station, where steam trains operate most weekends.

Ashby-de-la-Zouch Soap, crisp and biscuit making are the chief present-day concerns of this pleasant market town. The remains of the 15th-century castle are preserved near the centre of the town.

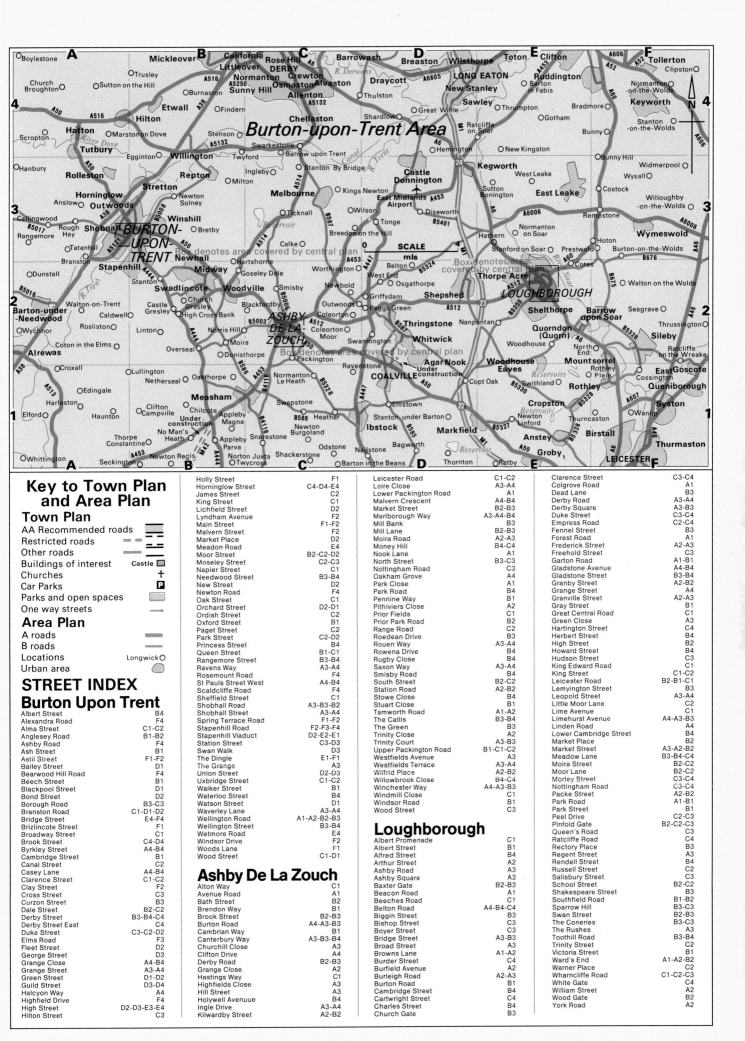

Key to Town Plan and Area Plan

Town Plan
AA Recommended roads
Restricted roads
Other roads
Buildings of interest   Castle
Churches   +
Car Parks   P
Parks and open spaces
One way streets

Area Plan
A roads
B roads
Locations   Longwick
Urban area

STREET INDEX

Burton Upon Trent

Albert Street	B4
Alexandra Road	F4
Alma Street	C1-C2
Anglesey Road	B1-B2
Ashby Road	F4
Ash Street	B1
Astil Street	F1-F2
Bailey Street	D1
Bearwood Hill Road	F4
Beech Street	B1
Blackpool Street	D1
Bond Street	D2
Borough Road	B3-C3
Branston Road	C1-D1-D2
Bridge Street	E4-F4
Brizlincote Street	F1
Broadway Street	C1
Brook Street	C4-D4
Byrkley Street	A4-B4
Cambridge Street	B1
Canal Street	C2
Casey Lane	A4-B4
Clarence Street	C1-C2
Clay Street	F2
Cross Street	C3
Curzon Street	B3
Dale Street	B2-C2
Derby Street	B3-B4-C4
Derby Street East	C4
Duke Street	C3-C2-D2
Elms Road	F3
Fleet Street	D2
George Street	D3
Grange Close	A4-B4
Grange Street	A3-A4
Green Street	D1-D2
Guild Street	D3-D4
Halcyon Way	A4
Highfield Drive	F4
High Street	D2-D3-E3-E4
Hilton Street	C3
Holly Street	F1
Horninglow Street	C4-D4-E4
James Street	C2
King Street	C1
Lichfield Street	D2
Lyndham Avenue	F2
Main Street	F1-F2
Malvern Street	F2
Market Place	D2
Meadon Road	E4
Moor Street	B2-C2-D2
Moseley Street	C2-C3
Napier Street	C1
Needwood Street	B3-B4
New Street	D2
Newton Road	F4
Oak Street	C1
Orchard Street	D2-D1
Ordish Street	C2
Oxford Street	B1
Paget Street	C2
Park Street	C2-D2
Princess Street	B4
Queen Street	B1-C1
Rangemore Street	B3-B4
Ravens Way	A3-A4
Rosemount Road	F4
St Pauls Street West	A4-B4
Scaldcliffe Road	F4
Sheffield Street	C1
Shobhall Road	A3-B3-B2
Shobhall Street	A3-A4
Spring Terrace Road	F1-F2
Stapenhill Road	F2-F3-F4
Stapenhill Viaduct	D2-E2-E1
Station Street	C3-D3
Swan Walk	D3
The Dingle	E1-F1
The Grange	A3
Union Street	D2-D3
Uxbridge Street	C1-C2
Walker Street	B1
Waterloo Street	B4
Watson Street	D1
Waverley Lane	A3-A4
Wellington Road	A1-A2-B2-B3
Wellington Street	B3-B4
Wetmore Road	E4
Windsor Drive	F2
Woods Lane	F1
Wood Street	C1-D1

Ashby De La Zouch

Alton Way	C1
Avenue Road	A1
Bath Street	B2
Brendon Way	B1
Brook Street	B2-B3
Burton Road	A4-A3-B4
Cambrian Way	B1
Canterbury Way	A3-B3-B4
Churchill Close	A3
Clifton Drive	A4
Derby Road	B2-B3
Grange Close	A2
Hastings Way	C1
Highfields Close	A3
Hill Street	A3
Holywell Avenue	A3
Ingle Drive	A3-A4
Kilwardby Street	A2-B2
Leicester Road	C1-C2
Loire Close	A3-A4
Lower Packington Road	A1
Malvern Crescent	A4-B4
Market Street	B2-B3
Marlborough Way	A3-A4-B4
Mill Bank	B3
Mill Lane	B2-B3
Moira Road	A2-A3
Money Hill	B4-C4
Nook Lane	A1
North Street	B3-C3
Nottingham Road	C3
Oakham Grove	A4
Park Close	A1
Park Road	B4
Pennine Way	B1
Pithiviers Close	A2
Prior Fields	C1
Prior Park Road	B2
Range Road	C2
Roedean Drive	B3
Rouen Way	A3-A4
Rowena Drive	B4
Rugby Close	B4
Saxon Way	A3-A4
Smisby Road	A2
South Street	B2-C2
Station Road	A2-B2
Stowe Close	B4
Stuart Close	B1
Tamworth Road	A1-A2
The Callis	B3-B4
The Green	B3
Trinity Close	A2
Trinity Court	A3-B3
Upper Packington Road	B1-C1-C2
Westfields Avenue	A3
Westfields Terrace	A3-A4
Wilfrid Place	A2-B2
Willowbrook Close	B4-C4
Winchester Way	A4-A3-B3
Windmill Close	C1
Windsor Road	B1
Wood Street	C3

Loughborough

Albert Promenade	C1
Albert Street	B1
Alfred Street	B4
Arthur Street	A2
Ashby Road	A3
Ashby Square	A3
Baxter Gate	B2-B3
Beacon Road	A1
Beeches Road	C1
Belton Road	A4-B4-C4
Biggin Street	B3
Bishop Street	C3
Boyer Street	A3-B3
Bridge Street	A3
Broad Street	A1-A2
Browns Lane	C4
Burder Street	A2
Burfield Avenue	A2-A3
Burleigh Road	B1
Burton Road	B4
Cambridge Street	C4
Cartwright Street	B4
Charles Street	B3
Church Gate	C3-C4
Clarence Street	A1
Colgrove Road	B3
Dead Lane	A3-A4
Derby Road	A3-B3
Derby Square	C3-C4
Duke Street	C2-C4
Empress Road	B3
Fennel Street	A1
Forest Road	A2-A3
Frederick Street	C3
Freehold Street	A1-B1
Garton Road	A4-B4
Gladstone Avenue	B3-B4
Gladstone Street	A2-B2
Granby Street	A4
Grange Street	A2-A3
Granville Street	B1
Gray Street	C1
Great Central Road	A3
Green Close	C4
Hartington Street	B4
Herbert Street	B2
High Street	B4
Howard Street	C3
Hudson Street	C1
King Edward Road	C1-C2
King Street	B2-B1-C1
Leicester Road	B3
Lemyington Street	A3-A4
Leopold Street	C2
Little Moor Lane	C1
Lime Avenue	A4-A3-B3
Limehurst Avenue	A4
Linden Road	B4
Lower Cambridge Street	B2
Market Place	A3-A2-B2
Market Street	B3-B4-C4
Meadow Lane	B2-C2
Moira Street	B2-C2
Moor Lane	C3-C4
Morley Street	C3-C4
Nottingham Road	A2-B2
Packe Street	A1-B1
Park Road	B1
Park Street	C2-C3
Peel Drive	C3
Pinfold Gate	B2-C2-C3
Queen's Road	C4
Ratcliffe Road	B3
Rectory Place	A3
Regent Street	B4
Rendell Street	C2
Russell Street	C3
Salisbury Street	B2-C2
School Street	B3
Shakespeare Street	B1-B2
Southfield Road	B3-C3
Sparrow Hill	B2-B3
Swan Street	B3-C3
The Coneries	A3
The Rushes	B3-B4
Toothill Road	C2
Trinity Street	B1
Victoria Street	A1-A2-B2
Ward's End	C2
Warner Place	C1-C2-C3
Wharncliffe Road	A4
White Gate	C4
William Street	A2
Wood Gate	B2
York Road	A2

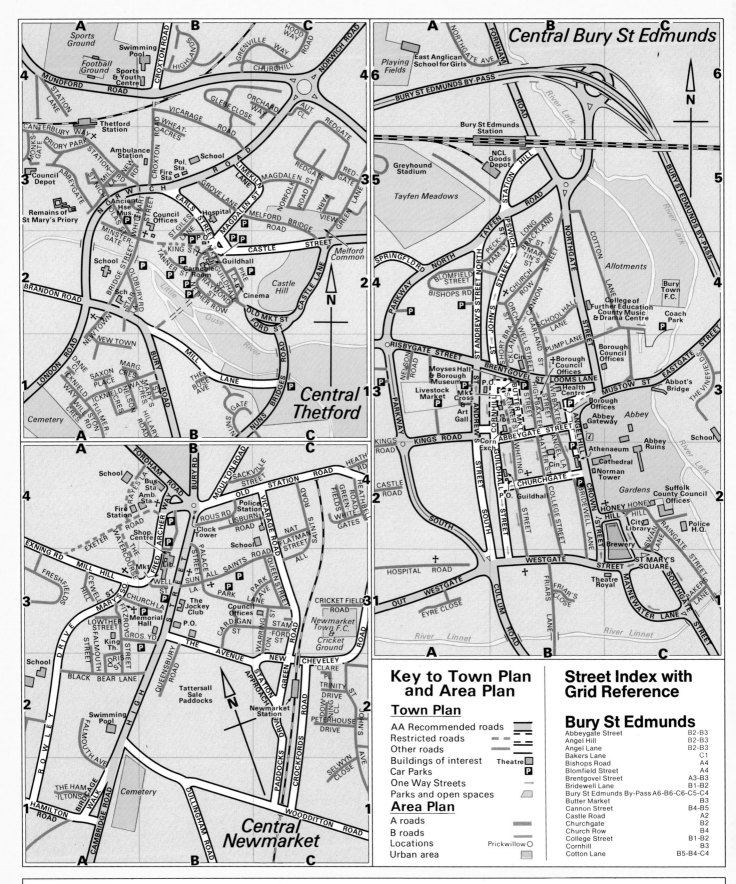

Central Thetford

Central Bury St Edmunds

Central Newmarket

Key to Town Plan and Area Plan

Town Plan

AA Recommended roads
Restricted roads
Other roads
Buildings of interest — Theatre
Car Parks — P
One Way Streets →
Parks and open spaces

Area Plan

A roads
B roads
Locations — Prickwillow O
Urban area

Street Index with Grid Reference

Bury St Edmunds

Street	Grid Ref
Abbeygate Street	B2-B3
Angel Hill	B2-B3
Angel Lane	B2-B3
Bakers Lane	C1
Bishops Road	A4
Blomfield Street	A4
Brentgovel Street	A3-B3
Bridewell Lane	B1-B2
Bury St Edmunds By-Pass	A6-B6-C6-C5-C4
Butter Market	B3
Cannon Street	B4-B5
Castle Road	A2
Churchgate	B2
Church Row	B4
College Street	B1-B2
Cornhill	B3
Cotton Lane	B5-B4-C4

Bury St Edmunds

This is one of the architectural gems of East Anglia with its streets of Georgian and earlier houses on the Norman grid pattern. The Norman Abbey ruins are set in attractive grounds with a magnificent gateway, and the cathedral church of St Edmunds-bury is adjacent to a massive Norman tower. Also worth seeing are the Guildhall (13th-century and later), the Athenaeum, the colonnaded Corn Exchange (1862) and the 1711 Pentecostal Church. Moyses Hall and Borough Museum goes back to the 12th century and the rebuilt Market Cross and Art Gallery to the 17th. Angel Corner has a fine display of clocks and watches, and St Mary's Church holds Mary Tudor's tomb.

Newmarket Headquarters of British horse racing, breeding and training for nearly 400 years, this is the home of the Jockey Club (founded 1750), the National Stud and the National Horseracing Museum. The racecourse has the world's longest 'straight'.

Thetford was once a Saxon cathedral city and seat of early kings. London overspill sparked off expansion in the 1960s, but Georgian and medieval buildings can still be seen in the town, as well as a Norman castle mound, 12th-century priory remains and Iron Age earthworks. *Rights of Man* author Thomas Paine was born here in 1737. The 15th-century Ancient House offers local history exhibits and the Museum of Childhood Treasures.

74

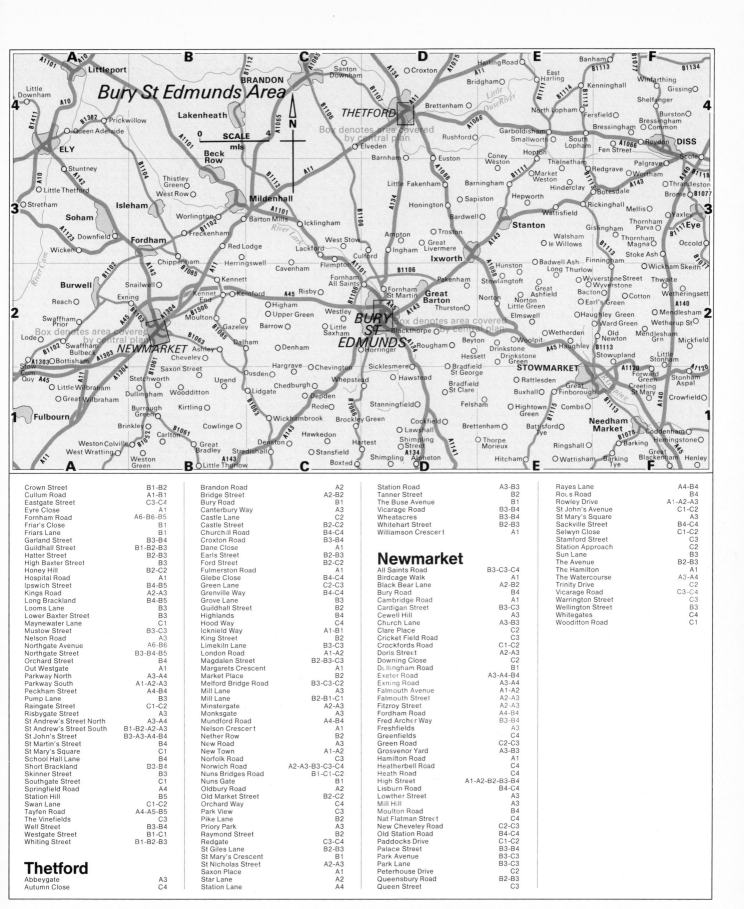

Bury St Edmunds Area

THETFORD

BURY ST EDMUNDS

NEWMARKET

Box denotes area covered by central plan

SCALE mls

Crown Street	B1-B2
Cullum Road	A1-B1
Eastgate Street	C3-C4
Eyre Close	A1
Fornham Road	A6-B6-B5
Friar's Close	B1
Friars Lane	B1
Garland Street	B3-B4
Guildhall Street	B1-B2-B3
Hatter Street	B2-B3
High Baxter Street	B3
Honey Hill	B2-C2
Hospital Road	A1
Ipswich Street	B4-B5
Kings Road	A2-A3
Long Brackland	B4-B5
Looms Lane	B3
Lower Baxter Street	B3
Maynewater Lane	C1
Mustow Street	B3-C3
Nelson Road	A3
Northgate Avenue	A6-B6
Northgate Street	B3-B4-B5
Orchard Street	B4
Out Westgate	A1
Parkway North	A3-A4
Parkway South	A1-A2-A3
Peckham Street	A4-B4
Pump Lane	B3
Raingate Street	C1-C2
Risbygate Street	A3
St Andrew's Street North	A3-A4
St Andrew's Street South	B1-B2-A2-A3
St John's Street	B3-A3-A4-B4
St Martin's Street	B4
St Mary's Square	C1
School Hall Lane	B4
Short Brackland	B3-B4
Skinner Street	B3
Southgate Street	C1
Springfield Road	A4
Station Hill	B5
Swan Lane	C1-C2
Tayfen Road	A4-A5-B5
The Vinefields	C3
Well Street	B3-B4
Westgate Street	B1-C1
Whiting Street	B1-B2-B3

Thetford

Abbeygate	A3
Autumn Close	C4

Brandon Road	A2
Bridge Street	A2-B2
Bury Road	B1
Canterbury Way	A3
Castle Lane	C2
Castle Street	B2-C2
Churchill Road	B4-C4
Croxton Road	B3-B4
Dane Close	A1
Earls Street	B2-B3
Ford Street	B2-C2
Fulmerston Road	A1
Glebe Close	B4-C4
Green Lane	C2-C3
Grenville Way	B4-C4
Grove Lane	B3
Guildhall Street	B2
Highlands	B4
Hood Way	C4
Icknield Way	A1-B1
King Street	B2
Limekiln Lane	B3-C3
London Road	A1-A2
Magdalen Street	B2-B3-C3
Margarets Crescent	A1
Market Place	B2
Melford Bridge Road	B3-C3-C2
Mill Lane	A3
Mill Lane	B2-B1-C1
Minstergate	A2-A3
Monksgate	A3
Mundford Road	A4-B4
Nelson Crescent	A1
Nether Row	B2
New Road	A3
New Town	A1-A2
Norfolk Road	C3
Norwich Road	A2-A3-B3-C3-C4
Nuns Bridges Road	B1-C1-C2
Nuns Gate	B1
Oldbury Road	A2
Old Market Street	B2-C2
Orchard Way	C4
Park View	C3
Pike Lane	B2
Priory Park	A3
Raymond Street	B2
Redgate	C3-C4
St Giles Lane	B2-B3
St Mary's Crescent	B1
St Nicholas Street	A2-A3
Saxon Place	A1
Star Lane	A2
Station Lane	A4

Station Road	A3-B3
Tanner Street	B2
The Buse Avenue	B1
Vicarage Road	B3-B4
Wheatacres	B3-B4
Whitehart Street	B2-B3
Williamson Crescent	A1

Newmarket

All Saints Road	B3-C3-C4
Birdcage Walk	A1
Black Bear Lane	A2-B2
Bury Road	B4
Cambridge Road	A1
Cardigan Street	B3-C3
Cewell Hill	A3
Church Lane	A3-B3
Clare Place	C2
Cricket Field Road	C3
Crockfords Road	C1-C2
Doris Street	A2-A3
Downing Close	C2
Dullingham Road	B1
Exeter Road	A3-A4-B4
Exning Road	A3-A4
Falmouth Avenue	A1-A2
Falmouth Street	A2-A3
Fitzroy Street	A2-A3
Fordham Road	A4-B4
Fred Archer Way	B3-B4
Freshfields	A3
Greenfields	C4
Green Road	C2-C3
Grosvenor Yard	A3-B3
Hamilton Road	A1
Heatherbell Road	C4
Heath Road	C4
High Street	A1-A2-B2-B3-B4
Lisburn Road	B4-C4
Lowther Street	A3
Mill Hill	A3
Moulton Road	B4
Nat Flatman Street	C4
New Cheveley Road	C2-C3
Old Station Road	B4-C4
Paddocks Drive	C1-C2
Palace Street	B3-B4
Park Avenue	B3-C3
Park Lane	B3-C3
Peterhouse Drive	C2
Queensbury Road	B2-B3
Queen Street	C3

Rayes Lane	A4-B4
Rous Road	B4
Rowley Drive	A1-A2-A3
St John's Avenue	C1-C2
St Mary's Square	A3
Sackville Street	B4-C4
Selwyn Close	C1-C2
Stamford Street	C3
Station Approach	C2
Sun Lane	B3
The Avenue	B2-B3
The Hamilton	A1
The Watercourse	A3-A4
Trinity Drive	C2
Vicarage Road	C3-C4
Warrington Street	C3
Wellington Street	B3
Whitegates	C4
Wooditton Road	C1

BURY ST EDMUNDS
Overlooked by Moyses Hall, market stalls still crowd the Cornhill and Buttermarket twice a week, and have been a feature of the town for several centuries.

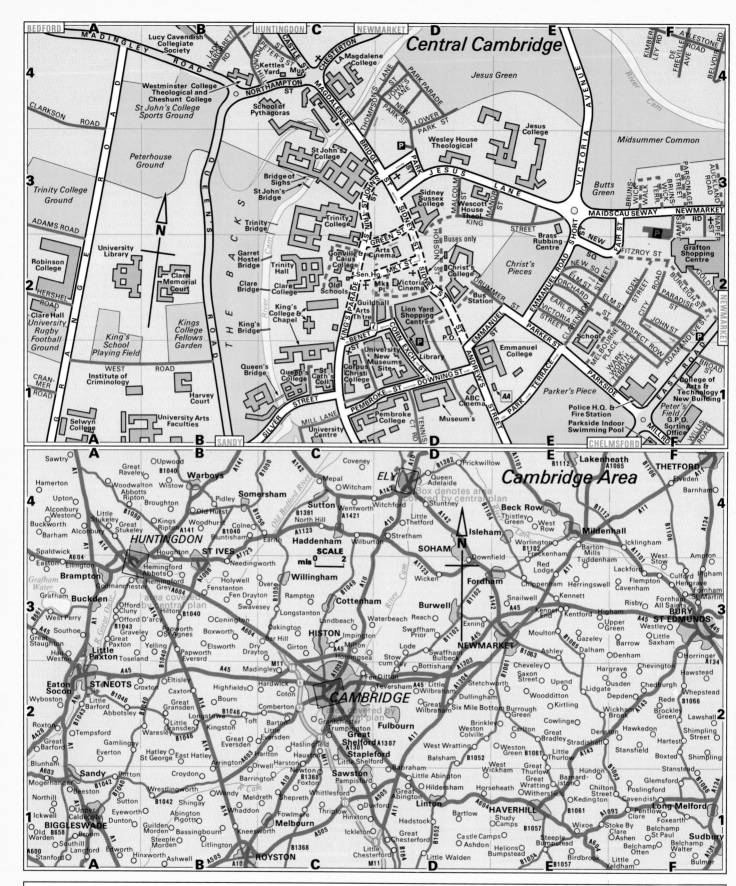

Cambridge

Few views in England, perhaps even in Europe, are as memorable as that from Cambridge's Backs towards the colleges. Dominating the scene, in every sense, is King's College Chapel. One of the finest Gothic buildings anywhere, it was built in three stages from 1446 to 1515.

No one would dispute that the chapel is Cambridge's masterpiece, but there are dozens of buildings here that would be the finest in any other town or city. Most are colleges, or are attached to colleges, and it is the university which permeates every aspect of Cambridge's landscape and life. In all there are 33 university colleges in the city, and nearly all have buildings and features of great interest. Cambridge's oldest church is St Bene't's, with a Saxon tower; its most famous is the Church of the Holy Sepulchre, one of only four round churches of its kind.

Huntingdon and **Ely** are both within easy driving distance of Cambridge. Oliver Cromwell and Samuel Pepys were pupils at Huntingdon Grammar School. The building is now a Cromwell museum. Ely also has strong Cromwellian connections – he and his family lived here for ten years. Ely's outstanding feature is the cathedral, a Norman foundation crowned by a stately octagonal lantern tower which contains the Stained Glass Museum.

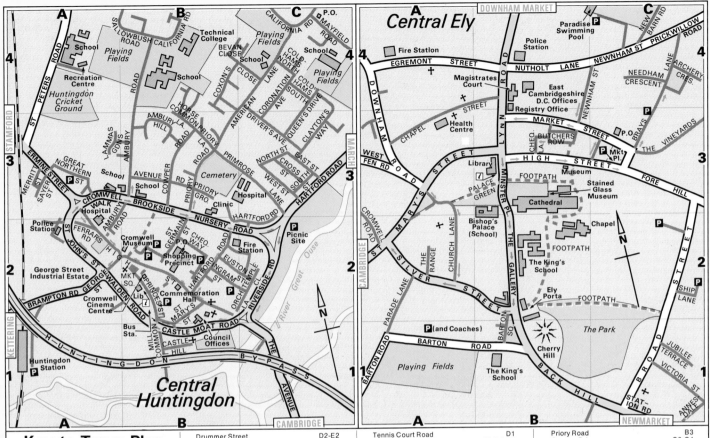

Central Huntingdon

Central Ely

CAMBRIDGE
Behind the gracious university college buildings beautiful lawns and gardens known as the Backs sweep down to the River Cam which, spanned by little bridges and shaded by willows, provides an idyllic setting for punting.

77

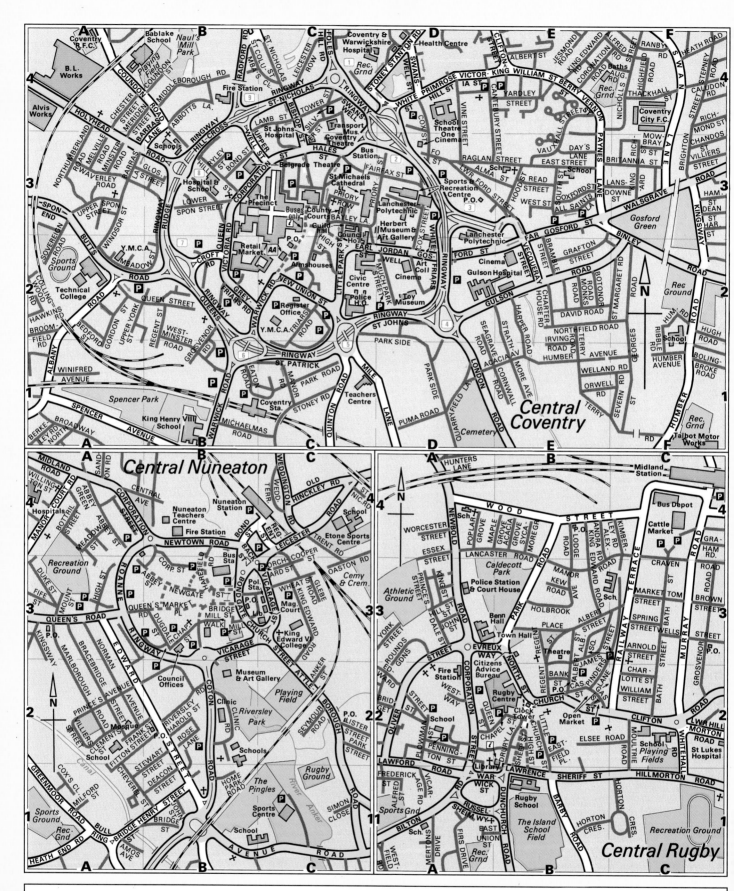

Coventry

Few British towns were as battered by the Blitz as Coventry. A raid in November 1940 flattened most of the city and left the lovely cathedral church a gaunt shell with only the tower and spire still standing. Rebuilding started almost immediately. Symbolising the creation of the new from the ashes of the old is Sir Basil Spence's cathedral, completed in 1962 beside the bombed ruins.

A few medieval buildings have survived intact in the city. St Mary's Guildhall is a finely restored 14th-century building with an attractive minstrels' gallery. Whitefriars Monastery now serves as a local museum. The Herbert Art Gallery and Museum has several collections. Coventry is an important manufacturing centre – most notably for cars – and it is also a university city with the fine campus of the University of Warwick some four miles from the centre.

Nuneaton is an industrial town to the north of Coventry with two distinguished old churches – St Nicholas' and St Mary's. Like Coventry it was badly damaged in the war and its centre has been rebuilt.

Rugby was no more than a sleepy market town until the arrival of the railway. Of course it did have the famous Rugby School, founded in 1567 and one of the country's foremost educational establishments. The railway brought industry – still the town's mainstay.

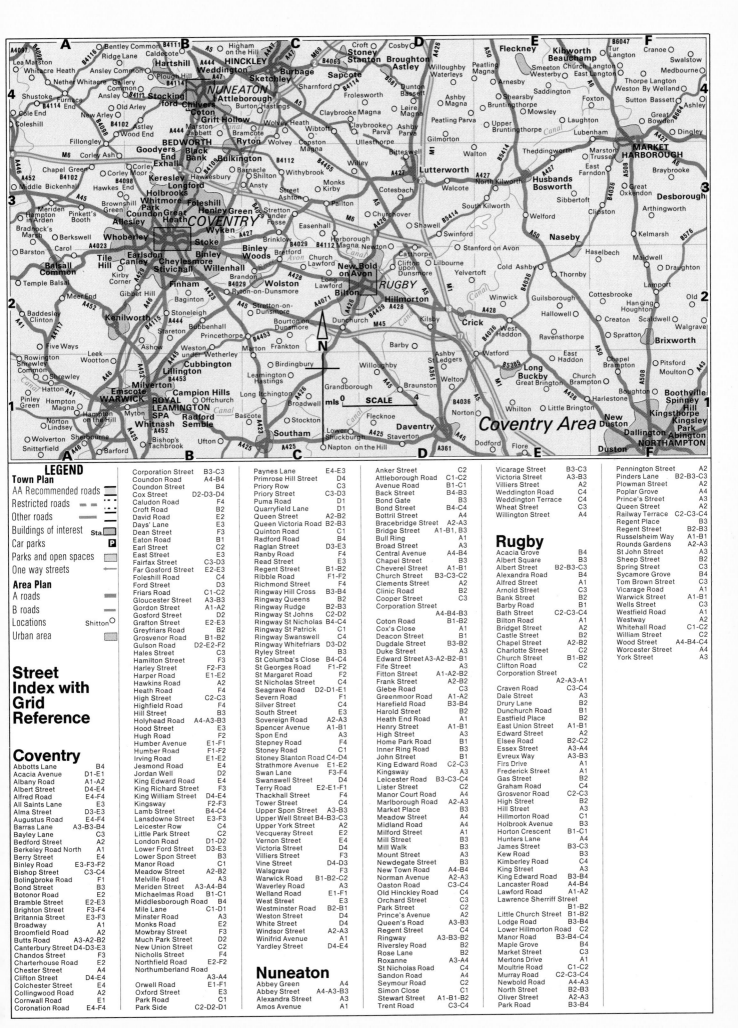

Street Index with Grid Reference

Coventry

Abbotts Lane B4
Acacia Avenue D1-E1
Albany Road A1-A2
Albert Street D4-E4
Alfred Road E4-F4
All Saints Lane E3
Alma Street D3-E3
Augustus Road E4-F4
Barras Lane A3-B3-B4
Bayley Lane C3
Bedford Street A2
Berkeley Road North A1
Berry Street E4
Binley Road E3-F3-F2
Bishop Street C3-C4
Bolingbroke Road F1
Bond Street B3
Botonor Road E2
Bramble Street E2-E3
Brighton Street F3-F4
Britannia Street E3-F3
Broadway A1
Broomfield Road A2
Butts Road A3-A2-B2
Canterbury Street D4-D3-E3
Chandos Street F3
Charterhouse Road E2
Chester Street A4
Clifton Street D4-E4
Colchester Street E4
Collingwood Road A2
Cornwall Road E1
Coronation Road E4-F4
Corporation Street B3-C3
Coundon Road A4-B4
Coundon Street B4
Cox Street D2-D3-D4
Caludon Road F4
Croft Road B2
David Road E2
Days' Lane E3
Dean Street F3
Eaton Road B1
Earl Street C2
East Street E3
Fairfax Street C3-D3
Far Gosford Street E2-E3
Foleshill Road C4
Ford Street D3
Friars Road C1-C2
Gloucester Street A3-B3
Gordon Street A1-A2
Gosford Street D2
Grafton Street E2-E3
Greyfriars Road B2
Grosvenor Road B1-B2
Gulson Road D2-E2-F2
Hales Street C3
Hamilton Street F3
Harley Street F2-F3
Harper Road E1-E2
Hawkins Road A2
Heath Road F4
High Street C2-C3
Highfield Road F4
Hill Street B3
Holyhead Road A4-A3-B3
Hood Street E3
Hugh Road F2
Humber Avenue E1-F1
Humber Road F1-F2
Irving Road E1-E2
Jesmond Road E4
Jordan Well D2
King Edward Road E4
King Richard Street F3
King William Street D4-E4
Kingsway F2-F3
Lamb Street B4-C4
Lansdowne Street E3-F3
Leicester Row C4
Little Park Street C3
London Road D1-D2
Lower Ford Street D3-E3
Lower Spon Street B3
Manor Road C1
Meadow Street A2-B2
Melville Road A3
Meriden Street A3-A4-B4
Middlesborough Road B4
Mile Lane C1-D1
Minster Road A3
Monks Road E2
Mowbray Street F3
Much Park Street D2
New Union Street C2
Nicholls Street F4
Northfield Road E2-F2
Northumberland Road A3-A4
Orwell Road E1-F1
Oxford Street E3
Park Road C1
Park Side C2-D2-D1
Paynes Lane E4-E3
Primrose Hill Street D4
Priory Row C3
Priory Street C3-D3
Puma Road D1
Quarryfield Lane D1
Queen Street A2-B2
Queen Victoria Road B2-B3
Quinton Road C1
Radford Road B4
Raglan Street D3-E3
Ranby Road F4
Read Street E3
Regent Street B1-B2
Ribble Road F1-F2
Richmond Street F4
Ringway Hill Cross B3-B4
Ringway Queens B2
Ringway Rudge B2-B3
Ringway St Johns C2-D2
Ringway St Nicholas B4-C4
Ringway St Patrick C1
Ringway Swanswell C4
Ringway Whitefriars D3-D2
Ryley Street D3
St Columba's Close B4-C4
St Georges Road F1-F2
St Margaret Road F2
St Nicholas Street C4
Seagrave Road D2-D1-E1
Severn Road F1
Silver Street C4
South Street E3
Sovereign Road A2-A3
Spencer Avenue A1-B1
Spon End A3
Stepney Road F4
Stoney Road C1
Stoney Stanton Road C4-D4
Strathmore Avenue E1-E2
Swan Lane F3-F4
Swanswell Street C4
Terry Road E2-E1-F1
Thackhall Street E3
Tower Street C4
Upper Spon Street A3-B3
Upper Well Street B4-B3-C3
Upper York Street A2
Vecqueray Street E2
Vernon Street E4
Victoria Street D4
Villiers Street F3
Vine Street D4-E3
Walsgrave F3
Warwick Road B1-B2-C2
Waverley Road A3
Welland Road E1-F1
West Street E3
Westminster Road B2-B1
Weston Street D4
White Street D4
Windsor Street A2-A3
Winifrid Avenue A1
Yardley Street D4-E4

Nuneaton

Abbey Green A4
Abbey Street A4-A3-B3
Alexandra Street A3
Amos Avenue A1
Anker Street C2
Attleborough Road C1-C2
Avenue Road B1-C1
Back Street B4-B3
Bond Gate B3
Bond Street B4-C4
Bottril Street A4
Bracebridge Street A2-A3
Bridge Street A1-B1, B3
Bull Ring A1
Broad Street A3
Central Avenue A4-B4
Chapel Street B3
Cheverel Street A1-B1
Church Street B3-C3-C2
Clements Street A2
Clinic Road B2
Cooper Street C3
Corporation Street A4-B4-B3
Coton Road B1-B2
Cox's Close A1
Deacon Street B1
Dugdale Street B3-B2
Duke Street A3
Edward Street A3-A2-B2-B1
Fife Street A3
Fitton Street A1-A2-B2
Frank Street A2-B2
Glebe Road C3
Greenmoor Road A1-A2
Harefield Road B3-B4
Harold Street B2
Heath End Road A1
Henry Street A1-B1
High Street A3
Home Park Road B1
Inner Ring Road B3
John Street B1
King Edward Road C2-C3
Kingsway A3
Leicester Road B3-C3-C4
Lister Street C2
Manor Court Road A4
Marlborough Road A2-A3
Market Place B3
Meadow Street A4
Midland Road A4
Milford Street A1
Mill Street B3
Mill Walk B3
Mount Street A3
Newdegate Street B3
New Town Road A4-B4
Norman Avenue A2-A3
Oaston Road C3-C4
Old Hinckley Road C4
Orchard Street C3
Park Street C2
Prince's Avenue A2
Queen's Road A3-B3
Regent Street A3
Ringway A3-B3-B2
Riversley Road B2
Rose Lane B2
Roxanne A3-A4
St Nicholas Road C4
Sandon Road A3
Seymour Road C2
Simon Close C1
Stewart Street A1-B1-B2
Trent Road C3-C4
Vicarage Street B3-C3
Victoria Street A3-B3
Villiers Street A2
Weddington Road C4
Weddington Terrace C4
Wheat Street C3
Willington Street A4

Rugby

Acacia Grove B4
Albert Square B3
Albert Street B2-B3-C3
Alexandra Road B4
Alfred Street A1
Arnold Street C3
Bank Street B2
Barby Road B1
Bath Street C2-C3-C4
Bilton Road A1
Bridget Street A2
Castle Street B2
Chapel Street A2-B2
Charlotte Street C2
Church Street B1-B2
Clifton Road C2
Corporation Street A2-A3-A1
Craven Road C3-C4
Dale Street A3
Drury Lane B2
Dunchurch Road B1
Eastfield Place B2
East Union Street A1-B1
Edward Street A2
Elsee Road B2-C2
Essex Street A3-A4
Evreux Way A3-B3
Firs Drive A1
Frederick Street A1
Gas Street B2
Graham Road C4
Grosvenor Road C2-C3
High Street B2
Hill Street A3
Hillmorton Road C1
Holbrook Avenue B3
Horton Crescent B1-C1
Hunters Lane A4
James Street B3-C3
Kew Road B3
Kimberley Road C4
King Street A3
King Edward Road B3-B4
Lancaster Road A4-B4
Lawford Road A4
Lawrence Sherriff Street B1-B2
Little Church Street B1-B2
Lodge Road B3-B4
Lower Hillmorton Road C2
Manor Road B3-B4-C4
Maple Grove A3
Market Street C3
Mertons Drive A2
Moultrie Road C1-C2
Murray Road C2-C3-C4
Newbold Road A4-A3
North Street B2-B3
Oliver Street A2-A3
Park Road B3-B4
Pennington Street A2
Pinders Lane B2-B3-C3
Plowman Street A2
Poplar Grove A4
Prince's Street A3
Queen Street A2
Railway Terrace C2-C3-C4
Regent Place B3
Regent Street B2-B3
Russelsheim Way A1-B1
Rounds Gardens A2-A3
St John Street A3
Sheep Street B2
Spring Street C3
Sycamore Grove B4
Tom Brown Street C3
Vicarage Road A1
Warwick Street A1-B1
Wells Street C3
Westfield Road A1
Westway A2
Whitehall Road C1-C2
William Street C2
Wood Street A4-B4-C4
Worcester Street A4
York Street A3

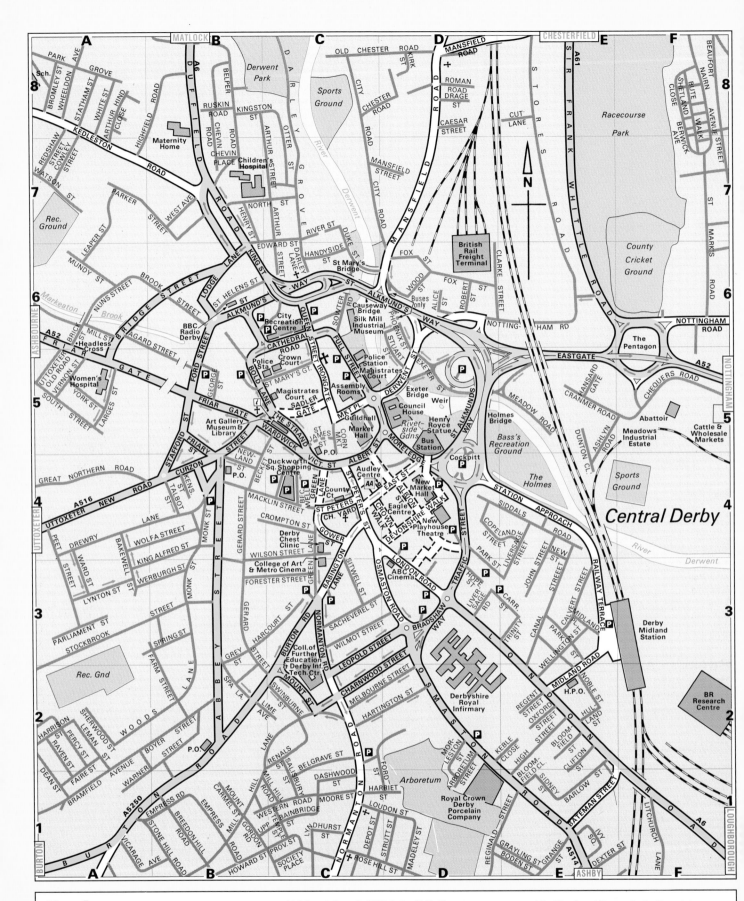

Derby

Present-day Derby, designated a city in 1977, is a product of the Industrial Revolution. During the 19th century the Midland Railway made its headquarters in the ancient country town, bringing with it prosperity and considerable new building. Around the old Market Place stand the Guildhall, which is now used as a concert hall, the Market Hall, and the façade of the old Assembly Rooms which burnt down in 1963. Later Rolls-Royce established its car manufacturing works here and one of the company's founders, Sir Henry Royce, is commemorated in the Arboretum, laid out by Joseph Loudon. Rolls-Royce aero engines can be seen in the Industrial Museum, appropriately housed in England's first silk mill, set up in 1717 on the banks of the Derwent.

Despite this strong industrial influence, for many people Derby means only one thing – porcelain. The Royal Crown Derby Porcelain Company produced work of such excellence that George III granted it the right to use the Crown insignia. A museum on the premises houses a treasure-trove of Crown Derby.

Derby's cathedral, All Saint's, was built during Henry VIII's reign but, except for its 178ft-high pinnacled tower, was rebuilt in 1725 by James Gibb. The tomb of Bess of Hardwick, who died in 1607, can be seen inside.

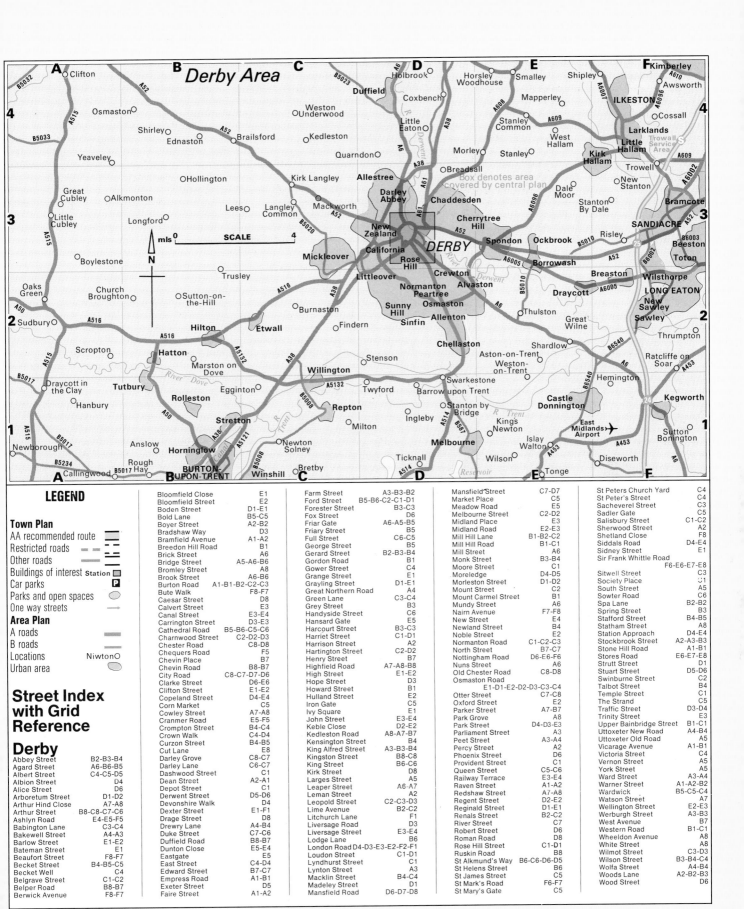

Derby Area

A B C D E F

LEGEND

Town Plan
AA recommended route
Restricted roads
Other roads
Buildings of interest Station 🔲
Car parks P
Parks and open spaces
One way streets

Area Plan
A roads
B roads
Locations Niwton○
Urban area

Street Index with Grid Reference

Derby

Abbey Street	B2-B3-B4
Agard Street	A6-B6-B5
Albert Street	C4-C5-D5
Albion Street	D4
Alice Street	D6
Arboretum Street	D1-D2
Arthur Hind Close	A7-A8
Arthur Street	B8-C8-C7-C6
Ashlyn Road	E4-E5-F5
Babington Lane	C3-C4
Bakewell Street	A4-A3
Barlow Street	E1-E2
Bateman Street	E1
Beaufort Street	F8-F7
Becket Street	B4-B5-C5
Becket Well	C4
Belgrave Street	C1-C2
Belper Road	B8-B7
Berwick Avenue	F8-F7
Bloomfield Close	E1
Bloomfield Street	E2
Boden Street	D1-E1
Bold Lane	B5-C5
Boyer Street	A2-B2
Bradshaw Way	D3
Bramfield Avenue	A1-A2
Breedon Hill Road	B1
Brick Street	A6
Bridge Street	A5-A6-B6
Bromley Street	A8
Brook Street	A6-B6
Burton Road	A1-B1-B2-C2-C3
Bute Walk	F8-F7
Caesar Street	D8
Calvert Street	E3
Canal Street	E3-E4
Carrington Street	D3-E3
Cathedral Road	B5-B6-C5-C6
Charnwood Street	C2-D2-D3
Chester Road	C8-D8
Chequers Road	F5
Chevin Place	B7
Chevin Road	B8-B7
City Road	C8-C7-D7-D6
Clarke Street	D6-E6
Clifton Street	E1-E2
Copeland Street	D4-E4
Corn Market	C5
Cowley Street	A7-A8
Cranmer Road	E5-F5
Crompton Street	B4-C4
Crown Walk	C4-D4
Curzon Street	B4-B5
Cut Lane	E8
Darley Grove	C8-C7
Darley Lane	C6-C7
Dashwood Street	C1
Dean Street	A2-A1
Depot Street	C1
Derwent Street	D5-D6
Devonshire Walk	D4
Dexter Street	E1-F1
Drage Street	D8
Drewry Lane	A4-B4
Duke Street	C7-C6
Duffield Road	B8-B7
Dunton Close	E5-E4
Eastgate	E5
East Street	C4-D4
Edward Street	B7-C7
Empress Road	A1-B1
Exeter Street	D5
Faire Street	A1-A2

Farm Street	A3-B3-B2
Ford Street	B5-B6-C2-C1-D1
Forester Street	B3-C3
Fox Street	D6
Friar Gate	A6-A5-B5
Friary Street	B5
Full Street	C6-C5
George Street	B2-B3-B4
Gerard Street	B2-B3-B4
Gordon Road	B1
Gower Street	C4
Grange Street	E1
Grayling Street	D1-E1
Great Northern Road	A4
Green Lane	C3-C4
Grey Street	B3
Handyside Street	C6
Hansard Gate	E5
Harcourt Street	B3-C3
Harriet Street	C1-D1
Harrison Street	A2
Hartington Street	C2-D2
Henry Street	B7
Highfield Road	A7-A8-B8
High Street	E1-E2
Hope Street	D3
Howard Street	B1
Hulland Street	E2
Iron Gate	C5
Ivy Square	E1
John Street	E3-E4
Keble Close	D2-E2
Kedleston Road	A8-A7-B7
Kensington Street	B4
King Alfred Street	A3-B3-B4
Kingston Street	B8-C8
King Street	B6-C6
Kirk Street	D8
Larges Street	A5
Leaper Street	A6-A7
Leman Street	A2
Leopold Street	C2-C3-D3
Lime Avenue	B2-C2
Litchurch Lane	F1
Liversage Road	D3
Liversage Street	E3-E4
Lodge Lane	B6
London Road	D4-D3-E3-E2-F2-F1
Loudon Street	C1-D1
Lyndhurst Street	C1
Lynton Street	A3
Macklin Street	B4-C4
Madeley Street	D1
Mansfield Road	D6-D7-D8

Mansfield Street	C7-D7
Market Place	C5
Meadow Road	E5
Melbourne Street	C2-D2
Midland Place	E3
Midland Road	E2-E3
Mill Hill Lane	B1-B2-C2
Mill Hill Road	B1-C1
Mill Street	A6
Monk Street	B3-B4
Moore Street	C1
Moreledge	D4-D5
Morleston Street	D1-D2
Mount Street	C2
Mount Carmel Street	B1
Mundy Street	A6
Nairn Avenue	F7-F8
New Street	E4
Newland Street	B4
Noble Street	E2
Normanton Road	C1-C2-C3
North Street	B7-C7
Nottingham Road	D6-E6-F6
Nuns Street	A6
Old Chester Road	C8-D8
Osmaston Road	E1-D1-E2-D2-D3-C3-C4
Otter Street	C7-C8
Oxford Street	E2
Parker Street	A7-B7
Park Grove	A8
Park Street	D4-D3-E3
Parliament Street	A3
Peet Street	A3-A4
Percy Street	A2
Phoenix Street	D6
Provident Street	C1
Queen Street	C5-C6
Railway Terrace	E3-E4
Raven Street	A1-A2
Redshaw Street	A7-A8
Regent Street	D2-E2
Reginald Street	D1-E1
Renals Street	B2-C2
River Street	C7
Robert Street	D6
Roman Road	D8
Rose Hill Street	C1-D1
Ruskin Road	B8
St Alkmund's Way	B6-C6-D6-D5
St Helens Street	B6
St James Street	C5
St Mark's Road	F6-F7
St Mary's Gate	C5

St Peters Church Yard	C4
St Peter's Street	C4
Sacheverel Street	C3
Sadler Gate	C5
Salisbury Street	C1-C2
Sherwood Street	A2
Shetland Close	F8
Siddals Road	D4-E4
Sidney Street	E1
Sir Frank Whittle Road	F6-E6-E7-E8
Sitwell Street	C3
Society Place	C1
South Street	A5
Sowter Road	C6
Spa Lane	B2-B2
Spring Street	B3
Stafford Street	B4-B5
Statham Street	A8
Station Approach	D4-E4
Stockbrook Street	A2-A3-B3
Stone Hill Road	A1-B1
Stores Road	E6-E7-E8
Strutt Street	D1
Stuart Street	D5-D6
Swinburne Street	C2
Talbot Street	B4
Temple Street	C1
The Strand	C5
Traffic Street	D3-D4
Trinity Street	E3
Upper Bainbridge Street	B1-C1
Uttoxeter New Road	A4-B4
Uttoxeter Old Road	A5
Vicarage Avenue	A1-B1
Victoria Street	C4
Vernon Street	A5
York Street	A5
Ward Street	A3-A4
Warner Street	A1-A2-B2
Wardwick	B5-C5-C4
Watson Street	A7
Wellington Street	E2-E3
Werburgh Street	A3-B3
West Avenue	B7
Western Road	B1-C1
Wheeldon Avenue	A8
White Street	A8
Wilmot Street	C3-D3
Wilson Street	B3-B4-C4
Wolfa Street	A4-B4
Woods Lane	A2-B2-B3
Wood Street	D6

DERBY
The 1907 Silver Ghost, one of Rolls Royce's first cars, was produced just before the company moved its factory to Derby. Cars were their sole product until World War I when the first aero engine was designed.

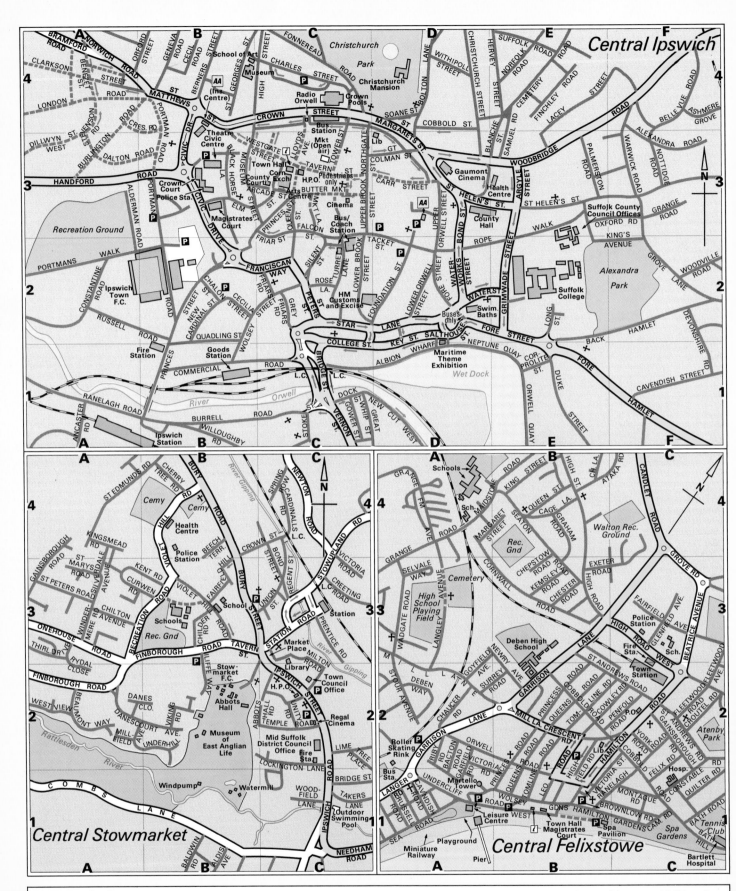

Ipswich

In the Middle Ages England became rich from wool, and East Anglia in particular prospered. Ipswich shared in the wealth, being the port from which wool was exported to Europe. Twelve medieval churches survive in Ipswich, a remarkable number for a town of its size, and all of them have features of beauty and interest. Of the town's nonconformist chapels, the 17th-century Unitarian

is outstanding. Unfortunately, many of Ipswich's ancient secular buildings were swept away during the 1960s fever for clearances, precincts and redevelopment; however, some of the finest survive. Best is Ancient House, dating back to 1567 and embellished on the outside with complex decorative plasterwork. Other fine buildings can be seen in Lower Brook Street and Fore Street. Christchurch Mansion dates from 1548 and now houses a museum.

Felixstowe is a seaside resort with Edwardian characteristics, a commercial centre, and a container port. Its handsome promenade is nearly two miles long.

Stowmarket has an excellent country life museum – the Museum of East Anglian Life. Among its exhibits are reconstructed buildings, agricultural machinery and domestic items. The town itself is a shopping and market centre for the rich arable farmlands of Central Suffolk.

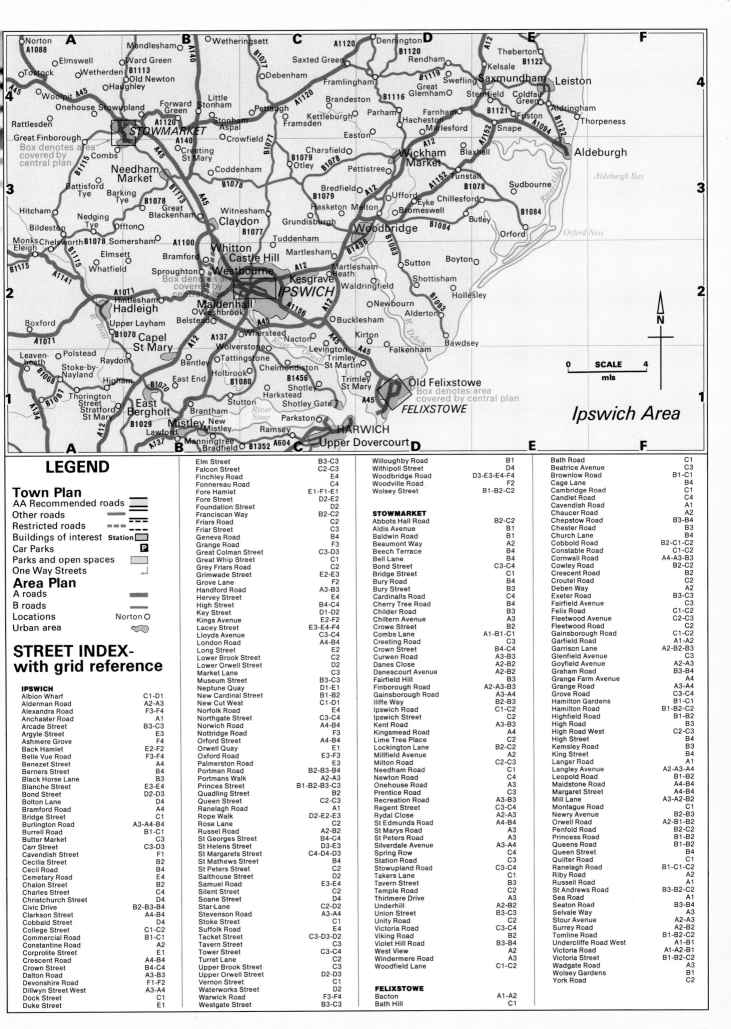

LEGEND

Town Plan
- AA Recommended roads
- Other roads
- Restricted roads
- Buildings of interest — Station
- Car Parks — P
- Parks and open spaces
- One Way Streets

Area Plan
- A roads
- B roads
- Locations — Norton ○
- Urban area

STREET INDEX- with grid reference

IPSWICH

Albion Wharf	C1-D1
Alderman Road	A2-A3
Alexandra Road	F3-F4
Anchaster Road	A1
Arcade Street	B3-C3
Argyle Street	E3
Ashmere Grove	F4
Back Hamlet	E2-F2
Belle Vue Road	F3-F4
Benezet Street	A4
Berners Street	B4
Black Horse Lane	B3
Blanche Street	E3-E4
Bond Street	D2-D3
Bolton Lane	D4
Bramford Road	A4
Bridge Street	C1
Burlington Road	A3-A4-B4
Burrell Road	B1-C1
Butter Market	C3
Carr Street	C3-D3
Cavendish Street	F1
Cecilia Street	B2
Cecil Road	B4
Cemetary Road	E4
Chalon Street	B2
Charles Street	C4
Christchurch Street	D4
Civic Drive	B2-B3-B4
Clarkson Street	A4-B4
Cobbald Street	D4
College Street	C1-C2
Commercial Road	B1-C1
Constantine Road	A2
Corprolite Street	E1
Crescent Road	A4-B4
Crown Street	B4-C4
Dalton Road	A3-B3
Devonshire Road	F1-F2
Dillwyn Street West	A3-A4
Dock Street	C1
Duke Street	E1

Elm Street	B3-C3
Falcon Street	C2-C3
Finchley Road	E4
Fonnereau Road	C4
Fore Hamlet	E1-F1-E1
Fore Street	D2-E2
Foundation Street	D2
Franciscan Way	B2-C2
Friars Road	C2
Friar Street	C3
Geneva Road	B4
Grange Road	F3
Great Colman Street	C3-D3
Great Whip Street	C1
Grey Friars Road	C2
Grimwade Street	E2-E3
Grove Lane	F2
Handford Road	A3-B3
Hervey Street	E4
High Street	B4-C4
Key Street	D1-D2
Kings Avenue	E2-F2
Lacey Street	E3-E4-F4
Lloyds Avenue	C3-C4
London Road	A4-B4
Long Street	E2
Lower Brook Street	C2
Lower Orwell Street	D2
Market Lane	C3
Museum Street	B3-C3
Neptune Quay	D1-E1
New Cardinal Street	B1-B2
New Cut West	C1-D1
Norfolk Road	E4
Northgate Street	C3-C4
Norwich Road	A4-B4
Nottridge Road	F3
Orford Street	A4-B4
Orwell Quay	E1
Oxford Road	E3-F3
Palmerston Road	E3
Portman Road	B2-B3-B4
Portmans Walk	A2-A3
Princes Street	B1-B2-B3-C3
Quadling Street	B2
Queen Street	C2-C3
Ranelagh Road	A1
Rope Walk	D2-E2-E3
Rose Lane	C2
Russel Road	A2-B2
St Georges Street	B4-C4
St Helens Street	D3-E3
St Margarets Street	C4-D4-D3
St Mathews Street	B4
St Peters Street	C2
Salthouse Street	D2
Samuel Road	E3-E4
Silent Street	C2
Soane Street	D4
Star-Lane	C2-D2
Stevenson Road	A3-A4
Stoke Street	C1
Suffolk Road	E4
Tacket Street	C3-D3-D2
Tavern Street	C3
Tower Street	C3-C4
Turret Lane	C2
Upper Brook Street	C3
Upper Orwell Street	D2-D3
Vernon Street	C1
Waterworks Street	D2
Warwick Road	F3-F4
Westgate Street	B3-C3

Willoughby Road	B1
Withipoll Street	D4
Woodbridge Road	D3-E3-E4-F4
Woodville Road	F2
Wolsey Street	B1-B2-C2

STOWMARKET

Abbots Hall Road	B2-C2
Aldis Avenue	B1
Baldwin Road	B1
Beaumont Way	A2
Beech Terrace	B4
Bell Lane	B4
Bond Street	C3-C4
Bridge Street	C1
Bury Road	B4
Bury Street	B3
Cardinalls Road	C4
Cherry Tree Road	B4
Childer Road	B3
Chiltern Avenue	A3
Crowe Street	B2
Combs Lane	A1-B1-C1
Creeting Road	C3
Crown Street	B4-C4
Curwen Road	A3-B3
Danes Close	A2-B2
Danescourt Avenue	A2-B2
Fairfield Hill	B3
Finborough Road	A2-A3-B3
Gainsborough Road	A3-A4
Iliffe Way	B2-B3
Ipswich Road	C1-C2
Ipswich Street	C2
Kent Road	A3-B3
Kingsmead Road	A4
Lime Tree Place	C2
Lockington Road	B2-C2
Millfield Avenue	A2
Milton Road	C2-C3
Needham Road	C1
Newton Road	C4
Onehouse Road	A3
Prentice Road	C3
Recreation Road	A3-B3
Regent Street	C3-C4
Rydal Close	A2-A3
St Edmunds Road	A4-B4
St Marys Road	A3
St Peters Road	A3
Silverdale Avenue	A3-A4
Spring Row	C4
Station Road	C3
Stowupland Road	C3-C4
Takers Lane	C1
Tavern Street	B3
Temple Road	C2
Thirlmere Drive	A3
Underhill	A2-B2
Union Street	B3-C3
Unity Road	C2
Victoria Road	C3-C4
Viking Way	B2
Violet Hill Road	B3-B4
West View	A2
Windermere Road	A3
Woodfield Lane	C1-C2

FELIXSTOWE

Bacton	A1-A2
Bath Hill	C1

Bath Road	C1
Beatrice Avenue	C3
Brownlow Road	B1-C1
Cage Lane	B4
Cambridge Road	C1
Candlet Road	C4
Cavendish Road	A1
Chaucer Road	A2
Chepstow Road	B3-B4
Chester Road	B3
Church Lane	B4
Cobbold Road	B2-C1-C2
Constable Road	C1-C2
Cornwall Road	A4-A3-B3
Cowley Road	B2-C2
Crescent Road	B2
Croutel Road	C2
Deben Way	A2
Exeter Road	B3-C3
Fairfield Avenue	C3
Felix Road	C1-C2
Fleetwood Avenue	C2-C3
Fleetwood Road	C2
Gainsborough Road	C1-C2
Garfield Road	A1-A2
Garrison Lane	A2-B2-B3
Glenfield Avenue	C3
Goyfield Avenue	A2-A3
Graham Road	B3-B4
Grange Farm Avenue	A4
Grange Road	A3-A4
Grove Road	C3-C4
Hamilton Gardens	B1-C1
Hamilton Road	B1-B2-C2
Highfield Road	B1-B2
High Road	B3
High Road West	C2-C3
High Street	B4
Kemsley Road	B3
King Street	B4
Langer Road	A1
Langley Avenue	A2-A3-A4
Leopold Road	B1-B2
Maidstone Road	A4-B4
Margaret Street	A4-B4
Mill Lane	A3-A2-B2
Montague Road	C1
Newry Avenue	B2-B3
Orwell Road	A2-B1-B2
Penfold Road	B2-C2
Princess Road	B1-B2
Queens Road	B1-B2
Queen Street	B4
Quilter Road	C1
Ranelagh Road	B1-C1-C2
Riby Road	A2
Russell Road	A1
St Andrews Road	B3-B2-C2
Sea Road	B1
Seaton Road	B3-B4
Selvale Way	A3
Stour Avenue	A2-A3
Surrey Road	A2-B2
Tomline Road	B1-B2-C2
Undercliffe Road West	A1-B1
Victoria Road	A1-A2-B1
Victoria Street	B1-B2-C2
Wadgate Road	A3
Wolsey Gardens	B1
York Road	C2

83

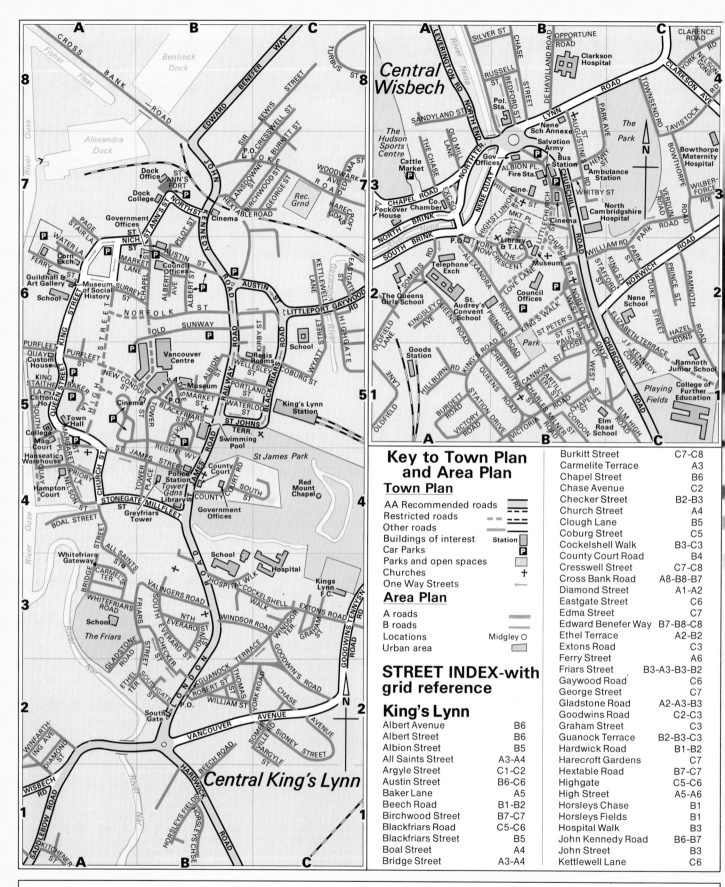

Key to Town Plan and Area Plan

Town Plan

AA Recommended roads	
Restricted roads	
Other roads	
Buildings of interest	Station
Car Parks	P
Parks and open spaces	
Churches	+
One Way Streets	←

Area Plan

A roads	
B roads	
Locations	Midgley ○
Urban area	

STREET INDEX-with grid reference

King's Lynn

Albert Avenue	B6
Albert Street	B6
Albion Street	B5
All Saints Street	A3-A4
Argyle Street	C1-C2
Austin Street	B6-C6
Baker Lane	A5
Beech Road	B1-B2
Birchwood Street	B7-C7
Blackfriars Road	C5-C6
Blackfriars Street	B5
Boal Street	A4
Bridge Street	A3-A4

Burkitt Street	C7-C8
Carmelite Terrace	A3
Chapel Street	B6
Chase Avenue	C2
Checker Street	B2-B3
Church Street	A4
Clough Lane	B5
Coburg Street	C5
Cockelshell Walk	B3-C3
County Court Road	B4
Cresswell Street	C7-C8
Cross Bank Road	A8-B8-B7
Diamond Street	A1-A2
Eastgate Street	C6
Edma Street	C7
Edward Benefer Way	B7-B8-C8
Ethel Terrace	A2-B2
Extons Road	C3
Ferry Street	A6
Friars Street	B3-A3-B3-B2
Gaywood Road	C6
George Street	C7
Gladstone Road	A2-A3-A3
Goodwins Road	C2-C3
Graham Street	C3
Guanock Terrace	B2-B3-C3
Hardwick Road	B1-B2
Harecroft Gardens	C7
Hextable Road	B7-C7
Highgate	C5-C6
High Street	A5-A6
Horsleys Chase	B1
Horsleys Fields	B1
Hospital Walk	B3
John Kennedy Road	B6-B7
John Street	B3
Kettlewell Lane	C6

King's Lynn

Pilgrims on their way to Walsingham would stop at the 15th-century Red Mount Chapel in the Walks at King's Lynn, and commercial prominence really began here as far back as the 13th century, when this Great Ouse port had connections with the German trading towns of the Hanseatic League. Prosperity continued until well into the 18th century, and although modern expansion has brought new shopping, sports and entertainment facilities to the town centre, a number of medieval buildings survive, including the Guild Hall of St George (now a theatre) and the Guild Hall of Holy Trinity. St Margaret's Church still has portions of its Norman tower. The Lynn Museum in Old Market Street looks at the history of the area, and is complemented by the Museum of Social History in King Street.

Wisbech is at the heartland of soft fruit cultivation, and is especially known for its strawberries. Set in the low-lying fens and linked to the Wash by the River Nene, it has some fine examples of Georgian architecture in the North and South Brinks which line the river on either side. Eighteenth-century Peckover House now belongs to the National Trust; also of interest is the Clarkson Memorial in Bridge Street, erected in memory of Thomas Clarkson, who campaigned for the abolition of slavery.

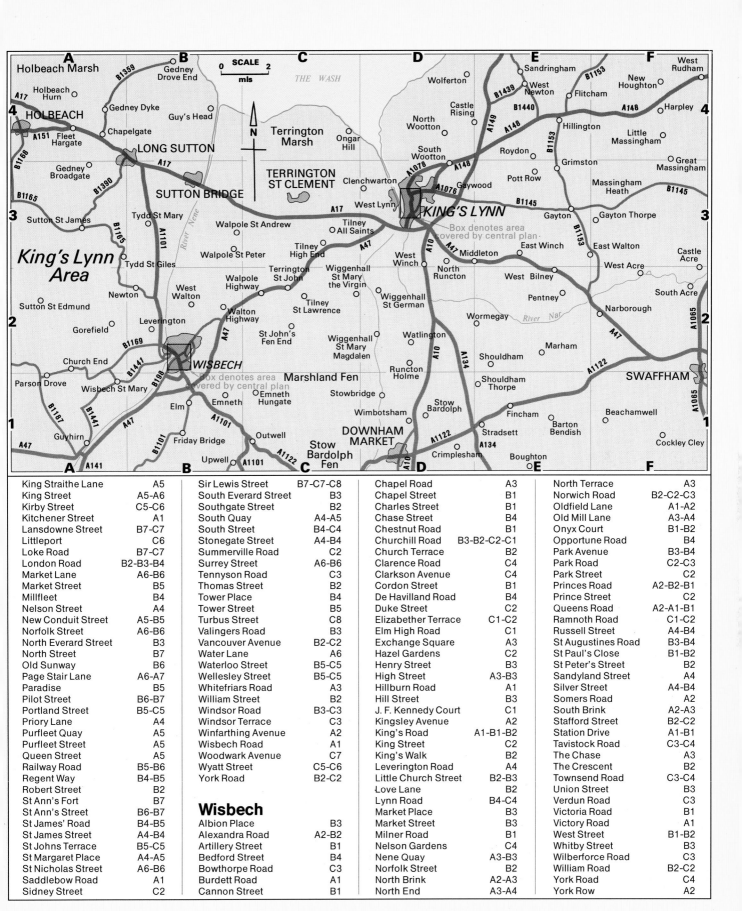

King Straithe Lane	A5	Sir Lewis Street	B7-C7-C8	Chapel Road
King Street	A5-A6	South Everard Street	B3	Chapel Street

King's Lynn Area

King Straithe Lane	A5
King Street	A5-A6
Kirby Street	C5-C6
Kitchener Street	A1
Lansdowne Street	B7-C7
Littleport	C6
Loke Road	B7-C7
London Road	B2-B3-B4
Market Lane	A6-B6
Market Street	B5
Millfleet	B4
Nelson Street	A4
New Conduit Street	A5-B5
Norfolk Street	A6-B6
North Everard Street	B3
North Street	B7
Old Sunway	B6
Page Stair Lane	A6-A7
Paradise	B5
Pilot Street	B6-B7
Portland Street	B5-C5
Priory Lane	A4
Purfleet Quay	A5
Purfleet Street	A5
Queen Street	A5
Railway Road	B5-B6
Regent Way	B4-B5
Robert Street	B2
St Ann's Fort	B7
St Ann's Street	B6-B7
St James' Road	B4-B5
St James Street	A4-B4
St Johns Terrace	B5-C5
St Margaret Place	A4-A5-A4
St Nicholas Street	A6-B6
Saddlebow Road	A1
Sidney Street	C2

Sir Lewis Street	B7-C7-C8
South Everard Street	B3
Southgate Street	B2
South Quay	A4-A5
South Street	B4-C4
Stonegate Street	A4-B4
Summerville Road	C2
Surrey Street	A6-B6
Tennyson Road	C3
Thomas Street	B2
Tower Place	B4
Tower Street	B5
Turbus Street	C8
Valingers Road	B3
Vancouver Avenue	B2-C2
Water Lane	A6
Waterloo Street	B5-C5
Wellesley Street	B5-C5
Whitefriars Road	A3
William Street	B2
Windsor Road	B3-C3
Windsor Terrace	C3
Winfarthing Avenue	A2
Wisbech Road	A1
Woodwark Avenue	C7
Wyatt Street	C5-C6
York Road	B2-C2

Wisbech

Albion Place	B3
Alexandra Road	A2-B2
Artillery Street	B1
Bedford Street	B4
Bowthorpe Road	C3
Burdett Road	A1
Cannon Street	B1

Chapel Road	A3
Chapel Street	B1
Charles Street	B1
Chase Street	B4
Chestnut Road	B1
Churchill Road	B3-B2-C2-C1
Church Terrace	B2
Clarence Road	C4
Clarkson Avenue	C4
Cordon Street	B1
De Havilland Road	B4
Duke Street	C2
Elizabether Terrace	C1-C2
Elm High Road	C1
Exchange Square	A3
Hazel Gardens	C2
Henry Street	B3
High Street	A3-B3
Hillburn Road	A1
Hill Street	B3
J. F. Kennedy Court	C1
Kingsley Avenue	A2
King's Road	A1-B1-B2
King Street	C2
King's Walk	B2
Leverington Road	A4
Little Church Street	B2-B3
Love Lane	B3
Lynn Road	B4-C4
Market Place	B3
Market Street	B3
Milner Road	B1
Nelson Gardens	C4
Nene Quay	A3-B3
Norfolk Street	B2
North Brink	A2-A3
North End	A3-A4

North Terrace	A3
Norwich Road	B2-C2-C3
Oldfield Lane	A1-A2
Old Mill Lane	A3-A4
Onyx Court	B1-B2
Opportune Road	B4
Park Avenue	B3-B4
Park Road	C2-C3
Park Street	C2
Princes Road	A2-B2-B1
Prince Street	C2
Queens Road	A2-A1-B1
Ramnoth Road	C1-C2
Russell Street	A4-B4
St Augustines Road	B3-B4
St Paul's Close	B1-B2
St Peter's Street	B2
Sandyland Street	A4
Silver Street	A4-B4
Somers Road	A2
South Brink	A2-A3
Stafford Street	B2-C2
Station Drive	A1-B1
Tavistock Road	C3-C4
The Chase	A3
The Crescent	B2
Townsend Road	C3-C4
Union Street	B3
Verdun Road	C3
Victoria Road	B1
Victory Road	A1
West Street	B1-B2
Whitby Street	B3
Wilberforce Road	C3
William Road	B2-C2
York Road	C4
York Row	A2

KINGS LYNN
Designed by local architect Henry Bell and dating back to 1683, the elegant Old Customs House bears witness to a longstanding importance as a trading centre serving both the Midlands (via inland waterways) and Europe.

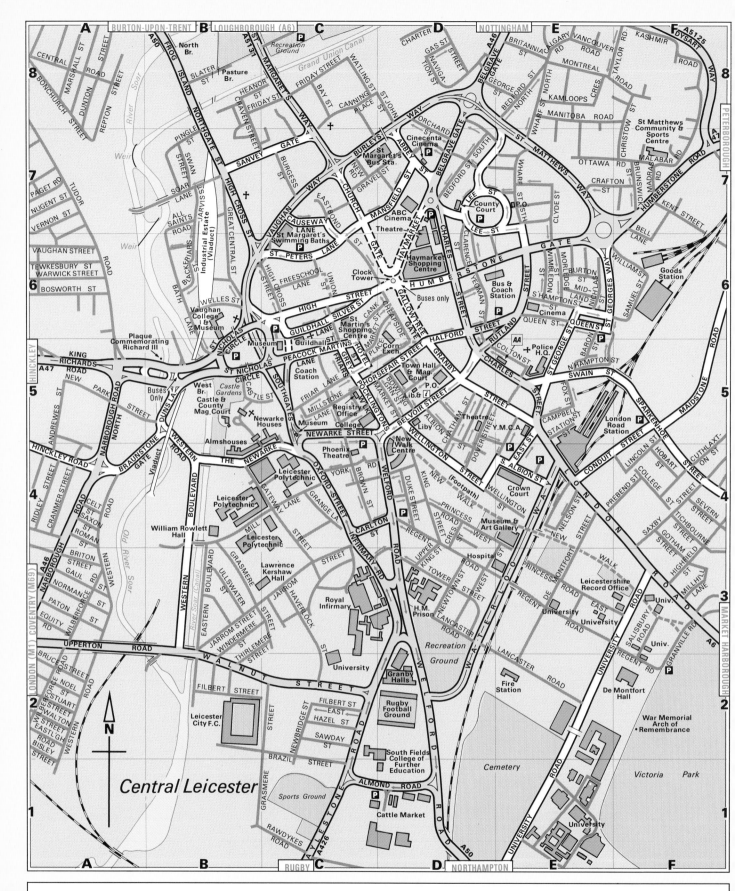

Leicester

A regional capital in Roman times, Leicester has retained many buildings from its eventful and distinguished past. Today the city is a thriving modern place, a centre for industry and commerce, serving much of the Midlands. Among the most outstanding monuments from the past is the Jewry Wall, a great bastion of Roman masonry. Close by are remains of the Roman baths and

several other contemporary buildings. Attached is a museum covering all periods from prehistoric times to 1500. Numerous other museums include the Wygston's House Museum of Costume, with displays covering the period 1769 to 1924; Newarke House, with collections showing changing social conditions in Leicester through four hundred years; and Leicestershire Museum and Art Gallery, with collections of drawings, paintings, ceramics, geology and natural history.

The medieval Guildhall has many features of interest, including a great hall, library and police cells. Leicester's castle, although remodelled in the 17th century, retains a 12th-century great hall. The Church of St Mary de Castro, across the road from the castle, has features going back at least as far as Norman times; while St Nicholas's Church is even older, with Roman and Saxon foundations. St Martin's Cathedral dates mainly from the 13th to 15th centuries and has a notable Bishop's throne.

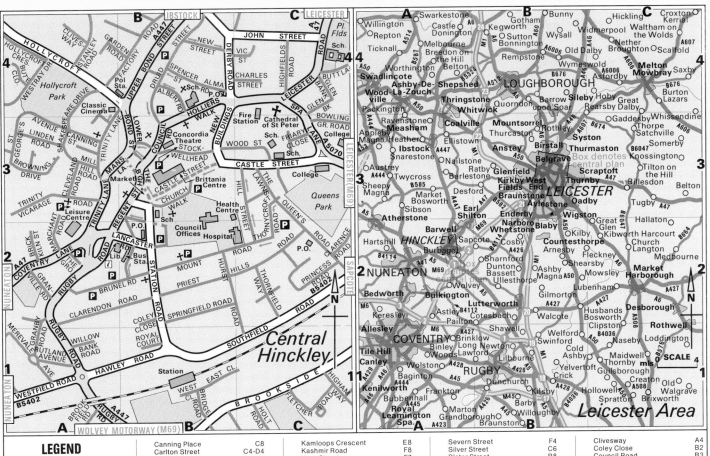

LEGEND

Town Plan

AA Recommended route
Restricted roads
Other roads
Buildings of interest
Car parks
Parks and open spaces

Area Plan

A roads
B roads
Locations   Creaton ○
Urban area

Street Index with Grid Reference

Leicester

Abbey Street	D7
Albion Street	D4-D5
All Saints Road	B7
Almond Road	C1-D1
Andrewes Street	A4-A5
Aylestone Road	C1-C2
Baron Street	E5-E6
Bath Lane	B5-B6
Bay Street	C8
Bedford Street North	E8
Bedford Street South	D7
Belgrave Gate	D7-D8-E8
Bell Lane	F6-F7
Belvoir Street	D5
Bisley Street	A1-A2
Blackfriars Street	B6
Bonchurch Street	A7-A8
Bosworth Street	A6
Bowling Green Street	D5
Braunstone Gate	A4-B4-B5
Brazil Street	C1-C2
Britannia Street	E8
Briton Street	A3
Brown Street	C4
Bruce Street	A2
Brunswick Street	F7
Burgess Street	C7
Burleys Way	C7-D7-D8
Burton Street	E6
Calgary Road	E8
Campbell Street	E5
Cank Street	C6-D6

Canning Place	C8
Carlton Street	C4-D4
Castle Street	B5-C5
Celt Street	A4
Central Road	A8
Charles Street	D7-D6-D5-E5
Charter Street	D8
Chatham Street	D4-D5
Cheapside	D5-D6
Christow Street	F7-F8
Church Gate	C7-C6-D6
Clarence Street	D6-D7
Clyde Street	E6-E7
College Street	F4
Colton Street	D5-E5
Conduit Street	E4-F4-F5
Crafton Street	E7-F7
Cranmer Street	A4
Craven Street	B7-B8
Crescent Street	D4
Cuthlaxton Street	F4-F5
De Montfort Street	E3-E4
Dover Street	D4-D5
Duke Street	D4
Duns Lane	B5
Dunton Street	A8
Dysart Way	F7-F8
East Bond Street	C6-C7-D6
East Street	E4-E5
Eastern Boulevard	B3-B4
Eastleigh Road	A2
Equity Road	A3
Filbert Street	B2-C2
Filbert Street East	C2
Fox Street	E5
Freeschool Lane	C6
Friar Lane	C5
Friday Street	B8-C8
Frog Island	B8
Gallowtree Gate	D6
Gas Street	D8
Gateway Street	B4-C4-C3
Gaul Street	A3
George Street	D8-E8
Gotham Street	F3-F4
Granby Street	D5-E5
Grange Lane	C4
Granville Road	F2-F3
Grasmere Street	B4-B3-C3-C2-C1-B1
Gravel Street	C7-D7
Great Central Street	B6-B7
Greyfriars	C5
Guildhall Lane	C6
Halford Street	D5-D6-E6
Haverlock Street	C2-C3
Haymarket	D6-D7
Hazel Street	C2
Heanor Street	B8-C8
High Cross Street	B7-B6-C6
Highfield Street	F3
High Street	C6-D6
Hinckley Road	A4
Hobart Street	F4
Horsefair Street	C5-D5
Hotel Street	C5
Humberstone Gate	D6-E6
Humberstone Road	F7
Infirmary Road	C4-C3-D3
Jarrom Street	B3-C3
Jarvis Street	B7

Kamloops Crescent	E8
Kashmir Road	F8
Kent Street	F7
King Richards Road	A5
King Street	D5
Lancaster Road	D3-E3-E2
Lee Street	D6-D7-E7
Lincoln Street	F4-F5
London Road	E5-E4-F4-F3
Madras Road	F7
Maidstone Road	F5-F6
Malabar Road	F7
Manitoba Road	E8-F8
Mansfield Street	C7-D7
Market Place	C5-C6-D6
Market Street	D5
Marshall Street	A8
Midland Street	E6
Mill Hill Lane	F3
Mill Lane	B4-C4
Millstone Lane	C5
Morledge Street	E6
Montreal Road	E8-F8
Narborough Road	A3-A4
Narborough Road North	A4-A5
Navigation Street	D8
Nelson Street	E4
Newarke Street	C5
Newbridge Street	C2
New Park Street	A5-B5
New Road	C7
Newtown Street	D3
Nicholas Street	E6
Noel Street	A2
Northampton Street	E5
Northgate Street	B7-B8
Norman Street	A3
Nugent Street	A7
Orchard Street	D7-D8
Ottawa Road	E7-F7
Oxford Street	C4
Paget Road	A7
Paton Street	A3
Peacock Lane	C5
Pingle Street	B7
Pocklingtons Walk	C5-D5
Prebend Street	E4-F4
Princess Road East	E3-F3
Princess Road West	D4-E4
Queen Street	E6
Rawdykes Road	B1-C1
Regent Road	D4-D3-E3-F3-F2
Repton Street	A7-A8
Ridley Street	A4
Roman Street	A4
Rutland Street	D5-E5-E6
St George Street	E5-E6
St Georges Way	E6-F6
St John Street	D8
St Margaret's Way	B8-C8-C7
St Martins	C5
St Mathews Way	E7
St Nicholas Circle	B6-B5-C5
St Peters Lane	C6
Salisbury Road	F2-F3
Samuel Stuart	F6
Sanvey Gate	B7-C7
Sawday Street	C2
Saxby Street	F4
Saxon Street	A4

Severn Street	F4
Silver Street	C6
Slater Street	B8
Soar Lane	B7
South Albion Street	E4
Southampton Street	E6
Southgates	C5
Sparkenhoe Street	F4-F5
Station Street	E5
Stuart Street	A2
Swain Street	E5-F5
Swan Street	B7
The Newarke	B4-C4
Taylor Road	E8-F8
Tewkesbury Street	A6
Thirlemere Street	B2-B3-C3
Tichbourne Street	F3-F4
Tower Street	D3
Tudor Road	A5-A6-A7-A8
Ullswater Street	B3
Union Street	C6
University Road	E1-E2-E3-F3
Upper King Street	D3-D4
Upperton Road	A3-B3-B2
Vancouver Road	E8
Vaughan Way	C6-C7
Vaughan Street	A6
Vernon Street	A6-A7
Walnut Street	B3-B2-C2
Walton Street	A2
Warwick Street	A6
Waterloo Way	D2-D3-E3-E4
Watling Street	C8
Welford Road	D1-D2-D3-D4
Welles Street	B6
Wellington Street	D4-E4-D5
Western Boulevard	B3-B4
Western Road	A1-A2-A3-A4-B4-B5
West Street	D3-E3-E4
Wharf Street North	E7-E8
Wharf Street South	E7
Wilberforce Road	A2-A3
William Street	F6
Wimbledon Street	E6
Windermere Street	B2-B3-C3
Yeoman Street	D6
York Road	C4

Hinckley

Albert Road	B4
Alma Road	B4
Bowling Green Road	C3
Brick Kiln Street	A2
Bridge Road	B1
Brookfield Road	B1-C1
Brookside	A3
Browning Drive	A3
Brunel Road	A2-B2
Bute Close	A4
Butt Lane	C4
Canning Street	A3
Castle Street	B3-C3
Charles Street	C4
Church Walk	B3
Clarence Road	C2
Clarendon Road	A2-B2
Cleveland Road	A3

Clivesway	A4
Coley Close	B2
Council Road	B3
Coventry Lane	A2
Derby Road	B4
Druid Street	B3-B4
East Close	B1-C1
Factory Road	A4-B4
Fletcher Road	C1
Friary Close	C3
Garden Road	A4-B4
Glen Bank	C4
Granby Road	A1-A2
Granville Road	A2
Hawley Road	A1-B1
Higham Way	C1
Highfields Road	C4
Hill Street	C2-C3
Holliers Walk	B3-B4
Hollycroft	C4
Hollycroft Crescent	A4
Holt Road	C1
Hurst Road	B2-C1-C2
John Street	C4
Lancaster Road	A2-B2
Leicester Road	C4
Linden Road	A3
Lower Bond Street	B3-B4
Mansion Lane	A3-B3
Marchant Road	A2-A3
Merevale Avenue	A1
Mill Hill Road	A3
Mount Road	B2-C2
New Buildings	B3-B4
New Street	B4
Priest Hills Road	B2-C2
Princess Road	C2
Queens Road	C2-C3
Regent Street	A2-B2-A3-A3
Royal Court	C3
Rugby Road	A2-A1-B1
Rutland Avenue	A1
St George's Avenue	A3-A4
Shakespeare Drive	A3-A4
Southfield Road	B1-C1-C2
Spa Lane	C3-C4
Spencer Street	B4
Springfield Road	B2
Stanley Road	A4
Station Road	B1-B2
Stockwellhead	B3
The Borough	B3
The Grove	A2
The Lawns	C3
Thornfield Way	C2
Thornycroft Road	C2-C3
Trinity Lane	A2-A3-A4-B3
Trinity Vicarage Road	A3
Upper Bond Street	B4
Victoria Street	C4
West Close	B1
Westray Drive	A4
Westfield Road	A1
Willow Bank Road	A1
Wood Street	B3-C3

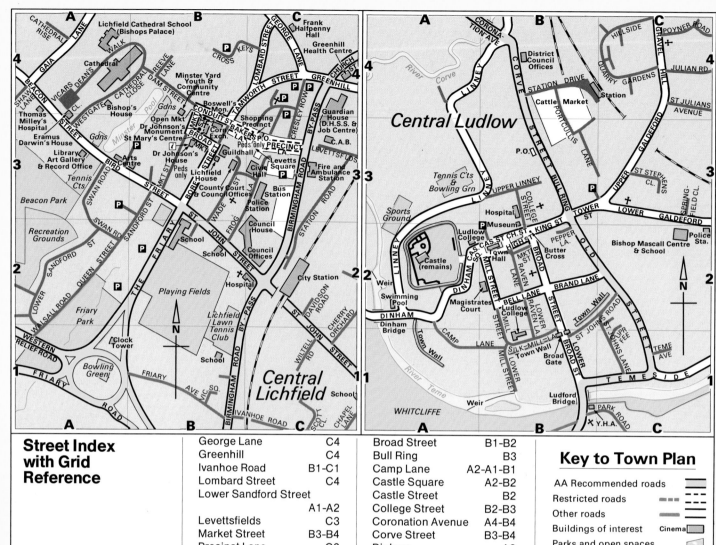

Street Index with Grid Reference

Lichfield

Bakers Lane	B3-C3
Beacon Street	A3-A4
Bird Street	A3-B3
Birmingham Road By-Pass	B1-B2-C2-C3-C4
Bore Street	B3
Broad Market	B3
Cathedral Close	A4-B4
Cathedral Rise	A4
Chapel Lane	C1
Cherry Orchard	C1-C2
Church Street	C4
Conduit Street	B3-B4
Cresley Row	C3-C4
Crosskeys	B4-C4
Dam Street	B4
Davidson Road	C2
Dean's Walk	A4-B4
Friary Avenue	B1
Friary Road	A1-B1
Frog Lane	B2-B3-C3
Gaia Lane	A4

George Lane	C4
Greenhill	C4
Ivanhoe Road	B1-C1
Lombard Street	C4
Lower Sandford Street	A1-A2
Levettsfields	C3
Market Street	B3-B4
Precinct Lane	C3
Queen Street	A2
Reeve Lane	B4
St John Street	B3-B2-C2-C1
Sandford Street	A2-B2-B3
Scott Close	C1
Shaw Lane	A4
Station Road	C2-C3
Swan Road	A2-A3
Tamworth Street	B3-B4-C4
The Friary	A2-B2-B3
Vicars Close	A4
Victoria Square	B1
Wade Street	B2-B3
Walsall Road	A1-A2
Western Relief Road	A1
Westgate	A3-A4
Wittell Road	C1

Ludlow

Bell Lane	B2
Brand Lane	B2-C2
Broad Street	B1-B2
Bull Ring	B3
Camp Lane	A2-A1-B1
Castle Square	A2-B2
Castle Street	B2
College Street	B2-B3
Coronation Avenue	A4-B4
Corve Street	B3-B4
Dinham	A2
Gravel Hill	C4
High Street	B2
Hillside	C4
Julian Road	C4
King Street	B2-B3
Linney	A2-A3-B3-A3-A4-B4
Lower Broad Street	B1
Lower Galdeford	C2-C3
Lower Mill Street	B1
Lower Raven Lane	B1-B2
Market Street	B2
Mill Street	B1-B2
Old Street	B3-B2-C2-C1
Park Road	B1-C1
Pepper Lane	B2
Portcullis Lane	B4-B3-C3
Poyner Road	C4
Quarry Gardens	C4
Raven Lane	B2
St Johns Lane	C1-C2
St Johns Road	B1-B2-C2
St Julians Avenue	C4
St Stephens Close	C3

Silk Mill Lane	B1
Springfield Close	C3
Station Drive	B4
Teme Avenue	C1
Temeside	B1-C1
Tower Street	B3-C3
Upper Fee	C1-C2
Upper Galdeford	C3-C4
Upper Linney	B3

Key to Town Plan

AA Recommended roads	
Restricted roads	
Other roads	
Buildings of interest	Cinema
Parks and open spaces	
Car Parks	P
Churches	†

Lichfield Three graceful spires known as the 'Ladies of the Vale' soar up from Lichfield's Cathedral of St Mary and St Chad. Constructed in the 13th century and combining early English and decorated Gothic styles, the Cathedral is the most outstanding feature of this attractive city, which has retained a distinctly rural appearance despite a good deal of industrial expansion.

Most distinguished son of Lichfield is Dr Samuel Johnson and his father's 18th-century house in Market Square (which served the family as a dwelling and a bookshop) has been restored and converted into a museum. Johnson's birthday (18 September) is commemorated on the nearest Saturday by a procession from the Guild Hall.

Ludlow, built on a steep hill washed on two sides by the Rivers Corve and Teme, has, since earliest times, been recognised as a strategic site, and the Normans were quick to take advantage of this. Their castle, now an impressive ruin crowning the hilltop, looks out over the Welsh Marches. The town beneath is a charming mixture of wide Georgian streets and narrow medieval alleyways where 18th-century brick and stucco rubs shoulders with half-timbered Tudor buildings with leaning walls and steeply-pitched roofs. The most famous of all the timbered buildings is the Feathers Hotel, although it has plenty of competitors, and the dignified stone Butter Cross houses the town's museum.

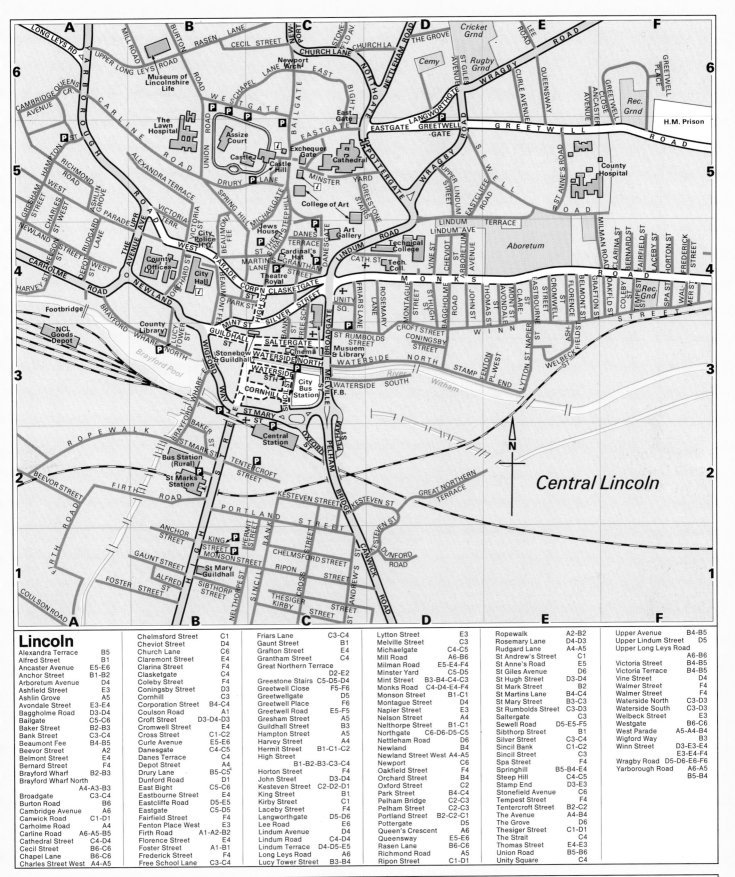

Lincoln

Alexandra Terrace	B5		
Alfred Street	B1		
Ancaster Avenue	E5-E6		
Anchor Street	B1-B2		
Arboretum Avenue	D4		
Ashfield Street	E3		
Ashlin Grove	A5		
Avondale Street	E3-E4		
Bagholme Road	D3-D4		
Bailgate	C5-C6		
Baker Street	B2-B3		
Bank Street	B3-C4		
Beaumont Fee	B4-B5		
Beevor Street	A2		
Belmont Street	E4		
Bernard Street	F4		
Brayford Wharf	B2-B3		
Brayford Wharf North			
	A4-A3-B3		
Broadgate	C3-C4		
Burton Road	B6		
Cambridge Avenue	A6		
Canwick Road	C1-D1		
Carholme Road	A4		
Carline Road	A6-A5-B5		
Cecil Street	B6-C6		
Chapel Lane	B6-C6		
Charles Street West	A4-A5		

Chelmsford Street	C1		
Cheviot Street	D4		
Church Lane	C6		
Claremont Street	E4		
Clarina Street	F4		
Clasketgate	C4		
Coleby Street	F4		
Coningsby Street	D3		
Cornhill	C3		
Corporation Street	B4-C4		
Croft Street	D3-D4-D3		
Cromwell Street	E4		
Cross Street	C1-C2		
Curle Avenue	E5-E6		
Danesgate	C4-C5		
Danes Terrace	C4		
Depot Street	A4		
Drury Lane	B5-C5		
Dunford Road	D1		
East Bight	C5-C6		
Eastbourne Street	E4		
Eastcliffe Road	D5-E5		
Fairfield Street	F4		
Fenton Place West	E3		
Firth Road	A1-A2-B2		
Florence Street	F4		
Foster Street	A1-B1		
Frederick Street	F4		
Free School Lane	C3-C4		

Friars Lane	C3-C4		
Gaunt Street	B1		
Grafton Street	E4		
Grantham Street	C4		
Great Northern Terrace			
	D2-E2		
Greestone Stairs	C5-D5-D4		
Greetwell Close	F5-F6		
Greetwellgate	D5		
Greetwell Place	F6		
Greetwell Road	E5-F5		
Gresham Street	A5		
Guildhall Street	B3		
Hampton Street	A5		
Harvey Street	A4		
Hermit Street	B1-C1-C2		
High Street			
	B1-B2-B3-C3-C4		
Horton Street	F4		
John Street	D3-D4		
Kesteven Street	C2-D2-D1		
King Street	B1		
Kirby Street	C1		
Laceby Street	F4		
Langworthgate	D5-D6		
Lee Road	E6		
Lindum Avenue	D4		
Lindum Road	C4		
Lindum Terrace	D4-D5-E5		
Long Leys Road	A6		
Lucy Tower Street	B3-B4		

Lytton Street	E3		
Melville Street	C3		
Michaelgate	C4-C5		
Mill Road	A6-B6		
Milman Road	E5-E4-F4		
Minster Yard	C5-D5		
Mint Street	B3-B4-C4-C3		
Monks Road	C4-D4-E4-F4		
Monson Street	B1-C1		
Montague Street	D4		
Napier Street	E3		
Nelson Street	A4		
Nelthorpe Street	B1-C1		
Newland	B4		
Newland Street West	A4-A5		
Newport	C6		
Oakfield Street	F4		
Orchard Street	B4		
Oxford Street	C2		
Park Street	B4-C4		
Pelham Bridge	C2-C3		
Pelham Street	C2-C3		
Portland Street	B2-C2-C1		
Pottergate	D5		
Queen's Crescent	A6		
Queensway	E5-E6		
Rasen Lane	B6-C6		
Richmond Road	A5		
Ripon Street	C1-D1		

Ropewalk	A2-B2		
Rosemary Lane	D4-D3		
Rudgard Lane	A4-A5		
St Andrew's Street	C1		
St Anne's Road	E5		
St Giles Avenue	D6		
St Hugh Street	D3-D4		
St Mark Street	B2		
St Martins Lane	B4-C4		
St Mary Street	B3-C3		
St Rumbolds Street	D3-D3		
Saltergate	C3		
Sewell Road	D5-E5-F5		
Sibthorp Street	B1		
Silver Street	C3-C4		
Sincil Bank	C1-C2		
Sincil Street	C3		
Spa Street	F4		
Springhill	B5-B4-E4		
Steep Hill	C4-C5		
Stamp End	D3-E3		
Stonefield Avenue	C6		
Tempest Street	F4		
Tentercroft Street	B2-C2		
The Avenue	A4-B4		
The Grove	D6		
Thesiger Street	C1-D1		
The Strait	C4		
Thomas Street	E4-E3		
Union Road	B5-B6		
Unity Square	C4		

Upper Avenue	B4-B5		
Upper Lindum Street	D5		
Upper Long Leys Road			
	A6-B6		
Victoria Street	B4-B5		
Victoria Terrace	B4-B5		
Vine Street	D4		
Walmer North	F4		
Walmer Street	F4		
Waterside North	C3-D3		
Waterside South	C3-D3		
Welbeck Street	E3		
Westgate	B6-C6		
West Parade	A5-A4-B4		
Wigford Way	B3		
Winn Street	D3-E3-E4		
	E3-E4-F4		
Wragby Road	D5-D6-E6-F6		
Yarborough Road	A6-A5		
	B5-B4		

Lincoln

The striking triple-spired cathedral of Lincoln, the third largest in England, dominates the countryside for miles. Its impressive west front, decorated with many statues, is all that remains of the first cathedral the Normans built, and most of the rest dates from the 13th century. Among its treasures is one of the four extant original copies of Magna Carta.

Built on a rugged limestone plateau above the River Witham, the cobbled streets of the medieval city straggle down the sides of the hill past old houses built from the same local honey-coloured limestone as the cathedral. Modern Lincoln owes much to engineering industries, but few tentacles of change have crept into the heart of the city where the oldest inhabited house in England, Aaron's House, can be found. Other places of interest include the quaintly-named Cardinal's Hat

– thought to be named after Cardinal Wolsey who was Bishop of Lincoln for one year. Newport Arch, at the end of the picturesque street called Bailgate, is a relic from the Roman city of Lincoln – *Lindum Colonia*. It is the only Roman gateway in the country still open to traffic. Complementing the cathedral in size if not in majesty is the Norman castle. It is possible to walk along the battlements and the old prison chapel provides a grim insight into the punishment meted out in less enlightened times.

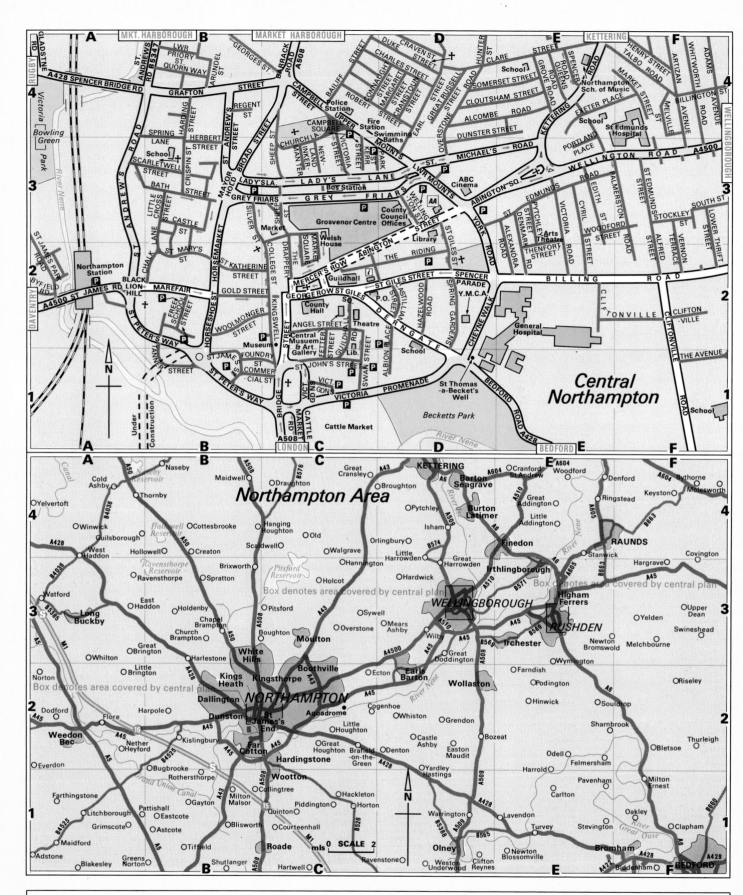

Northampton

The town's long connection with the boot and shoe trade started during the Civil War when Northampton made footwear for Cromwell's army. Now, although still internationally famous for this commodity, it is also an important light industry and distribution centre. Predictably, both the town's museums contain shoes, and include Queen Victoria's wedding shoes and Nijinsky's ballet shoes among their exhibits.

Northampton has a long and important history and its castle became a resting place for every English king from Henry I to Edward III. However, due to Charles II's destruction of the castle and the town walls, and a devastating fire in 1675, little remains of the medieval town. The vast market square – one of the largest in the country – dates from the days of the cattle drovers when Northampton was an important market centre, and many of the street names – such as Horsemarket and Mercer's Row – reflect the town's history.

Wellingborough stands in the valley of the River Nene; like Northampton, the manufacture of footwear is a well-established industry. The two churches of the town form an interesting contrast; All-Hallows retains traces of medieval workmanship and has a 17th-century house as well as a church hall, whilst St Mary's is a modern building designed by Sir Ninian Comper.

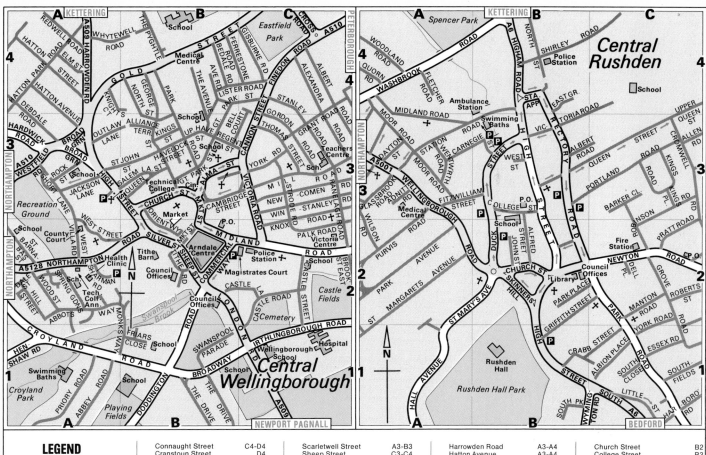

LEGEND

Town Plan
AA recommended route	
Restricted roads	
Other roads	
Buildings of interest	Library
Car parks	P
Parks and open spaces	

Area Plan
A roads	
B roads	
Locations	Winfarth
Urban area	

Street Index with Grid Reference

Northampton

Abington Square	D3-E3
Abington Street	C2-D2-D3
Adams Avenue	F4
Albion Place	D1-D2
Alcombe Road	D4-E4
Alexandra Road	E2-E3
Alfred Street	F2-F3
Angel Street	C2
Artizan Avenue	F3-F4
Arundel Street	B4
Bailiff Street	C4
Barrack Road	C4
Bath Street	A3-B3
Bedford Road	D1-E1
Billing Road	E2-F2
Billington Street	F4
Black Lion Hill	A2
Bridge Street	C1-C2
Broad Street	B3-B4-C4
Byfield Road	A2
Campbell Square	C4
Campbell Street	C4
Castle Street	B3
Castilian Street	D2
Cattle Market Road	C1
Chalk Lane	B2-B3
Charles Street	C4-D4
Cheyne Walk	D1-D2
Church Lane	C3-C4
Clare Street	D4-E4
Cliftonville	E2-F2
Cliftonville Road	F1-F2
Cloutsham Street	D4-E4
College Street	C2
Commercial Street	B1-C1
Connaught Street	C4-D4
Cranstoun Street	D4
Craven Street	D4
Crispin Street	B3
Cyril Street	E2-E3
Denmark Road	E2-E3
Derngate	C2-D2-D1
Duke Street	C4-D4
Dunster Street	D3-D4-E4
Earl Street	D3-D4
Edith Street	E3
Exeter Place	E4-F4
Fetter Street	C1-C2
Foundry Street	B1-C1
Free School Street	B2
George Row	C2
Georges Street	B4-C4
Gladstone Road	A4
Gold Street	B2-C2
Grafton Street	B4-C4
Great Russell Street	D4
Greyfriars	B3-C3-D3
Grove Road	E4
Guildhall Road	C1-C2
Harding Street	B4
Hazelwood Road	D2
Henry Street	F4
Herbert Street	B3
Horsemarket	B2-B3
Horseshoe Street	B1-B2
Hunter Street	D4
Inkerman Terrace	C3
Kerr Street	C3-C4
Kettering Road	E3-E4
Kingswell	C1-C2
Lady's Lane	B3-C3-D3
Little Cross Street	B3
Lower Mounts	D3
Lower Priory Street	B4
Lower Thrift Street	F2-F3
Marefair	A2-B2
Margaret Street	D4
Market Square	C2-C3
Market Street	E4-F4
Mayor Hold	B3
Melville Street	F4
Mercers Row	C2
Newland	C3
Overstone Road	D3-D4
Palmerston Road	F3-F2
Park Street	C3
Portland Place	E3-E4
Pytchley Street	E3
Queens Road	E4
Quorn Way	B4
Regent Street	B4
Robert Street	C4-D4
St Andrews Road	A2-A3-A4-B4
St Andrews Street	B3-B4
St Edmunds Road	D3-E3-F3
St Edmunds Street	F3
St Giles Square	C2
St Giles Street	C2-D2-D3
St James Road	A2
St James Park Road	A2-A3
St James Street	B1
St John's Street	C1
St Katherine Street	B2-C2
St Mary's Street	B2
St Michael's Road	D3-E3
St Peter's Way	A2-B2-B1-C1

Scarletwell Street	A3-B3
Sheep Street	C3-C4
Silver Street	B3-C3
Somerset Street	D4-E4
South Street	F3
Spencer Road	E4
Spencer Bridge Road	A4
Spencer Parade	D2
Spring Gardens	D3
Spring Lane	A4-B4-B3
Stockley Street	F3
Swan Street	C1-C2
The Avenue	F1
The Drapery	C2-C3
The Riding	C2-D2
Tanner Street	B1-B2
Talbot Road	E4-F4
Thenfoot Street	E2-E3
Upper Mounts	C4-C3-D3
Vernon Terrace	F2-F3
Victoria Gardens	C1
Victoria Promenade	C1-D1
Victoria Road	E2-E3
Victoria Street	C3-C4
Wellington Road	E3-F3
Wellington Street	D3
Whitworth Road	F3-F4
Woodford Street	E3-F3
Woolmonger Street	B2-C2
York Road	D3-D2

Wellingborough

Abbey Road	A1
Abbotts Way	A2
Albert Road	C3-C4
Alexandra Road	C3-C4
Alliance Terrace	B3
Alma Street	B3
Avenue Road	B4
Bedale Road	B4
Bell Court	B3-C3-C4
Broad Green	A3
Broadway	B1-C1
Brook Street East	C2
Cambridge Street	B3-C3
Cannon Street	C3-C4
Castle Lane	B2-C2
Castle Road	C1-C2
Castle Street	C2
Church Street	B3
Commercial Way	B2
Cross Road	C4
Croyland Road	A2-A1-B1
Dale Street	A2
Debdale Road	A3-A4
Doddington Road	B1-B2
Ferrestone Road	B4-C4
Finedon Road	C4
Friars Close	B1
George Street	B3-B4
Gisburne Road	C4
Gold Street	A4-B4-C4
Gordon Road	C3
Grant Road	C3-C4
Great Park Street	B3-B4-C4
Hardwick Road	A3

Harrowden Road	A3-A4
Hatton Avenue	A3-A4
Hatton Street	A4
Hatton Park Road	A4
Havelock Street	B3
Henshaw Road	A1
High Street	A3-B3-B2
Hill Street	A2
Irthlingborough Road	C1-C2
Jackson Lane	A3
Kings Street	B3
Knights Court	A4-B4
Knox Road	C2-C3
Lister Road	B4-C4
London Road	B1-B2-C2-C1
Market Street	B2-B3
Midland Road	B2-C2
Mill Road	C3
Monks Way	A1-B1-B2
Newcomen Road	C3
North Street	B3-B4
Northampton Road	A2-B2
Orient Road	C2-C3
Outlaw Lane	A3-B3
Palk Road	C2
Park Road	B3-B4
Priory Road	A1
Queen Street	B3
Ranelagh Road	C2-C3
Redwell Road	A4
Regent Street	B3-C3
Rock Street	A3
St Barnabas Street	A2
St John Street	A3-B3
Salem Court	A3-B3
Sharman Road	A2
Sheep Street	B2
Short Lane	A3
Silver Street	B2
Spring Gardens	A2
Stanley Road	C3-C4
Strode Road	C2-C3
Swanspool Parade	B1
The Avenue	B3-B4
The Drive	B1
The Pyghtle	B4
Thomas Street	C3
Titheburn Road	B2
Upper Havelock Street	B3
Victoria Road	C2-C3
West Street	A2
Westfield Road	A3
West Villa Road	A2
Whytewell Road	A4-B4
Winstanley Road	C3
Wood Street	A2
York Road	C3

Rushden

Adnitt Road	A2-A3
Albert Road	B3-C3
Albion Place	C1
Alfred Street	B2-B3
Allen Road	C3
Barker Close	C3
Carnegie Street	A3-B3

Church Street	B2
College Street	B3
Crabb Street	B1-C1
Cromwell Road	C2-C3
Dayton Street	A3
Dell Place	C2
Duck Street	B2-B3
East Grove	B4
Essex Road	C1
Fitzwilliam Street	A3-B3
Fletcher Road	A4
Glassbrook Road	A3
Griffith Street	B1-B2-C2
Grove Road	C1-C2
Hall Avenue	A1
Harborough Road	C1
High Street	B2-B3-B4
High Street South	B2-B1-C1
Higham Road	B4
John Street	B2
Kings Road	C3
Kings Place	C3
Little Street	C1
Manton Road	C2
Midland Road	A3-A4
Moor Road	A3-A4
Newton Road	C2
North Street	B4
Park Avenue	A2
Park Place	B2-C2
Park Road	C2-C1
Pemberton Street	A3-A4
Portland Road	B3-C3
Pratt Road	C2-C3
Purvis Road	A2-A3
Queen Street	B3-C3
Quorn Road	A4
Rectory Road	B2-B3-B4
Roberts Street	C2
Robinson Road	C2-C3
St Margarets Avenue	A1-A2
St Mary's Avenue	A1-A2-B2
Shirley Road	B4-C4
Skinners Hill	B2
South Close	C1
South Park	B1
Southfields	C1
Station Approach	A4
Station Road	A3-B3-B4
Upper Queen Street	C3-C4
Victoria Road	B3-B4-C4
Washbrook Road	A4-B4
Wellingborough Road	A3-A2-B2
Wentworth Road	A3
West Street	B3
Wilson Road	A2-A3
Woodland Road	A4
Wymington Road	B1-C1
York Road	C1-C2

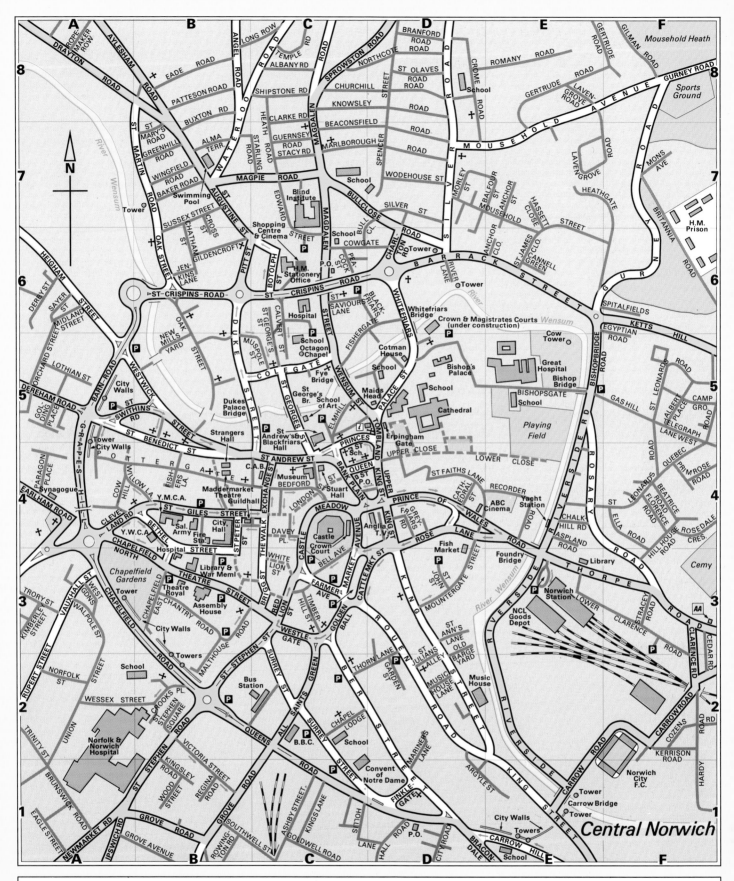

Norwich

Fortunately the heart has not been ripped out of Norwich to make way for some bland precinct, so its ancient character has been preserved. Narrow alleys run between the streets – sometimes opening out into quiet courtyards, sometimes into thoroughfares packed with people, sometimes into lanes which seem quite deserted. It is a unique place, with something of interest on every corner.

The cathedral was founded in 1096 by the city's first bishop, Herbert de Losinga. Among its most notable features are the nave, with its huge pillars, the bishop's throne (a Saxon survival unique in Europe) and the cloisters with their matchless collection of roof bosses. Across the city is the great stone keep of the castle, set on a mound and dominating all around it. It dates from Norman times, but was refaced in 1834. The keep now forms part of Norwich Castle Museum –

an extensive and fascinating collection. Other museums are Bridewell Museum – collections relating to local crafts and industries within a 14th-century building – and Strangers' Hall, a genuinely 'old world' house, rambling and full of surprises, both in its tumble of rooms and in the things which they contain. Especially picturesque parts of the city are Elm Hill – a street of ancient houses; Tombland – with two gateways into the Cathedral Close; and Pull's Ferry – a watergate by the river.

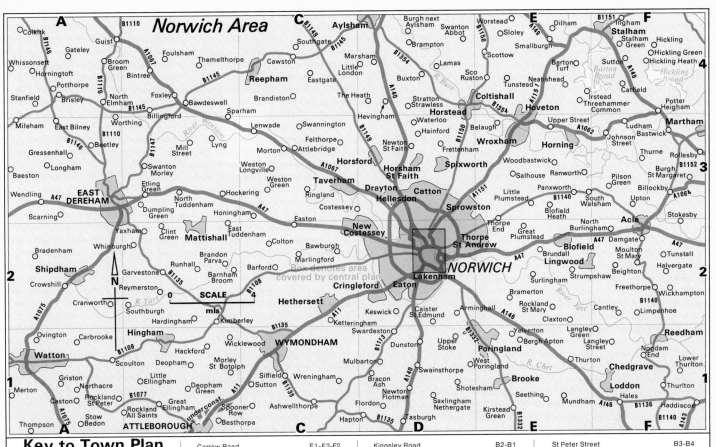

Norwich Area

Box denotes area covered by central plan

NORWICH

SCALE
mls

Key to Town Plan and Area Plan

Town Plan
AA Recommended roads
Restricted roads
Other roads
Buildings of interest — School
AA Service Centre — AA
Car Parks — P
Parks and open spaces
One Way Streets

Area Plan
A roads
B roads
Locations — East Rushton
Urban area

Street Index with Grid Reference

Norwich

Albany Road	C8
Albert Place	F5
All Saints Green	C2-C3
Alma Terrace	B7
Anchor Close	E6
Anchor Street	E7
Angel Road	B8
Argyle Street	D2-D1-E1
Ashby Street	C1
Aspland Road	E4
Aylesham Road	A8-B8
Baker Road	B7
Balfour Street	E7
Bank Plain	C4
Barn Road	A5
Barrack Street	D6-E6
Beaconsfield Road	C7-D7
Beatrice Road	F4
Bedford Street	C4
Bell Avenue	C3
Ber Street	C3-C2-D2-D1
Bethel Street	B4-B3
Bishopbridge Road	E5-E6
Bishopsgate	D5-E5
Blackfriars	C6-D6
Botolph Street	C6
Bracondale	D1-E1
Branford Road	E5
Brigg Street	C3
Britannia Road	F7-F6
Brunswick Road	A1
Bull Close	C6-C7-D7
Bull Close Road	C7-D7-D6
Buxton Road	B7-B8
Calvert Street	C6-C5
Camp Grove	F5
Cannell Green	E6
Carrow Hill	D1-E1

Carrow Road	E1-E2-F2
Castle Meadow Street	C3-C4
Cathedral Street	D4
Cattle Market	C4
Cedar Road	F3-F2
Chalkhill Road	E4
Chantry Road	B3
Chapelfield East	B3
Chapelfield North	A4-A3-B4-B3
Chapelfield Road	A3-B3-B2
Chapel Lodge	C2
Churchill Road	C8-D8
Charlton Road	D6
Chatham Street	B7-B6
City Road	D1
Clarence Road	F3-F2
Clarke Street	C7-C8
Cleveland Road	A4-B4
Colegate	B5-C5
Cowgate	C6-D6
Cow Hill	A4
Cozens Road	F2
Crome Road	D8-D7
Crooks Place	B2
Cross Street	B7-B6
Davey Place	C4
Derby Street	A6
Dereham Road	A5
Drayton Road	A8-B8
Duke Street	B6-B5-C5-C4
Eade Road	B8
Earlham Road	A4
Esdelle Street	B7-C7
Edward Street	C7-C6
Egyptian Road	E6-F6-F5
Ella Road	F4-F3
Elmhill	C5
Exchange Street	C4
Farmer Avenue	C3
Finkelgate	D1
Fishergate	C5-C6-D6
Fishers Lane	B4
Florence Road	F4
Garden Street	D2
Gas Hill	E5-F5
Gertrude Road	E7-E8-F8
Gildencroft	B6
Gilman Road	F8
Golden Ball	C3
Golding Place	A5
Goldwell Road	C1
Grapes Hill	A5-A4
Greenhill Road	B7
Greyfriars Road	D4
Grove Avenue	A1-B1
Grove Road	A1-B1-C1-C2
Gurney Road	E6-F6-F7-F8
Guernsey Road	C7
Hall Road	D1
Hardy Road	F1-F2
Hassett Close	E7
Heathgate	E7-F7
Heath Road	C8-C7
Heigham Street	A6-A5
Hill House Road	F3-F4
Hollis Lane	C1-D1
Ipswich Rpad	A1
Jenkins Lane	B6
Kerrison Road	F2
Ketts Hill	E6-F6-F5
Kimberley Street	A3
Kings Lane	C1

Kingsley Road	B2-B1
King Street	D4-D3-D2-E2-E1
Knowsley Road	C8-D8
Lavengrove Road	E8-E7-F7
London Street	C4
Long Row	B8-C8
Lothian Street	A5
Lower Clarence Road	E3-F3-F2
Lower Close	D4-E4
Magdalen Road	C7-C8
Magdalen Street	C7-C6-C5
Magpie Road	B7-C7
Malthouse Road	B2-B3
Mariners Lane	D1-D2
Market Avenue	C3-C4
Marlborough Road	C7-D7
Midland Street	A5-A6
Mons Avenue	F7
Morley Street	D7
Mountergate Street	D3-D4
Mousehold Avenue	D7-E7-E8-F8
Mousehold Street	D7-E7-E6-F6
Music House Lane	D2
Muspole Street	B5-C5
Newmarket Road	A1
New Mills Yard	B5
Norfolk Street	A2
Northcote Road	C8-D8
Oak Street	B6-B5
Old Barge Yard	D2-D3
Orchard Street	A5-A6
Palace Street	D5
Paragon Place	A4
Patteson Road	B8
Peacock Street	C6
Pitt Street	B6-C6
Pottergate	A4-B4
Prince of Wales Road	D4-E4-E3
Primrose Road	F4
Princes Street	C4-C5-D5
Quebec Road	F4-F5
Queens Road	B2-C2-C1
Queen Street	C4-D4
Recorder Road	E4
Red Lion Street	C3
Regina Road	B1
River Lane	D6
Riverside	E3-E2-E1
Riverside Road	E3-E4-E5
Romany Road	D8-E8
Ropemaker Row	A8
Rosary Road	E5-E4-F4-F3
Rosedale Crescent	F4
Rose Lane	D3-D4-E4
Rouen Road	C3-D3-D2
Rowington Road	B1
Rupert Street	A2-A3
St Andrew Street	C4
St Ann's Lane	D3
St Augustine Street	B7-B6
St Benedict Street	A5-B5-B4
St Crispins Road	B6-C6-D6
St Faiths Lane	D4
St George's Street	C6-C5-C4
St Giles Street	B4-C4
St James Close	E6
St John Street	D3
St Juliens Alley	D2-D3
St Leonards Road	E4-F4-F5
St Martin Road	A8-B8-A7-B7
St Mary's Road	B7
St Olaves Road	D8

St Peter Street	B3-B4
St Saviours Lane	C6
St Stephen Road	A1-B1-B2
St Stephen Street	B2-B3-C3
St Stephen Square	B2
St Swithins Road	A5-B5
Sayer Street	A6
Shipstone Road	B8
Silver Road	D6-D7-D8
Silver Street	D7
Southwell Street	B1-C1
Spencer Street	D7-D8
Spitalfields	E6-F6
Sprowston Road	C8-D8
Stacy Road	C7
Starling Road	B7-C7
Stracey Road	F3
Surrey Street	C3-C2-C1-D1
Sussex Street	B6-B7
The Walk	C3-C4
Telegraph Lane West	F5-F4
Temple Road	C8
Theatre Street	B3-C3
Thorne Lane	C2-D2-D3
Thorpe Road	E3-F3
Timberhill Street	C3
Tombland	D5-D4
Trinity Street	A2-A1
Trory Street	A3
Union Street	A1-A2-A3
Upper Close	D4
Upper King Street	D4
Vauxhall Street	A3
Victoria Street	B2-B1
Walpole Street	A3
Waterloo Road	B7-B8-C8
Whitefriars	D6-D5
White Lion Street	C3
Willow Lane	A4-B4
Wingfield Road	B7
Wensum Street	C5-D5
Wessex Street	A2-B2
West Gardens	A3
Westle Gate	C3
Westwick Street	A5-B5-B4
Wodehouse Street	D7
Wood Street	B1

93

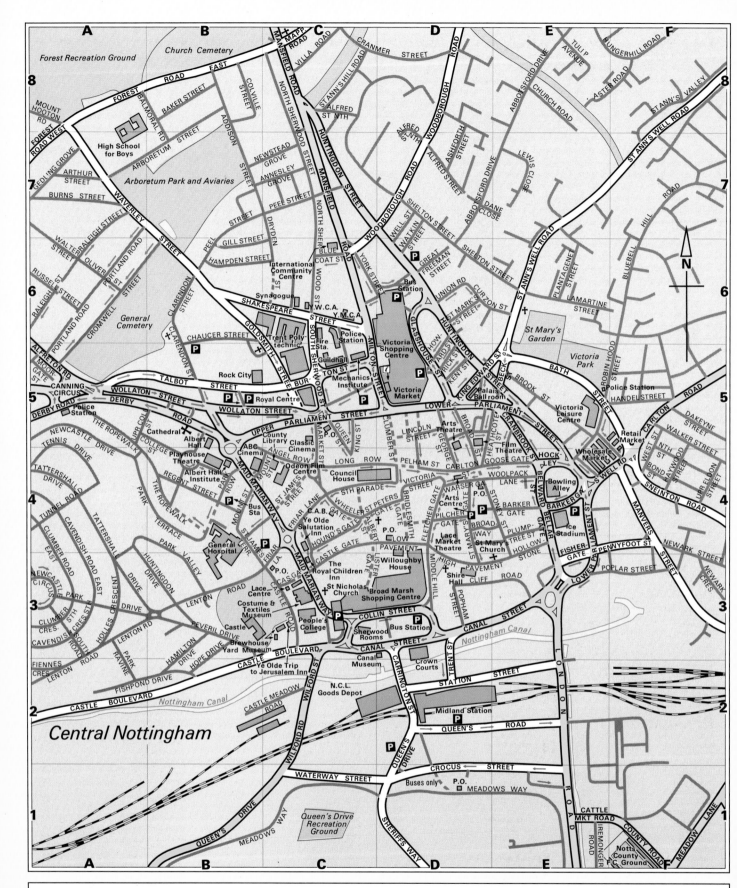

Nottingham

Hosiery and lace were the foundations upon which Nottingham's prosperity was built. The stockings came first – a knitting machine for these had been invented by a Nottinghamshire man as early as 1589 – but a machine called a 'tickler', which enabled simple patterns to be created in the stocking fabric, prompted the development of machine-made lace. The earliest fabric was

produced in 1768, and an example from not much later than that is kept in the city's Castlegate Costume and Textile Museum. In fact, the entire history of lacemaking is beautifully explained in this converted row of Georgian terraces. The Industrial Museum at Wollaton Park has many other machines and exhibits tracing the development of the knitting industry, as well as displays on the other industries which have brought wealth to the city – tobacco, pharmaceuticals,

engineering and printing. At Wollaton Hall is a natural history museum, while nearer the centre are the Canal Museum and the Brewhouse Yard Museum, a marvellous collection which shows items from daily life in the city up to the present day. Nottingham is not complete without mention of Robin Hood, the partly mythical figure whose statue is in the castle grounds. Although the castle itself has Norman foundations, the present structure is largely Victorian. It is now a museum.

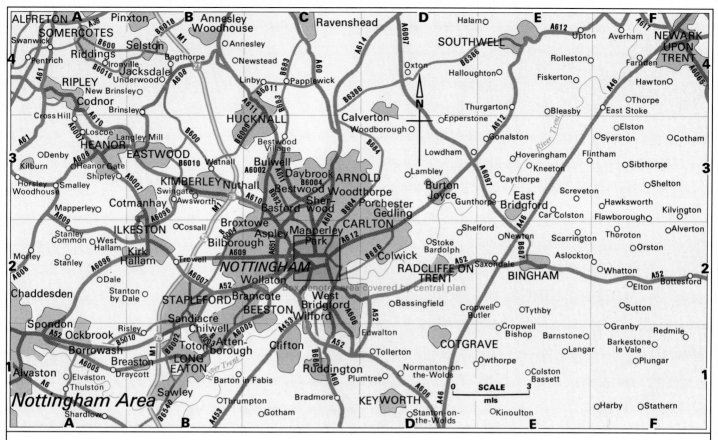

Key to Town Plan and Area Plan

Town Plan

AA Recommended roads	≡
Restricted roads	= = =
Other roads	═
Buildings of interest	Theatre ☐
Car Parks	Ⓟ
Parks and open spaces	▨
Churches	†
One Way Streets	→

Area Plan

A roads	▬
B roads	—
Locations	BagthorpeO
Urban area	▨

Street Index with Grid Reference

Nottingham

Abbotsford Drive	D7-D7-E7-E8
Addison Street	B7-B8
Albert Street	C4
Alfred Street	D7
Alfred Street North	C8, D7-D8
Alfreton Road	A5-A6
Angel Road	B5-B4-C4
Annesley Grove	B7-C7
Ashford Street	D7-D8
Aster Road	E8-F8
Arboretum Street	A7-B7-B8
Arthur Street	A7
Baker Street	B8
Balmoral Road	A8-B8-B7
Barker Gate	E4
Bath Gate	E5-F5
Beck Street	E5
Bellar Gate	E4
Belward Street	E4
Bluebell Hill Road	F6-F7
Bluecoat Street	C6
Bond Street	F4
Bridlesmith Gate	D4
Broad Street	D4-D5
Broadway	D4-E4
Brook Street	E5
Burns Street	A7
Burton Street	C5

Canal Street	C3-D3-E3
Canning Circus	A5
Carlton Road	F5
Carlton Street	D4
Carrington Street	D2-D3
Castle Boulevard	A2-B2-B3-C3
Castle Gate	C3-C4
Castle Market Road	E1-F1
Castle Meadow Road	B2-C2
Castle Road	C3
Cavendish Crescent South	A3
Cavendish Road East	A3-A4
Chaucer Street	B5-B6
Church Road	E8
Clarendon Street	B5-B6
Cliff Road	D3-E3
Clumber Crescent South	A3
Clumber Road East	A3-A4
Clumber Street	D4-D5
College Street	A5-B5-B4
Collin Street	C3-D3
Colville Street	B8
County Road	F1
Cranbrook Street	E4-E5
Cranmer Street	C8-D8
Crocus Street	D1-E1
Cromwell Street	A5-B6-C6
Curzon Street	D6-E6
Dane Close	D7-E7
Dakeyne Street	F5
Derby Road	A5-B5
Dryden Street	C6-C7
Fieness Crescent	A2
Fishergate	E3-E4
Fishpond Drive	A2-B2
Fletcher Gate	D4
Forest Road East	A8-B8-C8
Forest Road West	A7-A8
Friar Lane	C3-C4
Gedling Grove	A7
George Street	D4-D5
Gill Street	B6-C6
Glasshouse Street	D5-D6
Goldsmith Street	B6-C6-C5
Goose Gate	D4-E4
Great Freeman Street	D6
Hamilton Drive	B2-B3
Hampden Street	B6-C6
Handel Street	E5-F5
Haywood Street	F4-F5
High Pavement	D4-D3-E3
Hockley	E4
Holles Crescent	A3
Hollowstone	E3-E4
Hope Drive	B2-B3
Hound's Gate	C4

Howard Street	D5-D6
Hungerhill Road	E8-F8
Huntingdon Drive	A4-A3-B3
Huntingdon Drive	C8-C7-D7-D6-D5-E5
Huskisson Street	C6
Iremonger Road	E1
Kent Street	D5
King Edward Street	D5-E5
King Street	C4-C5
Lamartine Street	E6-F6
Lenton Road	A2-A3-B3
Lewis Close	E7
Lincoln Street	D5
Lister Gate	C3-C4
London Road	E1-E2-E3
Long Row	C4-D4
Lower Parliament Street	D5-E5-E4-E3
Low Pavement	C4-D4
Maid Marion Way	B4-C4-C3
Mansfield Street	C6-C7-C8
Manvers Street	F3-F4
Mapperley Road	C8
Market Street	C4-C5
Meadow Lane	F1
Meadows Road	B1-C1-D1-E1
Middle Hill	D3-D4
Milton Street	C6-C5-D5
Moorgate Street	A5
Mount Hooton Road	A8
Mount Street	B4-C4
Newark Crescent	F3
Newark Street	F3-F4
Newcastle Circus	A3
Newcastle Drive	A4-A5
Newstead Grove	B7-C7
North Street	F4-F5
North Sherwood Street	C6-C7-C8
Oliver Street	A6
Park Drive	A3-B3
Park Ravine	A2-A3
Park Row	B4
Park Terrace	A4-B4
Park Valley	A4-B4-B3
Peel Street	B6-B7-C7
Pelham Street	D4
Pennyfoot Street	E4-F4
Peveril Drive	B3
Pilcher Gate	D4
Plantagenet Street	E6
Plumptree Street	E4
Popham Street	D3
Poplar Street	E3-F3
Portland Road	A5-A6-A7
Queen's Drive	B1-C1, D1-D2
Queen's Road	D2-E2
Queen Street	C4-C5

Releigh Street	A6-A7
Regent Street	B4
Rick Street	D5
Robin Hood Street	E5-F5-F6
Russell Street	A6
St Ann's Hill Road	C8
St Ann's Valley	F7-F8
St Ann's Well Road	E5-E6-E7-F7-F8
St James Street	C4
St James Terrace	B4-B3-C3
St Mark's Street	D6
St Peters Gate	C4-D4
Shakespeare Street	B6-C6
Shelton Street	D7-D6-E6
Sherriffs Way	D1
Sneinton Road	F4
South Parade	C4-D4
South Road	A3
South Sherwood Street	C5-C6
Southwell Road	E4-F4
Station Street	D2-E2
Stony Street	D4-E4
Talbot Street	A5-B5-C5
Tattershall Drive	A4-A3-B3
Tennis Drive	A4-A5-A4
The Robewalk	A5-A4-B4
Trent Street	D2-D3
Tulip Avenue	A8
Tunnel Road	A4
Union Road	D6
Upper College Street	A5-B5
Upper Eldon Street	F4
Upper Parliament Street	B5-C5-D5
Victoria Street	D4
Villa Road	C8
Walker Street	F4-F5
Walter Street	A6-A7
Warser Gate	D4
Waterway Street	C1-D1
Watkin Street	D6-D7
Waverley Street	A8-A7-B7-B6
Wellington Street	D6-D7
West Street	F4-F5
Wheeler Gate	C4
Wilford Road	C1-C2
Wilford Street	C2-C3
Wollaton Street	A5-B5-C5
Woodborough Road	C6-C7-D7-D8
Woolpack Lane	D4-E4
York Street	C6-D6

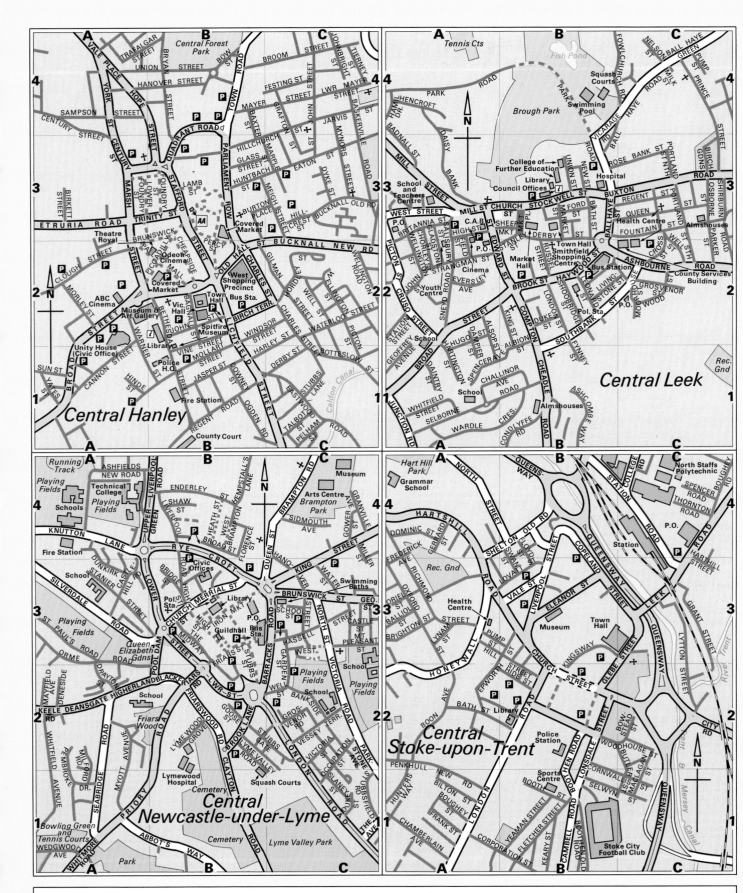

Stoke-on-Trent

Wedgwood, Spode and Royal Doulton are among the names that spring to mind with the mention of Stoke-on-Trent. Renowned for many years as the capital of the pottery industry, the town has numerous museums dealing with the industry's history as well as with leading figures involved in it, and tours of pottery factories can be arranged. On the sporting side, Stoke City, the local football team, which plays in the Canon League, boasts Sir Stanley Matthews amongst its former players.

Hanley is the birthplace of Arnold Bennet, who immortalised the Potteries in his stories about the 'Five Towns'. Born here too was Spitfire designer Reginald Mitchell, and the town has a museum devoted to his life and work. Another great attraction of Hanley for many is the fine woodland expanse of 90-acre Central Forest Park.

Leek was once renowned for silk and dye, but now attracts visitors to its antique shops. Amongst its interesting older buildings, Brindley Mill and Museum specialises in the work of 18th-century canal builder James Brindley.

Newcastle-under-Lyme boasts a fine old Guildhall and several inns dating from the 17th and 18th centuries. Keele University, to the south-west, has contributed to the town's cultural activities in recent years.

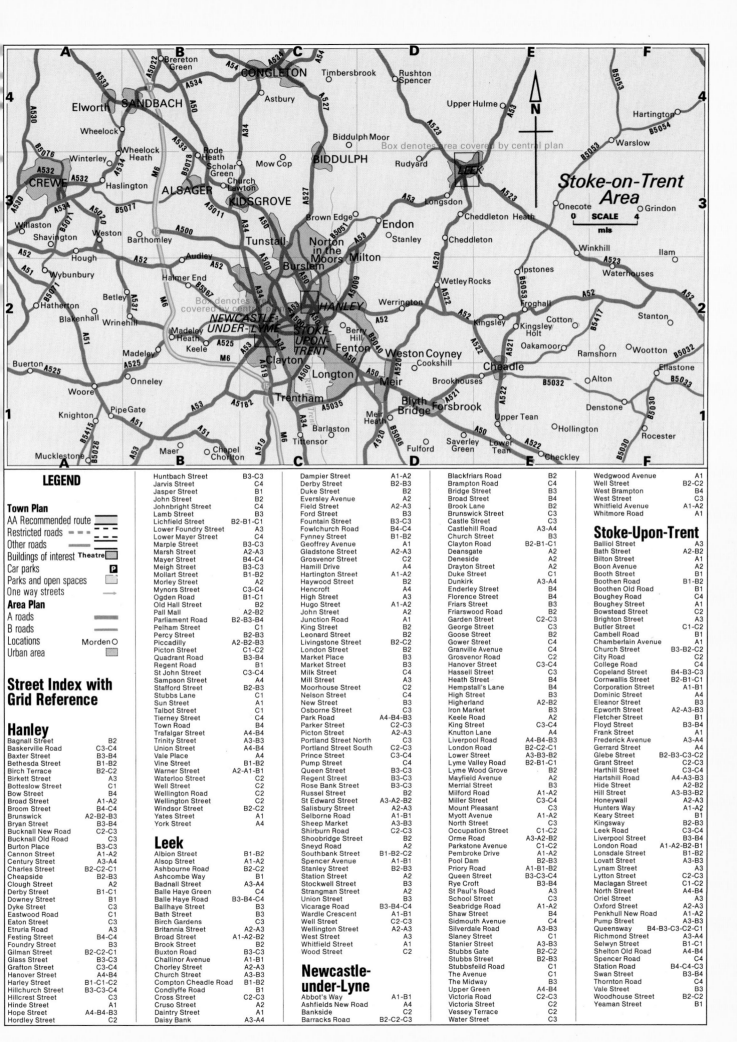

LEGEND

Town Plan
AA Recommended route
Restricted roads
Other roads
Buildings of interest   Theatre
Car parks   P
Parks and open spaces
One way streets

Area Plan
A roads
B roads
Locations   Morden O
Urban area

Street Index with Grid Reference

Hanley

Bagnall Street	B2
Baskerville Road	C3-C4
Baxter Street	B3-B4
Bethesda Street	B1-B2
Birch Terrace	B2-C2
Birkett Street	A3
Botteslow Street	C1
Bow Street	B4
Broad Street	A1-A2
Broom Street	B3-B4
Brunswick	A2-B2-B3
Bryan Street	B3-B4
Bucknall New Road	C2-C3
Bucknall Old Road	C3
Burton Place	B3-C3
Cannon Street	A1-A2
Century Street	A3-A4
Charles Street	B2-C2-C1
Cheapside	B2-B3
Clough Street	A2
Derby Street	B1-C1
Downey Street	B1
Dyke Street	C3
Eastwood Road	C1
Eaton Street	C3
Etruria Road	A3
Festing Street	B4-C4
Foundry Street	B3
Gilman Street	B2-C2-C1
Glass Street	B3-C3
Grafton Street	C3-C4
Hanover Street	A4-B4
Harley Street	B1-C1-C2
Hillchurch Street	B3-C3-C4
Hillcrest Street	C3
Hinde Street	A1
Hope Street	A4-B4-B3
Hordley Street	C2
Huntbach Street	B3-C3
Jarvis Street	C4
Jasper Street	B1
John Street	B2
Johnbright Street	C4
Lamb Street	B2
Lichfield Street	B2-B1-C1
Lower Foundry Street	A3
Lower Mayer Street	C4
Marple Street	B3-C3
Marsh Street	A2-A3
Mayer Street	B4-C4
Meigh Street	B3-C3
Mollart Street	B1-B2
Morley Street	A2
Mynors Street	C3-C4
Ogden Road	B1-C1
Old Hall Street	B2
Pall Mall	A2-B2
Parliament Road	B2-B3-B4
Pelham Street	C1
Percy Street	B2-B3
Piccadilly	A2-B2-B3
Picton Street	C1-C2
Quadrant Road	B3-B4
Regent Road	B1
St John Street	C3-C4
Sampson Street	A4
Stafford Street	B2-B3
Stubbs Lane	C1
Sun Street	A1
Talbot Street	C1
Tierney Street	C4
Town Road	B4
Trafalgar Street	A4-B4
Trinity Street	A3-B3
Union Street	A4-B4
Vale Place	A4
Vine Street	B1-B2
Warner Street	A2-A1-B1
Waterloo Street	C2
Well Street	C2
Wellington Road	C2
Wellington Street	C2
Windsor Street	B2-C2
Yates Street	A1
York Street	A4

Leek

Albion Street	B1-B2
Alsop Street	A1-A2
Ashbourne Road	B2-C2
Ashcombe Way	B1
Badnall Street	A3-A4
Balle Haye Green	C4
Balle Haye Road	B3-B4-C4
Ballhaye Street	B3
Bath Street	B3
Birch Gardens	B3
Britannia Street	A2-A3
Broad Street	A1-A2-B2
Brook Street	B2
Buxton Road	B3-C3
Challinor Avenue	A1-B1
Chorley Road	A2-A3
Church Street	A3-B3
Compton Cheadle Road	B1-B2
Condlyffe Road	B1
Cross Street	C2-C3
Cruso Street	A2
Daintry Street	A1
Daisy Bank	A3-A4
Dampier Street	A1-A2
Derby Street	B2-B3
Duke Street	B2
Eversley Avenue	A2
Field Street	A2-A3
Ford Street	B3
Fountain Street	B3-C3
Fowlchurch Road	B4-C4
Fynney Street	B1-B2
Geoffrey Avenue	A1
Gladstone Street	A2-A3
Grosvenor Street	C2
Hamill Drive	A4
Hartington Street	A1-A2
Haywood Street	B2
Hencroft	A4
High Street	A3
Hugo Street	A1-A2
John Street	A2
Junction Road	A1
King Street	B2
Leonard Street	B2
Livingstone Street	B2-C2
London Street	B2
Market Place	B3
Market Street	B3
Milk Street	C4
Mill Street	A3
Moorhouse Street	C2
Nelson Street	C4
New Street	B3
Osborne Street	C2
Park Road	A4-B4-B3
Parker Street	C2-C3
Picton Street	A2-A3
Portland Street North	C3
Portland Street South	C2-C3
Prince Street	C3-C4
Pump Street	C4
Queen Street	B3-C3
Regent Street	B3-C3
Rose Bank Street	B3-C3
Russel Street	B2
St Edward Street	A3-A2-B2
Salisbury Street	A2-A3
Selborne Road	A1-B1
Sheep Market	A3-B3
Shirburn Road	C2-C3
Shoobridge Street	B2
Sneyd Road	A2
Southbank Street	B1-B2-C2
Spencer Avenue	A1-B1
Stanley Street	B2-B3
Station Street	A2
Stockwell Street	B3
Strangman Street	A2
Union Street	B3
Vicarage Road	B3-B4-C4
Wardle Crescent	A1-B1
Well Street	C2-C3
Wellington Street	A2-A3
West Street	A1
Whitfield Street	A1
Wood Street	C2

Newcastle-under-Lyne

Abbot's Way	A1-B1
Ashfields New Road	A4
Bankside	C2
Barracks Road	B2-C2-C3
Blackfriars Road	B2
Brampton Road	C4
Bridge Street	B3
Broad Street	B4
Brook Lane	B2
Brunswick Street	C3
Castle Street	C3
Castlehill Road	A3-A4
Church Street	B3
Clayton Road	B2-B1-C1
Deansgate	A2
Deneside	A2
Drayton Street	A2
Duke Street	C1
Dunkirk	A3-A4
Enderley Street	B4
Florence Street	B4
Friars Street	B3
Friarswood Road	B2
Garden Street	C2-C3
George Street	C3
Goose Street	B2
Gower Street	C4
Granville Avenue	C4
Grosvenor Road	C2
Hanover Street	C3-C4
Hassell Street	C3
Heath Street	B4
Hempstall's Lane	B4
High Street	B3
Higherland	A2-B2
Iron Market	B3
Keele Road	A2
King Street	C3-C4
Knutton Lane	A4
Liverpool Road	A4-B4-B3
London Street	B2-C2-C1
Lower Street	A3-B3-B2
Lyme Valley Road	B2-B1-C1
Lyme Wood Grove	B2
Mayfield Avenue	A2
Merrial Street	B3
Milford Road	A1-A2
Miller Street	C3-C4
Mount Pleasant	C3
Myott Avenue	A1-A2
North Street	C3
Occupation Street	C1-C2
Orme Road	A3-A2-B2
Parkstone Avenue	C1-C2
Pembroke Drive	A1-A2
Pool Dam	B2-B3
Priory Road	A1-B1-B2
Queen Street	B3-C3-C4
Rye Croft	B3-B4
St Paul's Road	A3
School Street	C3
Seabridge Road	A1-A2
Shaw Street	B4
Sidmouth Avenue	C4
Silverdale Road	A3-B3
Slaney Street	C1
Stanier Street	A3-B3
Stubbs Gate	B2-C2
Stubbs Street	B2-B3
Stubbsfield Road	C1
The Avenue	C1
The Midway	B3
Upper Green	A4-B4
Victoria Road	C2-C3
Victoria Street	C2
Vessey Terrace	C2
Water Street	C3
Wedgwood Avenue	A1
Well Street	B2-C2
West Brampton	B4
West Street	C3
Whitfield Avenue	A1-A2
Whitmore Road	A1

Stoke-Upon-Trent

Balliol Street	A1
Bath Street	A2-B2
Bilton Street	A1
Boon Avenue	A2
Booth Street	B1
Boothen Road	B1-B2
Boothen Old Road	B1
Boughey Road	C4
Boughey Street	A1
Bowstead Street	C2
Brighton Street	A3
Butler Street	C1-C2
Cambell Road	B1
Chamberlain Avenue	A1
Church Street	B3-B2-C2
City Road	C2
College Road	C4
Copeland Street	B4-B3-C3
Cornwallis Street	B2-B1-C1
Corporation Street	A1-B1
Dominic Street	A4
Eleanor Street	B3
Epworth Street	A2-A3-B3
Fletcher Street	B1
Floyd Street	B3-B4
Frank Street	A1
Frederick Avenue	A3-A4
Gerrard Street	A4
Glebe Street	B2-B3-C3-C2
Grant Street	C2-C3
Harthill Street	C3-C4
Hartshill Road	A4-A3-B3
Hide Street	A2-B2
Hill Street	A3-B3-B2
Honeywall	A2-A3
Hunters Way	A1-A2
Keary Street	B1
Kingsway	B2-B3
Leek Road	C3-C4
Liverpool Road	B3-B4
London Road	A1-A2-B2-B1
Lonsdale Street	B1-B2
Lovatt Street	B3
Lynam Street	A3
Lytton Street	C2-C3
Maclagan Street	C1-C2
North Street	A4-B4
Oriel Street	A3
Oxford Street	A2-A3
Penkhull New Road	A1-A2
Pump Street	A3
Queensway	B4-B3-C3-C2-C1
Richmond Street	A3-A4
Selwyn Street	B1-C1
Shelton Old Road	A4-B4
Spencer Road	A4
Station Road	B4-C4-C3
Swan Street	B3-B4
Thornton Road	C4
Vale Street	B3
Woodhouse Street	B2-B3
Yeaman Street	B1

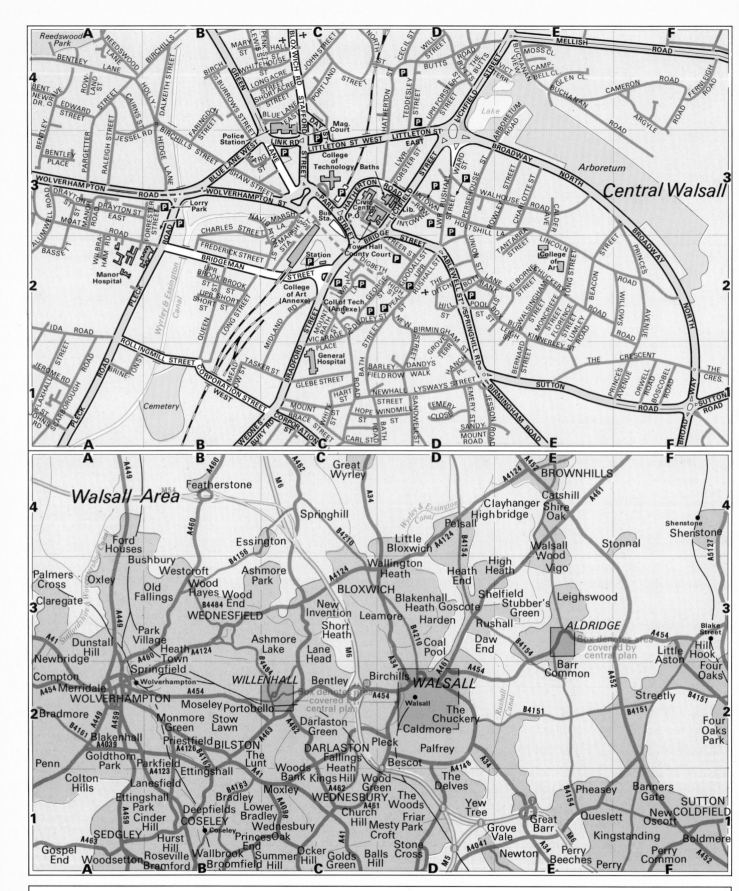

Walsall

Affectionately known as the 'Town of 100 Trades' because of its diversity of industries, Walsall is nevertheless a specialist in one area — leather manufacture. Saddles have been produced here since the 19th century, and all the British Army's saddles in World War I were Walsall-made.

A conservation area has been established at Church Hill, covering the Parish Church of St

Matthew (which dates back to the 12th century), and part of the town centre where Italian Renaissance style Taylor's Music Shop is just one of several fine Victorian buildings to be seen. Other places of interest are the Central Library's Local History Gallery, Belsize House, the birthplace of Jerome K. Jerome (now a museum dealing with his life and work) and the Garman Ryan Collection which has art donated by Lady Kathleen Epstein, widow of sculptor Sir Jacob. The

Walsall Illuminations appear each September.

Aldridge enjoys the contrasts of an industrial town set in pleasant rural surroundings. The oldest part of town, around the Parish Church, has been declared a conservation area.

Willenhall has kept its old 'Black Country' character, and the market place area is being restored in 19th-century style. A reputation for lock and key making is recalled in the local library's Lock Museum.

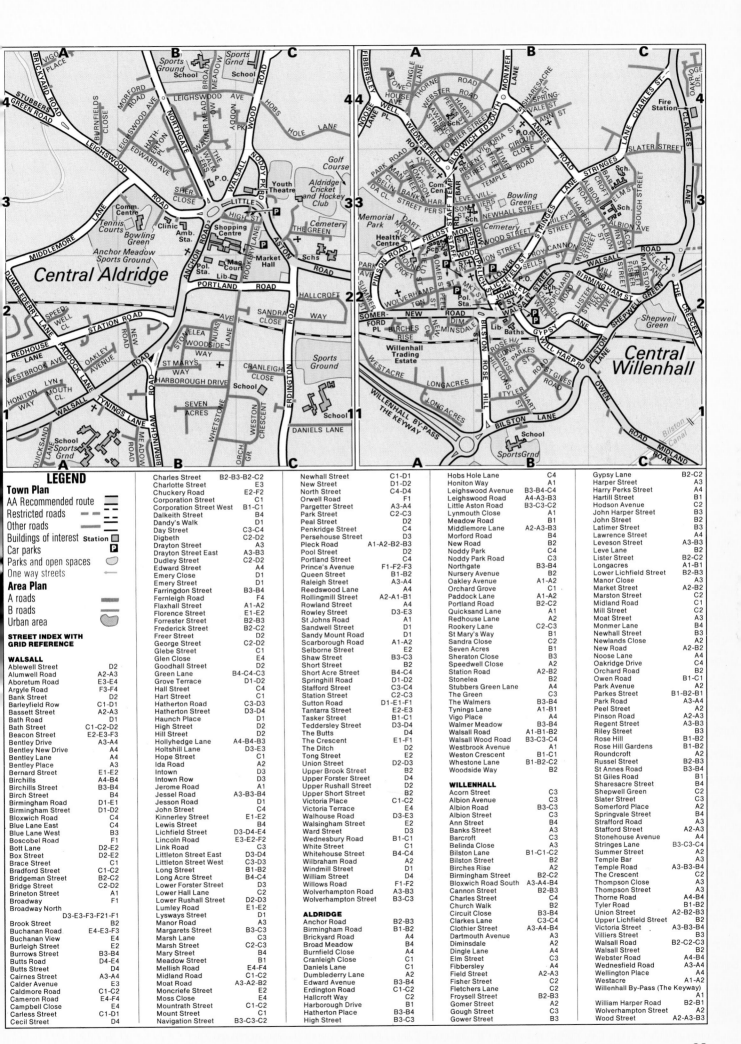

STREET INDEX WITH GRID REFERENCE

99

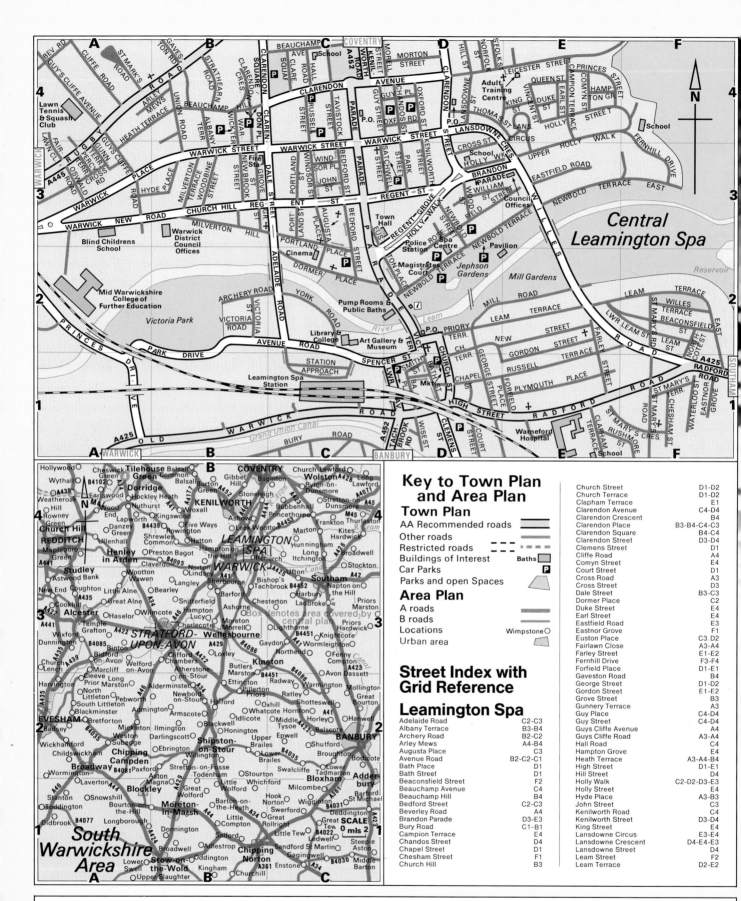

Key to Town Plan and Area Plan

Town Plan
AA Recommended roads ▬▬▬
Other roads ▬ ▬ ▬
Restricted roads ▬ ▬ ▬
Buildings of Interest   Baths ▢
Car Parks   🅿
Parks and open Spaces ◿

Area Plan
A roads ▬▬
B roads ▬▬
Locations   Wimpstone ○
Urban area ◿

Street Index with Grid Reference

Leamington Spa

Adelaide Road	C2-C3
Albany Terrace	B3-B4
Archery Road	B2-C2
Arley Mews	A4-B4
Augusta Place	C3
Avenue Road	B2-C2-C1
Bath Place	D1
Bath Street	D1
Beaconsfield Street	F2
Beauchamp Avenue	C4
Beauchamp Hill	B4
Bedford Street	C2-C3
Beverley Road	A4
Brandon Parade	D3-E3
Bury Road	C1-B1
Campion Terrace	E4
Chandos Street	D4
Chapel Street	D1
Chesham Street	F1
Church Hill	B3
Church Street	D1-D2
Church Terrace	D1-D2
Clapham Terrace	E1
Clarendon Avenue	C4-D4
Clarendon Crescent	B4
Clarendon Place	B3-B4-C4-C3
Clarendon Square	B4-C4
Clarendon Street	D3-D4
Clemens Street	D1
Cliffe Road	A4
Comyn Street	E4
Court Street	D1
Cross Road	A3
Cross Street	D3
Dale Street	B3-C3
Dormer Place	C2
Duke Street	E4
Earl Street	E4
Eastfield Road	E3
Eastnor Grove	F1
Euston Place	C3.D2
Fairlawn Close	A3-A4
Farley Street	E1-E2
Fernhill Drive	F3-F4
Forfield Place	D1-E1
Gaveston Road	B4
George Street	D1-D2
Gordon Street	E1-E2
Grove Street	B3
Gunnery Terrace	A3
Guy Place	C4-D4
Guy Street	C4-D4
Guys Cliffe Avenue	A4
Guys Cliffe Road	A3-A4
Hall Road	C4
Hampton Grove	E4
Heath Terrace	A3-A4-B4
High Street	D1-E1
Hill Street	D4
Holly Walk	C2-D2-D3-E3
Holly Street	E4
Hyde Place	A3-B3
John Street	C3
Kenilworth Road	C4
Kenilworth Street	D3-D4
King Street	E4
Lansdowne Circus	E3-E4
Lansdowne Crescent	D4-E4-E3
Lansdowne Street	D4
Leam Street	F2
Leam Terrace	D2-E2

Warwick

The old county town of the shire, Warwick lies in the shadow of its massive, historic castle which occupies the rocky ridge above the River Avon. Thomas Beauchamp and his son built the huge towers and curtain walls in the 14th century, but it was the Jacobean holders of the earldom, the Grevilles, who transformed the medieval stronghold into a nobleman's residence. In 1694,

the heart of the town was almost completely destroyed by fire and the few medieval buildings that survived lie on the outskirts of the present 18th-century centre. Of these Oken House, now a doll museum, and Lord Leycester's Hospital, almshouses dating back to the 14th century, are particularly striking.

Stratford-upon-Avon, as the birthplace of William Shakespeare, England's most famous poet and playwright, is second only to London as a

tourist attraction. This charming old market town is a living memorial to him; his plays are performed in the Royal Shakespeare Theatre which dominates the river bank, a waxwork museum specialises in scenes from his works, and his childhood home in Henley Street is a museum.

Leamington Spa, an inland spa on the River Leam, gained the prefix 'Royal' after Queen Victoria had visited it in 1838, and the town has been a fashionable health resort ever since.

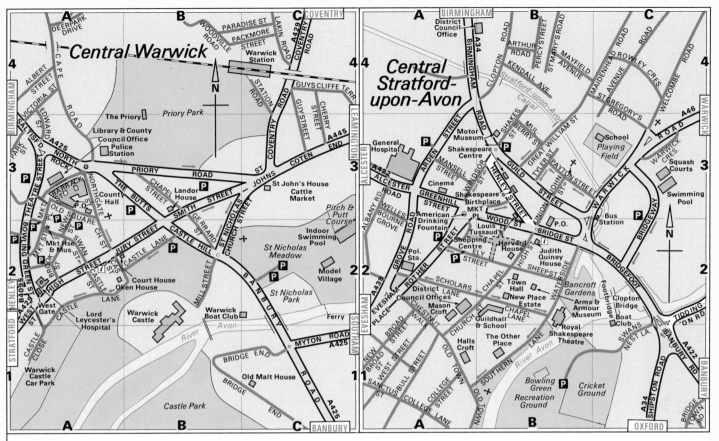

WARWICK
These pretty brick and timbered cottages standing in the shadow of the great medieval towers of Warwick Castle are among the few buildings in the town that survived a devastating fire in the late 17th century.

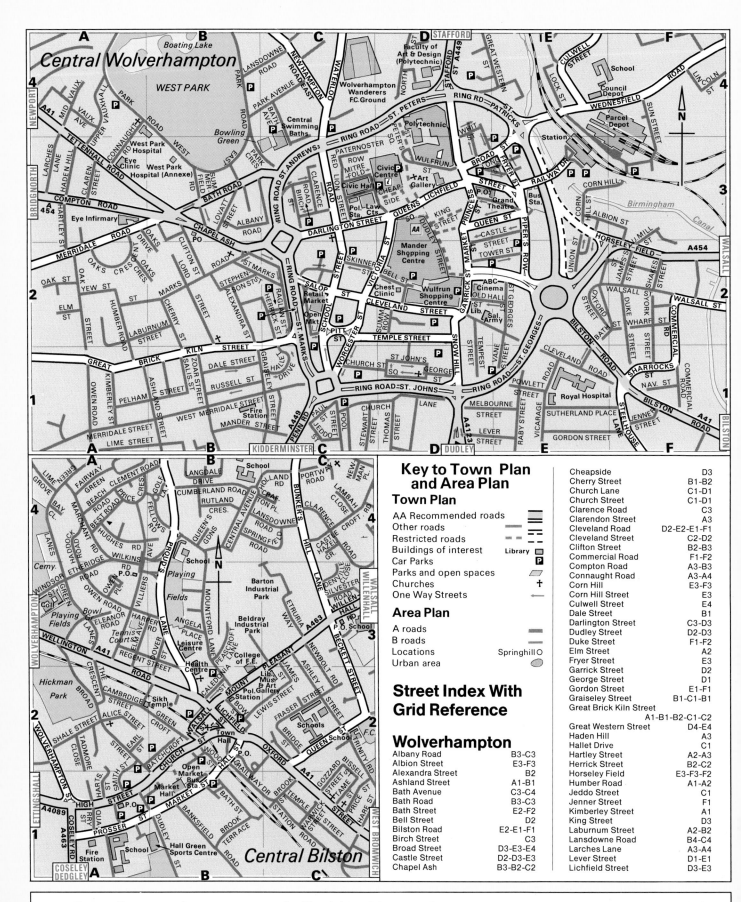

Central Wolverhampton

WEST PARK
Boating Lake
Bowling Green

Central Bilston

Key to Town Plan and Area Plan

Town Plan

AA Recommended roads	
Other roads	
Restricted roads	
Buildings of interest	Library
Car Parks	P
Parks and open spaces	
Churches	†
One Way Streets	←

Area Plan

A roads	
B roads	
Locations	Springhill O
Urban area	

Street Index With Grid Reference

Wolverhampton

Albany Road	B3-C3
Albion Street	E3-F3
Alexandra Street	B2
Ashland Street	A1-B1
Bath Avenue	C3-C4
Bath Road	B3-C3
Bath Street	E2-F2
Bell Street	D2
Bilston Road	E2-E1-F1
Birch Street	C3
Broad Street	D3-E3-E4
Castle Street	D2-D3-E3
Chapel Ash	B3-B2-C2
Cheapside	D3
Cherry Street	B1-B2
Church Lane	C1-D1
Church Street	C1-D1
Clarence Road	C3
Clarendon Street	A3
Cleveland Road	D2-E2-E1-F1
Cleveland Street	C2-D2
Clifton Street	B2-B3
Commercial Road	F1-F2
Compton Road	A3-B3
Connaught Road	A3-A4
Corn Hill	E3-F3
Corn Hill Street	E3
Culwell Street	E4
Dale Street	B1
Darlington Street	C3-D3
Dudley Street	D2-D3
Duke Street	F1-F2
Elm Street	A2
Fryer Street	E3
Garrick Street	D2
George Street	D1
Gordon Street	E1-F1
Graiseley Street	B1-C1-B1
Great Brick Kiln Street	A1-B1-B2-C1-C2
Great Western Street	D4-E4
Haden Hill	A3
Hallet Drive	C1
Hartley Street	A2-A3
Herrick Street	B2-C2
Horseley Field	E3-F3-F2
Humber Road	A1-A2
Jeddo Street	C1
Jenner Street	F1
Kimberley Street	A1
King Street	D3
Laburnum Street	A2-B2
Lansdowne Road	B4-C4
Larches Lane	A3-A4
Lever Street	D1-E1
Lichfield Street	D3-E3

Wolverhampton

Present-day Wolverhampton, capital of the Black Country, is a large and efficient town that belies its ancient origins. It was referred to as 'Heantun' in a 10th-century Royal charter, and the town coat of arms includes a cross ascribed to the Anglo-Saxon King Edgar.

In Victorian times Wolverhampton was widely known for its manufacture of chains, locks and nails, although the workshops were often tiny sheds in people's back yards. Today, many kinds of brass and iron products, as well as aircraft components, leave Wolverhampton's factories. Some different, but no less traditional, products of Midland craftsmen are displayed in the museum inside 19th-century Bantock House. These include japanned tin and papier-maché articles and painted enamels, as well as early Worcester porcelain.

Pre-dating Wolverhampton's industrial history by several hundred years is the carved shaft of Dane's Cross in St Peter's churchyard. Standing 14ft high, near a holed Bargain Stone, it was supposed to commemorate the defeat of the Danes in a local battle. The church mostly dates from the 15th century, and has a panelled tower and fine stone pulpit. There was an earlier monastery on the site, refounded in 994 by Lady Wulfruna, whose charter can now be seen in the vestry.

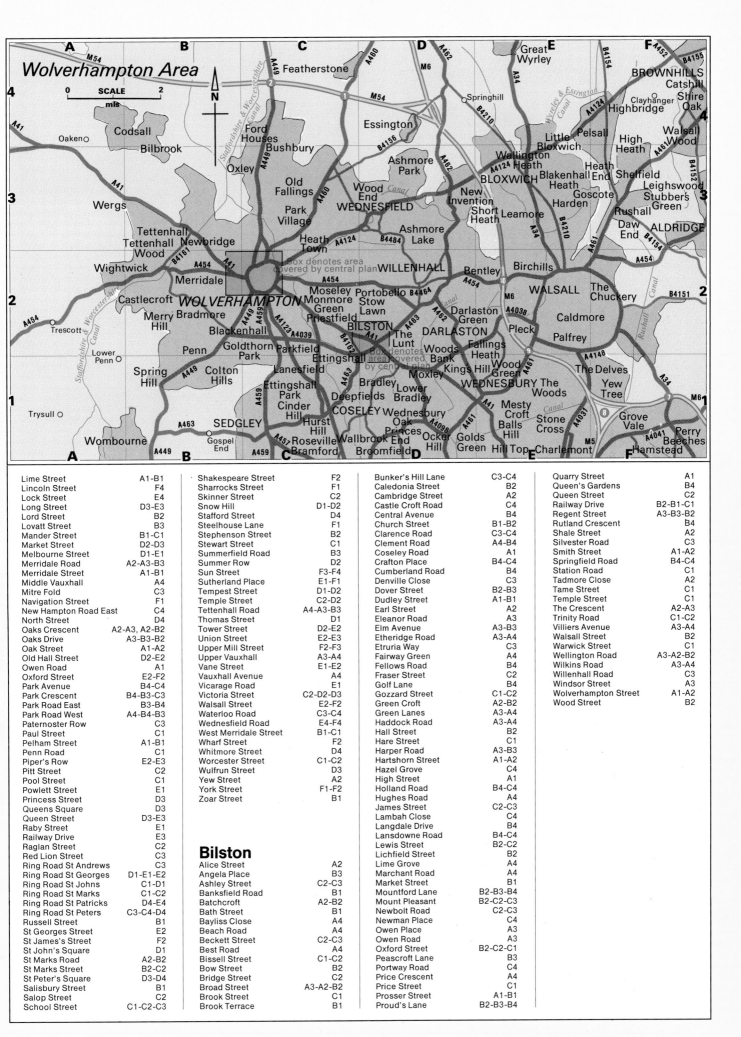

Wolverhampton Area

SCALE 0 - 2 mls

Lime Street	A1-B1
Lincoln Street	F4
Lock Street	E4
Long Street	D3-E3
Lord Street	B2
Lovatt Street	B3
Mander Street	B1-C1
Market Street	D2-D3
Melbourne Street	D1-E1
Merridale Road	A2-A3-B3
Merridale Street	A1-B1
Middle Vauxhall	A4
Mitre Fold	C3
Navigation Street	F1
New Hampton Road East	C4
North Street	D4
Oaks Crescent	A2-A3, A2-B2
Oaks Drive	A3-B3-B2
Oak Street	A1-A2
Old Hall Street	D2-E2
Owen Road	A1
Oxford Street	E2-F2
Park Avenue	B4-C4
Park Crescent	B4-B3-C3
Park Road East	B3-B4
Park Road West	A4-B4-B3
Paternoster Row	C3
Paul Street	C1
Pelham Street	A1-B1
Penn Road	C1
Piper's Row	E2-E3
Pitt Street	C2
Pool Street	C1
Powlett Street	E1
Princess Street	D3
Queens Square	D3
Queen Street	D3-E3
Raby Street	E1
Railway Drive	E3
Raglan Street	C2
Red Lion Street	C3
Ring Road St Andrews	C3
Ring Road St Georges	D1-E1-E2
Ring Road St Johns	C1-D1
Ring Road St Marks	C1-C2
Ring Road St Patricks	D4-E4
Ring Road St Peters	C3-C4-D4
Russell Street	B1
St Georges Street	E2
St James's Street	F2
St John's Square	D1
St Marks Road	A2-B2
St Marks Street	B2-C2
St Peter's Square	D3-D4
Salisbury Street	B1
Salop Street	C2
School Street	C1-C2-C3

Shakespeare Street	F2
Sharrocks Street	F1
Skinner Street	C2
Snow Hill	D1-D2
Stafford Street	D4
Steelhouse Lane	F1
Stephenson Street	B2
Stewart Street	C1
Summerfield Road	B3
Summer Row	D2
Sun Street	F3-F4
Sutherland Place	E1-F1
Tempest Street	D1-D2
Temple Street	C2-D2
Tettenhall Road	A4-A3-B3
Thomas Street	D1
Tower Street	D2-E2
Union Street	E2-E3
Upper Mill Street	F2-F3
Upper Vauxhall	A3-A4
Vane Street	E1-E2
Vauxhall Avenue	A4
Vicarage Road	E1
Victoria Street	C2-D2-D3
Walsall Street	E2-F2
Waterloo Road	C3-C4
Wednesfield Road	E4-F4
West Merridale Street	B1-C1
Wharf Street	F2
Whitmore Street	D4
Worcester Street	C1-C2
Wulfrun Street	D3
Yew Street	A2
York Street	F1-F2
Zoar Street	B1

Bilston

Alice Street	A2
Angela Place	B3
Ashley Street	C2-C3
Banksfield Road	B1
Batchcroft	A2-B2
Bath Street	B1
Bayliss Close	A4
Beach Road	A4
Beckett Street	C2-C3
Best Road	A4
Bissell Street	C1-C2
Bow Street	B2
Bridge Street	C2
Broad Street	A3-A2-B2
Brook Street	C1
Brook Terrace	B1

Bunker's Hill Lane	C3-C4
Caledonia Street	B2
Cambridge Street	A2
Castle Croft Road	C4
Central Avenue	B4
Church Street	B1-B2
Clarence Road	C3-C4
Clement Road	A4-B4
Coseley Road	A1
Crafton Street	B4-C4
Cumberland Road	B4
Denville Close	C3
Dover Street	B2-B3
Dudley Street	A1-B1
Earl Street	A2
Eleanor Road	A3
Elm Avenue	A3-B3
Etheridge Road	A3-A4
Etruria Way	C3
Fairway Green	A4
Fellows Road	B4
Fraser Street	C2
Golf Lane	B4
Gozzard Street	C1-C2
Green Croft	A2-B2
Green Lanes	A3-A4
Haddock Road	A3-A4
Hall Street	B2
Hare Street	C1
Harper Road	A3-B3
Hartshorn Street	A1-A2
Hazel Grove	C4
High Street	A1
Holland Road	B4-C4
Hughes Road	A4
James Street	C2-C3
Lambah Close	C4
Langdale Drive	B4
Lansdowne Road	B4-C4
Lewis Street	B2-C2
Lichfield Street	B2
Lime Grove	A4
Marchant Road	A4
Market Street	B1
Mountford Lane	B2-B3-B4
Mount Pleasant	B2-C2-C3
Newbolt Road	C2-C3
Newman Place	C4
Owen Place	A3
Owen Road	A3
Oxford Street	B2-C2-C1
Peascroft Lane	B3
Portway Road	A4
Price Crescent	A4
Price Street	C1
Prosser Street	A1-B1
Proud's Lane	B2-B3-B4

Quarry Street	A1
Queen's Gardens	B4
Queen Street	C2
Railway Drive	B2-B1-C1
Regent Street	A3-B3-B2
Rutland Crescent	B4
Shale Street	A2
Silvester Road	C3
Smith Street	A1-A2
Springfield Road	B4-C4
Station Road	C1
Tadmore Close	A2
Tame Street	C1
Temple Street	C1
The Crescent	A2-A3
Trinity Road	C1-C2
Villiers Avenue	A3-A4
Walsall Street	B2
Warwick Street	C1
Wellington Road	A3-A2-B2
Wilkins Road	A3-A4
Willenhall Road	C3
Windsor Street	A3
Wolverhampton Street	A1-A2
Wood Street	B2

103

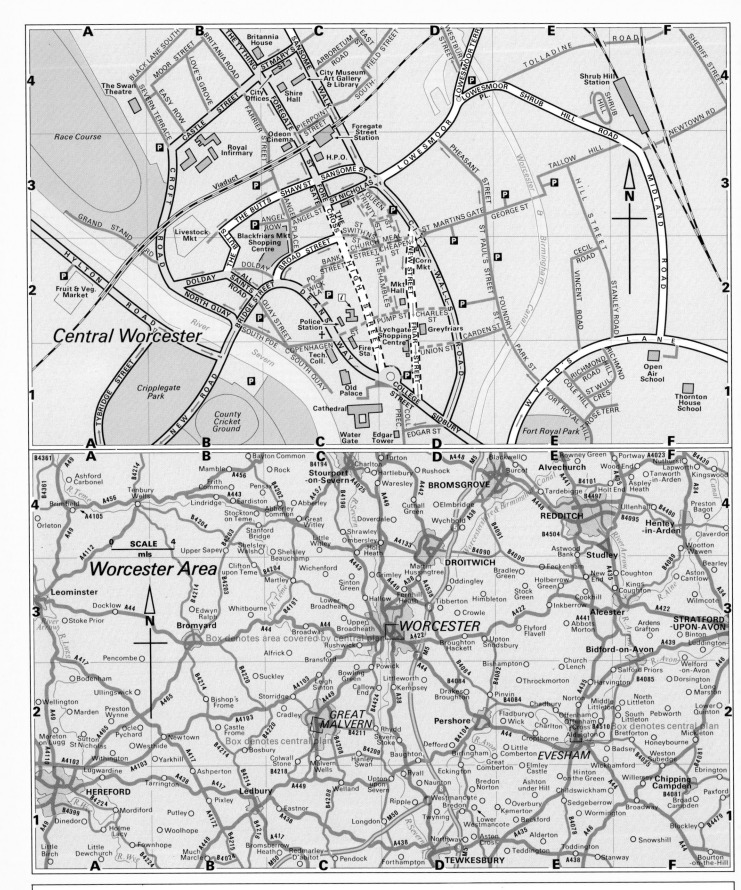

Worcester

County town and cathedral city, Worcester stands on the banks of the Severn in an area of rich agricultural land. Sadly, during the 1960s, the city suffered somewhat from ruthless redevelopment, but there is still much to interest the visitor, including The Commandery and the Tudor House, 15th-century buildings which both house museums. The cathedral, Worcester's oldest building, overlooks the river and the county cricket ground. It is one of the venues of the Three Choirs Festival, alternating with Gloucester and Hereford Cathedrals.

Worcester has become famous for its porcelain industry which was founded during the 18th century as an alternative to the ailing cloth trade. An exquisite collection of 'Royal Worcester' can be seen in the Dyson Perrins Museum.

Evesham is surrounded by the orchards that flourish in the fertile Vale of Evesham. It is an ancient market and light industrial town with two churches, a 16th-century bell-tower and the ruins of a Norman abbey all sharing the same grounds.

Malvern, famous for its mineral water, nestles at the foot of the Malvern Hills which are designated an Area of Outstanding Natural Beauty. Visitors have been drawn to this attractive town since Victorian times, and it retains much of the genteel elegance associated with bygone days.

104

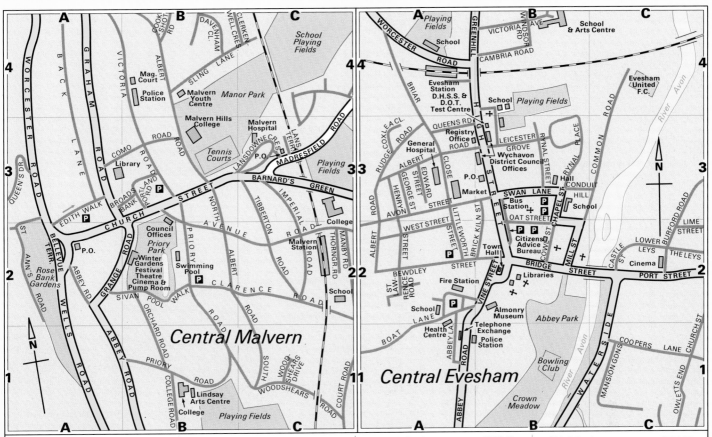

Central Malvern

Central Evesham

LEGEND

Town Plan
AA Recommended roads
Restricted roads
Other roads
Buildings of interest — Cinema
Car Parks — P
Parks and open spaces
One Way Streets

Area Plan
A roads
B roads
Locations — Suckley ○
Urban area

Street Index with Grid Reference

Worcester

All Saints Road	B2
Angel Place	C2-C3
Angel Row	B3-C3
Angel Street	C3
Arboreteum Road	C4
Bank Street	C2
Black Lane South	A4-B4
Bridge Street	B2-C2
Britania Road	B4
Broad Street	C2-C3
Carden Street	D2-E2
Castle Street	B3-B4
Cecil Road	E2
Charles Street	D2
Church Street	C2
City Wall Road	D1-D2-D3
Cole Hill	E1
College Precinct	D1
College Street	D1
Copenhagen Street	C1-C2
Croft Road	B3-B2
Deans Way	C1-C2
Dolday	B2-C2
East Street	C4
Easy Row	B4
Edgar Street	D1
Farrier Street	B4-C4-C3
Foregate	C3
Foregate Street	C4-C3
Fort Royal Hill	E1
Foundry Street	E2
Friar Street	D1-D2
George Street	D3-E3
Grand Stand Road	A3-A2-B2
High Street	C2-C1-D1
Hill Street	E2-E3
Hylton Road	A3-A2-B2-B1
Love's Grove	B4
Lowesmoor	D3-D4
Lowesmoor Place	D4-E4
Lowesmoor Terrace	D4
Meal Cheapen Street	D2
Midland Road	F2-F3
Moor Street	D2-D3
New Road	B1
New Street	D2-D3
Newton Road	F3-F4
North Quay	B2
Park Street	E1-E2
Pheasant Street	D3
Pierpoint Street	C4
Powick Lane	C2
Pump Street	C2-D2
Quay Street	B2-C2-C1
Queen Street	C3-D3
Richmond Hill	E1-F1
Richmond Road	E1
Rose Terrace	E1-F1
St Martin's Gate	D3
St Mary's Street	B4-C4
St Nicholas Street	C3
St Paul's Street	D3-D2-E2
St Swithuns Street	C2-C3
St Wulstans Crescent	E1-F1
Sansome Street	C3
Sansome Walk	C3
Severn Terrace	A4-B4-B3
Shaw Street	C3
Sheriff Street	F4
Shrub Hill	E4-F4
Shrub Hill Road	E4-E3-F3
Sidbury	D1
South Field Street	C4-D4
South Parade	B2-C2-C1
South Quay	C1
Stanley Road	E2-F2
Tallow Hill	E3-F3
The Butts	B2-B3-C3
The Cross	C3
The Shambles	D2
The Tything	B4
Tolladine Road	E4-F4
Trinity Street	C3-C2
Tybridge Street	A1-A2-B2-B1
Union Street	D1
Vincent Road	E1-E2
Westbury Street	D4
Wyld's Lane	E1-F1-F2

Malvern

Abbey Road	A2-A1-B1
Albert Road South	B2-C2-C1
Albert Road North	B4-B3-B2
Avenue Road	B3-B2-C2
Back Lane	A4-A3
Barnard's Green	C3
Bellevue Terrace	A2
Broads Bank	A3-A4
Church Street	A3-A2-B2-B3
Clarence Road	B2-C2
Clerkenwell Crescent	B4-C4
College Road	B1
Como Road	A3-B3
Cookshot Road	B4
Court Road	C1
Davenham Close	B4
Edith Walk	A2-A3
Graham Road	A4-A3
Grange Road	A2-B2
Imperial Road	C2-C3
Lansdowne Crescent	C3
Lansdowne Terrace	C3
Madresfield Road	C3-C4
Orchard Road	B1-B2
Portland Road	B3
Priory Road	B3-B2-B1
Queen's Drive	A3
St Ann's Road	A2-A3
Sivan Pool Walk	A3-B3
Thorn Grove Road	C3-C2
Tibberton Road	C3-C2
Victoria Road	A4-B4-B3
Wells Road	A2-A1
Woodshears Drive	C1
Woodshears Road	C1
Worcester Road	A4-A3-A2

Evesham

Abbey Road	A1-A2
Albert Road	A2-A3-B3
Avon Street	A2-A3-B3
Bewdley Street	A2-B2
Boat Lane	A1-A2-B2
Briar Close	A4-A3
Brick Kiln Street	B2-B3
Bridge Street	B2-C2
Burford Road	C2-C3
Cambria Road	B4
Castle Street	C2
Chapel Street	B2-B3
Church Street	C1-C2
Coopers Lane	C1
Common Road	B3-C3-C4
Conduit Hill	B3-C3
Cowl Street	B2
Coxlea Close	A3
Edward Street	A3
George Street	A3
Greenhill	A3-A4
Henry Street	A2-A3
Leicester Grove	B3
Lime Street	C2
Littleworth Street	A2-A3
Lower Leys	C2
Mansion Gardens	C1
Mill Street	B2-B3
Oat Street	B2
Owletts End	C1
Port Street	C2
Queens Road	A3
Rudge Road	A3
Rynal Place	B3
Rynal Street	B3
St Lawrence Road	A2
Swan Lane	B3
The Leys	C2
Victoria Avenue	B4
Vine Street	A2-B2
Waterside	B1-C1-C2
West Street	A2
Windsor Road	B4
Worcester Road	A4

WORCESTER
Worcester Cathedral, set high on the banks of the Severn with views across the Malvern Hills, has dominated the city for centuries. The chapter house, with its massive central column, is considered one of the finest in Britain.

Legend to Atlas

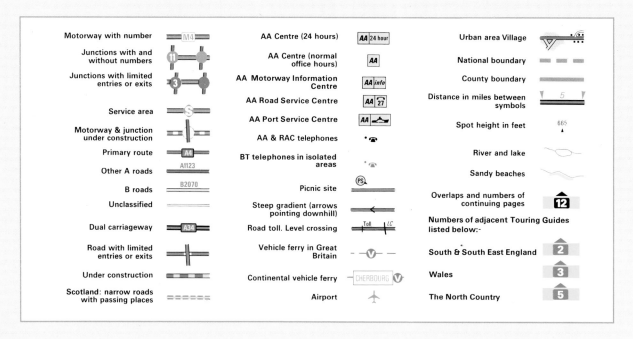

Motorway with number	M4	AA Centre (24 hours)	AA 24 hour	Urban area Village	
Junctions with and without numbers	11	AA Centre (normal office hours)	AA	National boundary	
Junctions with limited entries or exits	3	AA Motorway Information Centre	AA info	County boundary	
Service area	S	AA Road Service Centre	AA 27	Distance in miles between symbols	5
Motorway & junction under construction		AA Port Service Centre	AA	Spot height in feet	665
Primary route	A4	AA & RAC telephones			
Other A roads	A1123	BT telephones in isolated areas		River and lake	
B roads	B2070	Picnic site	PS	Sandy beaches	
Unclassified		Steep gradient (arrows pointing downhill)		Overlaps and numbers of continuing pages	12
Dual carriageway	A34	Road toll. Level crossing	Toll / LC	Numbers of adjacent Touring Guides listed below:-	
Road with limited entries or exits		Vehicle ferry in Great Britain	V	South & South East England	2
Under construction		Continental vehicle ferry	CHERBOURG V	Wales	3
Scotland: narrow roads with passing places		Airport		The North Country	5

🏛 Abbey or Cathedral		⚓ Coastal Launching Site		Nature Trail	
Ruined Abbey or Cathedral		Surfing		Wildlife Park (mammals)	
Castle		Climbing School		Wildlife Park (birds)	
House and Garden		County Cricket Ground		Zoo	
House		Gliding Centre		Forest Drive	
Garden		Artificial Ski Slope		Lighthouse	
Industrial Interest		Golf Course		Tourist Information Centre	
Museum or Collection		Horse Racing		Tourist Information Centre (summer only)	
Prehistoric Monument		Show Jumping/Equestrian Centre		Long Distance Footpath	
Famous Battle Site		Motor Racing Circuit		AA Viewpoint	
Preserved Railway or Steam Centre		Cave		Other Place of Interest	
Windmill		Country Park		Boxed symbols indicate tourist attractions in towns	
Sea Angling		Dolphinarium or Aquarium			

The National Grid

The National Grid provides a system of reference common to maps of all scales. The grid covers Britain with an imaginary network of 100 kilometre squares. Each square is identified by two letters, *eg* TR. Every 100 kilometre square is then sub-divided into 10 kilometre squares which appear as a network of blue lines on the map pages. These blue lines are numbered left to right ⓪-⑨ and bottom to top ⓪-⑨. These 10 kilometre squares can be further divided into tenths to give a place reference to the nearest kilometre.

Key to Road Maps

Outer Hebrides

Stornoway

Thurso
Wick

Ullapool

Banff
Inverness
Peterhead

Aberdeen

Shetland Islands

Portree

Fort William

Pitlochry

Perth
Dundee

Oban

Orkney Islands

Edinburgh

Largs
Glasgow

Berwick

Peebles

Campbeltown
Ayr

Dumfries

Newcastle upon Tyne

Stranraer

Workington

Middlesbrough

Kendal
Scarborough

Isle of Man

Lancaster

York

Douglas

Blackpool

Leeds
Hull

Liverpool

Grimsby

Caernarfon
Chester

Manchester	Sheffield	**28/29** Lincoln
24/25	**26/27**	

Stoke

14/15 Shrewsbury	**16/17**	**18/19** Nottingham Leicester	**20/21** King's Lynn Peterborough	**22/23** Norwich

Great Yarmouth

Aberystwyth

4/5	Birmingham Coventry **6/7** Worcester	Northampton **8/9**	**10/11** Cambridge	**12/13**

Fishguard
Carmarthen

2/3 Hereford

Gloucester

Felixstowe

Pembroke
Swansea

Cardiff
Bristol

Oxford

Reading

LONDON

Chelmsford

Maidstone

Barnstaple

Guildford

Dover
Folkestone

Salisbury

Taunton

Southampton

Brighton
Newhaven

Exeter
Weymouth
Bournemouth

Truro
Plymouth

Scilly Isles

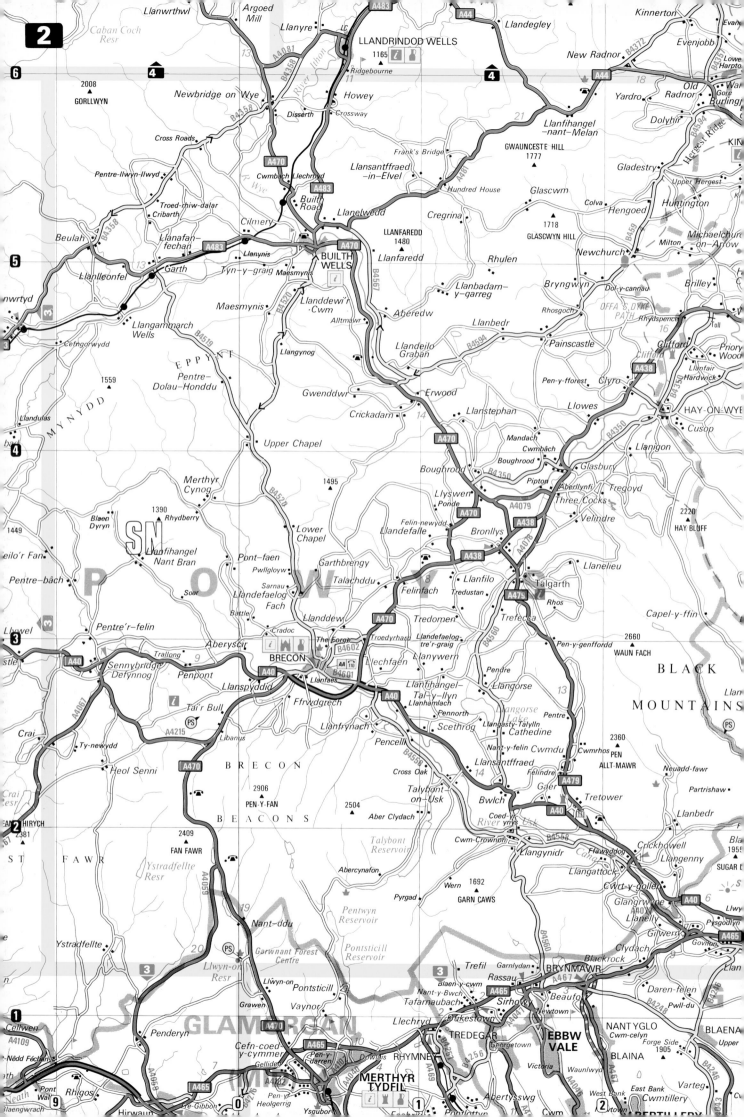

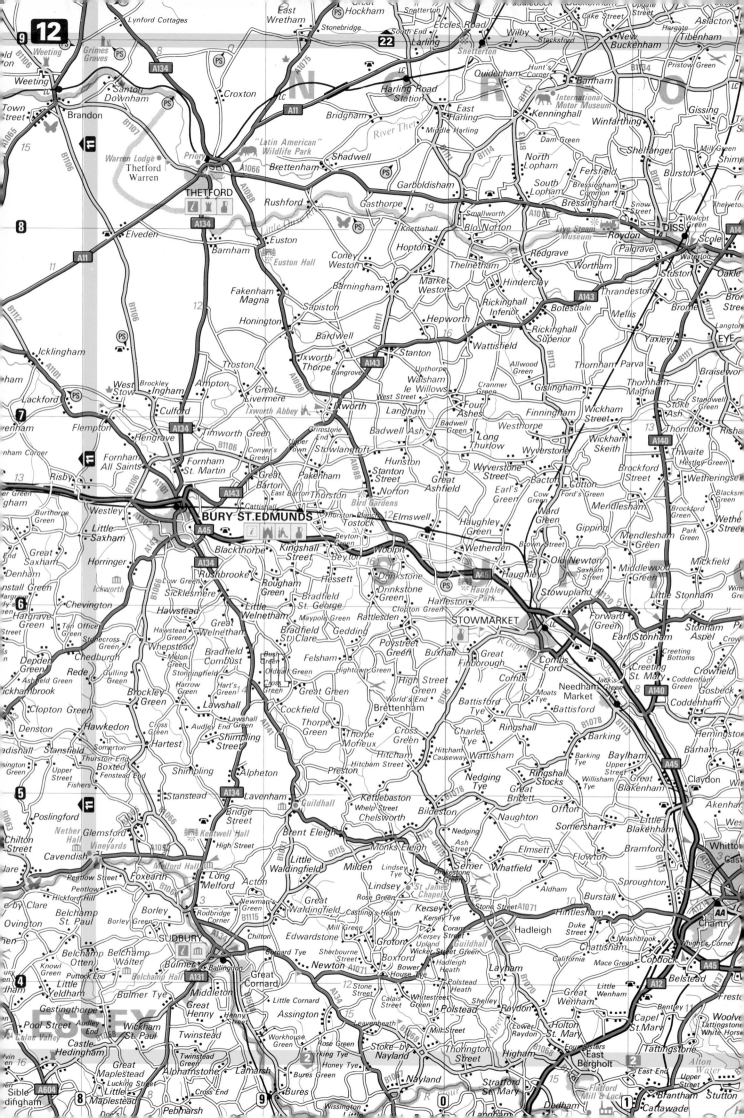

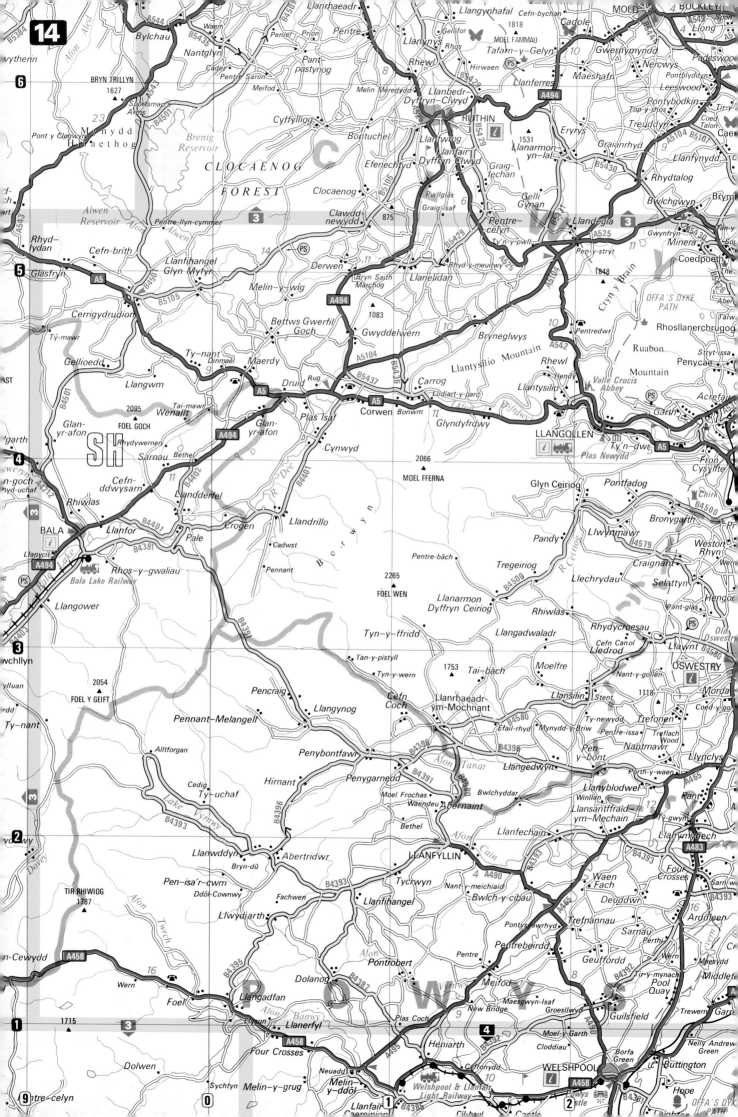

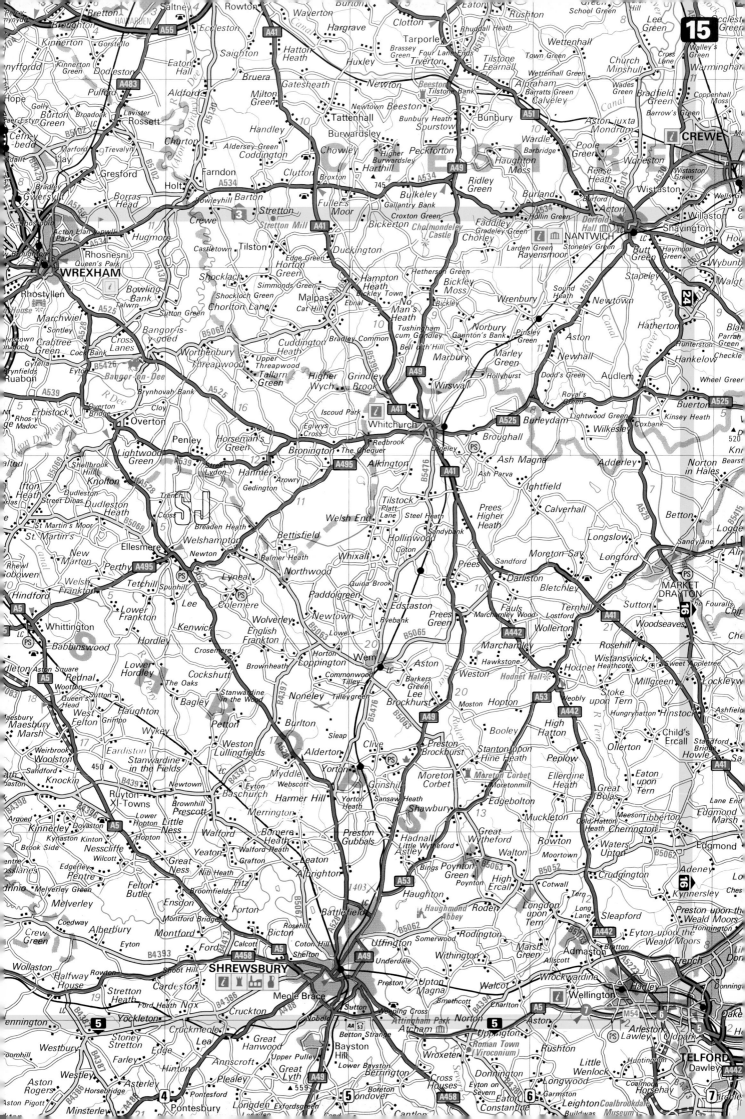

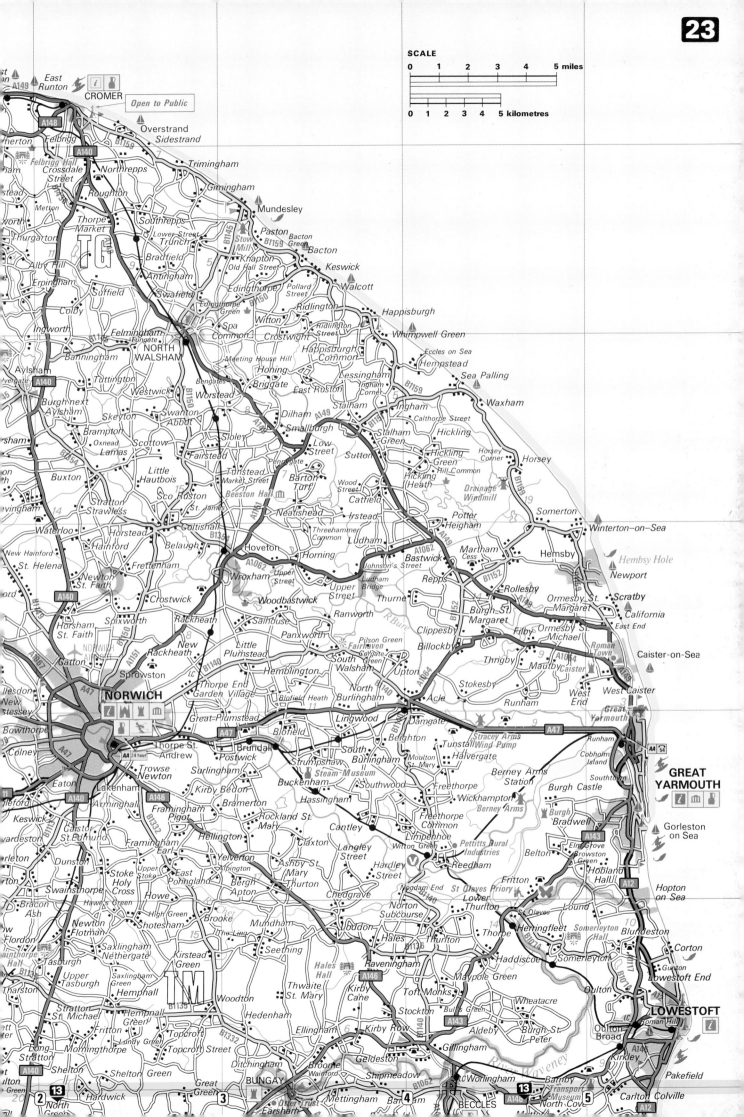

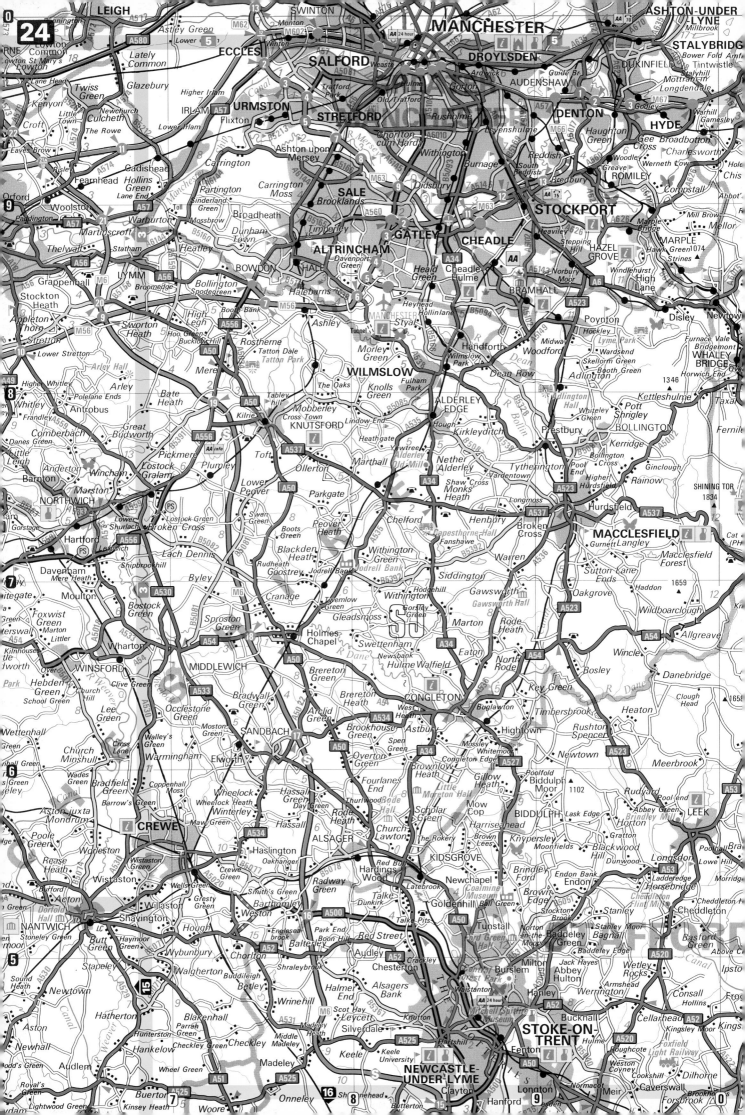

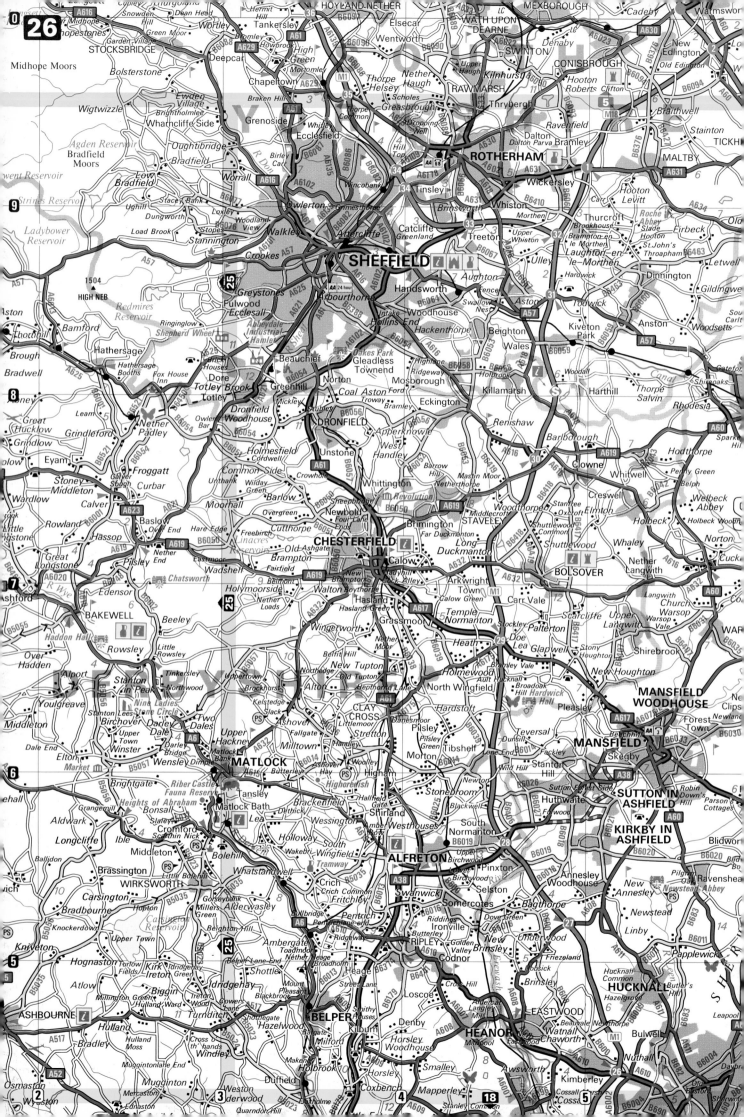

INDEX

As well as the page number of each place name the index also
includes an appropriate atlas page number together with a four figure
map reference (see National Grid explanation on page 106).

In a very few instances place names appear without a map reference.
This is because either they are not shown on the atlas or they lie just
outside the mapping area of the guide. However, each tour does
include a detailed map which highlights the location of all places
mentioned on the route.

136